ANGLISTIK UND ENGLISCHUNTERRICHT

Herausgegeben von
Gabriele Linke
Holger Rossow
Merle Tönnies

Band 88

CHRISTIAN LUDWIG
NICOLE MARUO-SCHRÖDER (Eds.)

"Tell Freedom I said Hello"

Issues in Contemporary Young Adult Dystopian Fiction

Universitätsverlag
WINTER
Heidelberg

Bibliografische Information der Deutschen Nationalbibliothek

Die Deutsche Nationalbibliothek verzeichnet diese Publikation in der Deutschen Nationalbibliografie; detaillierte bibliografische Daten sind im Internet über *http://dnb.d-nb.de* abrufbar.

Herausgeber:

Prof. Dr. Gabriele Linke
PD Dr. Holger Rossow
Prof. Dr. Merle Tönnies

Das Zitat stammt aus: DeStefano, Lauren. *Wither*. London: Harper Voyager, 2011, p. 210.

ISBN 978-3-8253-6875-3
ISSN 0344-8266

Imprimé en Allemagne · Printed in Germany
Druck: Memminger MedienCentrum, 87700 Memmingen

Gedruckt auf umweltfreundlichem, chlorfrei gebleichtem und alterungsbeständigem Papier

Den Verlag erreichen Sie im Internet unter:
www.winter-verlag.de

Contents

Part II: Didactic Explorations

List of Illustrations

Rüdiger Ahrens (Würzburg)

Preface

The subjects for the EFL classroom as taught in German schools are generally subdivided into three major areas:

1. linguistics referring to vocabulary and grammar in the United Kingdom ('Oxford Standard');
2. 'Cultural Studies' (and traditional *Landeskunde*) covering a variety of regions with English speaking populations;
3. literary texts of the English-speaking world.

These EFL curricular areas are presented in manifold variations as seen in textbooks, teaching materials, and in the global media in both oral and written forms. They are objectified in numberless teaching programs of school curricula due to the fact that English is considered to be the *lingua franca* world-wide. Numerous monographs about EFL teaching have been written in the last two centuries as English has gained a general status as the most requested modern language in Europe and the world. This status has been challenged from time to time depending on political situations in the home country or world-wide.

Although the first and second subject areas have undergone some methodological changes in the course of school history, they are generally considered to be relatively stable and consistent. The study of literary texts, in contrast, has undergone several changes and fractions including political and cultural fashions and shifts. Some teachers have banned literary texts from the EFL classroom altogether because they are considered too volatile as literary understanding is vulnerable to uncertainties of critical opinions and schools of thought. Others believe that learners are distracted by aesthetic predilections and are predisposed to be entertained or amused. The old Horatian formula stating that literature could "aut prodesse aut delectare" (either teach or delight) or in contemporary terms either contribute to cognition or affection has been misunderstood as an alternative and not as an additive principle. However, current didactic discussions recognize the complex determination of complimentary goals.

This dialectic determination of the effects of literary texts on learners of English has thrown open the door to interpretations which have been introduced into the EFL classroom. The present volume written for literary professionals contributes to the ongoing discussion by focussing on a particular literary genre which has been influencing the didactic debates for a long time. This discussion was started about five hundred years ago when Thomas More's *Utopia* saw the light of the day in 1516. The didactic function of the Utopia, or rather Eutopia as it described the future as a "good place" with positive connotations, was to invite reader emulation and served as an incentive for imitation. However, since the late 19th century, as seen for instance in Samuel Butler's satirical novels *Erewhon, or Over the Range* (1872) and *Erewhon Revisited* (1901), this didactic function has increasingly been replaced by a negative counterpart in the form of a dystopia. This turn-around brought about an abdication of the original "good place" in favour of a "bad place" as a deterrent to moral deterioration. The implicit discussion of negative warnings in dystopian texts points to the dangers of evolutionary possibilities in human history. Such literary texts used in the EFL classroom enhance a cautioning on the part of the learners, who are warned against the destruction of human life on this planet. Visions of endangered life affect above all students on the verge of adulthood in a vulnerable phase of their education. The reception of these dystopias by young adults might ultimately influence the social values of our present communities.

The essays published in this volume present students as well as teachers with analytical interpretations of a vast array of dystopian texts as well as films and posters based on these narratives. They are not intended to direct interpretative readings in a compulsory way, but allow for individual responses on the part of the students.

I strongly support the general intent of this volume and express my thanks to the authors of these essays and to the editors for the energy they put into compiling this volume. I hope that the new ideas incorporated in these writings will enter into the teaching of the EFL classroom of the future.

Würzburg, 2018

Christian Ludwig (Karlsruhe)
Nicole Maruo-Schröder (Koblenz)

"What, Indeed, Is the Matter with (Young Adult) Dystopia?" A Short Introduction

1. Introduction

Sitting down in the late spring of 2017 to write the introduction to this collection of essays, it is hard not to be discouraged by global events and to fall into a justifiably dystopian mood. Terrorist attacks seem to be on the rise all over the world. The suicide bombings in Manchester targeting a concert with a predominantly teenage audience is just the latest catastrophe in a series of similar events. Moreover, the fighting in Syria has developed into an increasingly large-scale conflict in which local citizens are suffering under the impact and consequences of larger global interests as confrontations are being fought, among other things, with chemical weapons. Donald Trump was elected President of the U.S. and so far has done nothing to mitigate the fears and anxieties that his presidential campaign created for many of us. On the contrary, considering his stance on climate change in connection with his close ties to the conventional energy industry or his decision to cut much-needed funding for the humanities, it is hard not to be overly pessimistic. Furthermore, developments such as the growing tendencies towards right-wing nationalism in the United States and all over Europe along with events like the "Brexit" in Great Britain, the ongoing refugee crisis that is only inadequately and unwillingly being dealt with by the EU, the political situation in Turkey, or mass migration due to climate change make us ponder what the future will look like for future generations.

Indeed, many of the conflicts that are visible today can be found (in one variation or another) in current young adult dystopian fiction whose teenage heroines and heroes fight for survival in a world ravaged by war, terrorism, environmental destruction, and the scarcity of food and water. It is rather striking how, with the turn of the millennium, the genre of young adult dystopian fiction has come into its own and even turned into a hype. Hence, we take up Ursula Heise's question "What Is the Matter with Dystopia?" as discussed in her eponymous article. In contrast to Heise however, we focus on the rather 'new' genre of young adult dystopia to see what it contributes to the current literary scene in terms of the topics and issues dealt with.[1] How does young adult fiction, with its focus on the process of growing up into a world ruled by 'authoritarian others' as well as often conflict-ridden relationships with peers, function in relation to the dystopian genre's focus on things gone wrong? How do these texts assess and deal with contemporary cultural developments and socio-political problems and conflicts? What do these new dystopian visions contribute to the long-standing narrative of the genre? And, even more importantly, what kind of potential does young adult dystopian fiction have – quite literally – for our future as a subject matter in the classroom?

Despite the fact that young adult fiction is still a rather neglected genre within academic discussions, and although the subgenre of young adult dystopia is quite new on the scene, there have been a number very good publications on the topic. Next to the groundbreaking (and early) collection *Utopian and Dystopian Writing for Children and Young Adults* (2003), edited by Carrie Hintz and Elaine Ostry, which highlights the significance of utopian and dystopian literature for children and young adults alike (covering texts from the eighteenth century onwards), we would like to draw attention to two more recent works: *Contemporary Dystopian Fiction for Young Adults: Brave New Teenagers* (2013), edited by Balaka Basu, Katherine R. Broad, and Carrie Hintz, which looks at recent genre examples to explore them as a "political, cultural, and aesthetic phenomenon" that combines pleasure and instruction for young people;[2] and *Female Rebellion in Young Adult Dystopian Fiction* (2014), edited by Sara K. Day, Miranda A. Green-Barteet, and Amy L. Montz, which focuses on the negotiation of gender and particularly femininity in newer publications of the genre. What our collection can contribute to the ongoing discussion is its twin focus of literary and cultural analysis of recent young adult dystopian fiction (part 1) as well as an exploration of its potential for teaching (part 2), each part being introduced by an overview article. A thread of continuity running through the contributions is the view that both despite and because of their popularity, these texts are worth looking at as they seem to have hit a nerve in readers of all ages. These novels and picturebooks do not simply negotiate current problematic issues and developments, but do so in ways that speak to (young) readers and engage them in ways different from the more 'classic' texts, as can be seen in the numerous fan-based websites devoted to young adult dystopian fiction. In the following, and as a basis for the collection, we briefly discuss "dystopia" and related concepts before giving an overview of the single contributions of this collection.

2. The Facets of Dystopia: A Brief Terminological Overview

Although attempts to define any genre routinely start with the disclaimer that the genre in question is difficult, if not impossible to define, a definition is, in the end, provided. Given the fact that the concept of "genre" is less a fixed category for sorting texts into distinct groups than more of a tool to see how a given text might compare to other similar texts in terms of structure, narrative patterns, characteristics, topoi and motifs etc., it is not surprising that a rigid definition is neither possible nor desirable. Moreover, historical changes as well as authorial (and reader) creativity contribute further to variations, deviations, and changes in the features that are said to define a genre. The same holds true for the genre of dystopia. Hence, what follows is not an attempt to define the genre, but to highlight certain discussions and questions that are important for the genre of dystopia.[3]

According to Heise, dystopias are a development of the twentieth century due the impact of two world wars and global conflicts of opposing political systems,[4] while dystopia's flip-side, utopia, has a much longer history. Its first occurrence, and also its history as a generic term, begins with Thomas More's eponymous work in 1516. In his *Utopia*, two meanings of the word come together: While utopia refers – via its derivation from Greek – to a "non-place," i.e. a place that does not exist, it is likewise a term for the narrative about such a place which comes with (changing) characteristics and patterns.[5] Moreover, the English language provided More with a pun that adds another meaning to the term: "Eutopia" means "the good place" and thus, the genre of utopia describes a good place while questioning (the possibility of) its existence at the same time.[6]

Similar to dystopia, utopia designates both a place – or the invention of a place – and a narrative form in which visions of such a place have been spread, i.e. "a non-existent society described in considerable detail and normally located in time and space."[7] The narrative form – the fictional design of a non-existent good place – comes with a didactic function usually meant as an incentive for the reader to take action, e.g. to help turn one's own society into a better place inspired by the fictional model.[8] Yet, as Elcena Madeline Davis Rogan points out, this is where things become more complicated. While she acknowledges that both meanings, utopia and eutopia, are present within More's work, she claims that the place described is, in fact, not the perfect place but that "it is rather an often satirical rendering of a non-place" meant to criticize existing structures and practices of More's society.[9] In other words, from the very beginning the term "utopia" has not only connoted the good or perfect place, but has also hinted at its potential for being, in fact, a negative place relating more or less obviously to the author's and readers' own place and time. What is present in any case is the didactic impetus of the narrative vision to function as a warning which invites readers to consider their own society critically. Should the described place be a eutopia – sometimes also called "positive utopia"[10] – it is often meant to provide features worthy of imitation.[11]

To make things even more complicated, what is considered to be a perfect place by one person, might be seen as its complete opposite by another. Hence, in readers' perception, an author's utopia can quickly become a "dystopia" – another word derived from Greek meaning "bad place."[12] Similarly, many dystopias were originally created as utopias by their founders and have, for a variety of reasons, developed into (more or less obvious) dystopian societies.[13] In analogy to the utopia, the dystopia has been defined as a society (or its depiction) to be considered "as considerably worse than the society in which the reader lived."[14] For this reason it is sometimes also called a "negative utopia" (in this collection, however, we use the term dystopia to describe such a place).[15]

Although dystopias describe decidedly bad places extrapolating current problems into the future as a warning, they are not devoid of hope. On the contrary, as Tom Moylan argues, they function as a warning thus containing the hope of betterment "in even the worst of times."[16] This stands in contrast to what is called the "anti-utopia," a genre that seeks to undermine the utopian genre's element of hope, considering it useless and often adding an ironic element to its vision of despair.[17] In contrast to this, "critical utopias" create positive social visions of better places yet indicate, according to Raffaela Baccolini and Tom Moylan, "a postmodern attitude of self-reflexivity" meaning being aware of the potential problems that each utopian vision automatically entails and thus creating "better but open futures" instead of stable, perfect places.[18]

The variety of terms show the historical changes in the (literary) visions of what a good place, and hence the future of the contemporaneous society, might look like as well as the changing attitudes towards the possibilities of creating such a place. They also reveal an awareness of the complexity entailed in dealing with social problems in the sense that there will never be a stable, coherent vision of 'the ideal place' acceptable for everybody. Hence, past and current visions of the future – whether as good, even perfect, or horrific places – are various and nuanced, even contradictory, emphasizing that the search for 'a better place' will be – indeed – an endless one that needs to be constantly tackled. In this sense, the future is happening now and the current wave of dystopian texts helps us to focus particularly on those areas of technology, scientific progress, social developments etc. that have the potential to develop into problems and threaten to turn our world into a dystopian one.

Consequently, just as societies always have to struggle with problems (problems that are, moreover, constantly changing), dystopia as a genre was never really 'dead' or 'gone.' Yet, it is quite striking how the genre had a resurgence around the millennium. The reasons for this are manifold and open to speculation. As has been done regarding the genre of disaster movies, the popularity of dystopias could be linked to both the millennial fear that accompanied the (Western) world's transition into the twenty-first century and the terrorist attacks of September 11, 2001 and their global aftermath. Similarly, an increase in both the experienced and visible consequences of climate change and more generally environmental destruction along with the realization that natural resources are not endless – accompanied by an astonishing refusal to adequately deal with such problems – might have influenced readers' interest in the dystopian genre. Increasingly rapid technological progress with consequences not easily surmised along with a growing gap between the rich and poor in almost all societies already show at least negative, if not dystopian, consequences and are likewise valid reasons for a turn of the zeitgeist to the genre in question. As with related genres such as disaster narratives or science fiction, utopian and dystopian texts sometimes reflect their zeitgeist in a very concrete way. In relation, it does not come as a surprise that the above mentioned developments and the anxieties attached to them will not just become visible in the genre, but also contribute to its popularity.

What seems new, however, is the decided turn towards young adult readers or rather, towards 'style' and plot structures that manage to address different audiences capturing older and younger readers alike. Economic considerations have certainly played a role as both authors and publishers try to take advantage of a newly discovered market. This market has perhaps become most visible with fantasy fiction such as J.K. Rowling's *Harry Potter* (1997 onwards) or Philip Pullman's *His Dark Materials* (1995 onwards) series. Moreover, the ever closer connection between the literary and film businesses contributes to this providing different media outlets to address and 'recruit' new reading and viewing communities. In a similar way, the franchise business must be mentioned here – it is probably no coincidence that the majority of young adult dystopias come in trilogies now (sometimes also featuring spin-off stories of minor characters) creating a prolonged way to earn money with a story and its characters.

Despite actually appealing to very diverse reading communities, the latest wave of dystopian fiction is marked by a decided turn to teenage and young adult heroines and (to a lesser extent) heroes, complete with patterns typical for the genre of young adult fiction, which is another reason for its popularity. Despite all its (relative) freedom as well as the chances and opportunities that Western society seems to offer young people, a rise in control, restrictions, surveillance and the necessity to conform has become visible. Thus, growing up today can actually feel very similar to living in a dystopian society. In relation, the rise in the genre's popularity seems to express youths' desire, in Scott Westerfeld's words, to "[b]rea[k] down the 'system.'"[19] Moreover, pure escapism from the more realistic everyday problems young people have to face as well as the clear-cut good vs. evil-structure at the heart of many dystopian texts can be seen as further reasons for the genre's popularity.[20]

As has been the case in literary history a number of times, the popularity of the genre has led (almost reflexively it seems) to criticism of its 'poor' quality, e.g. of its repetitive and simple storylines as well as its entertaining and unchallenging character in general. However, as all of our contributions argue, there is more to these texts than a simple but gripping storyline. Not only should we have a critical look at popular texts because of their appeal to (and thus potential influence on) a great number of readers; we should also take readers, their tastes, and their needs seriously and attempt to see what it is that makes these texts so relevant in the here and now. The current relevance of the genre is exemplified in the various (classroom) approaches to and readings of young adult dystopian fiction presented in this collection.

3. The Contributions

The collection is organized into two parts: The first part approaches young adult dystopian literature from a literary and cultural studies standpoint while the second has a more didactic impetus focusing on the genre's potential for teaching English as a foreign language. The collection's first section "Literary and Cultural Studies Perspectives" opens with Rüdiger Heinze's contribution "Through a Glass, Darkly: Contemporary Young Adult Dystopias," which provides orientation within the recent, very diverse field of young adult dystopian literature. Heinze compares this newest batch of dystopian fiction to the more established, 'classic' examples of the genre and finds, along with traditional traits and characteristics, the "right of exit," i.e. the possibility of leaving a society, to be a distinctive feature. His discussion and examples not only provide an overview of the wealth of storyworlds on the market, but also indicate the ways in which young adult dystopias both carry on and reinvent the genre's tradition, highlighting their political, social, and cultural acuity regarding problems and issues of contemporary (western) societies.

Nicole Maruo-Schröder's contribution "Technological Progress, Adult Power, and Teenage Bodies in 21st-Century Dystopias" explores current young adult dystopias from the specific angle of the body. Situated at the nexus between the aims and characteristics of young adult fiction as well as those of the dystopian genre, young adult dystopias use the body as a key site on which the struggle between the personal and the political is played out. In her discussion of Juliana Baggott's *Pure*, Lauren Oliver's *Delirium*, and Karen Sandler's *Tankborn*, she investigates the ways in which the individual body functions not only as a 'battleground' for morally and ethically controversial questions, but also more generally as a catalyst for political enlightenment and action.

The next contribution "Withering Bodies: Objectifying the Female Adolescent Body in Lauren DeStefano's *Chemical Garden* Trilogy" by

Sarah Schäfer-Althaus shifts the focus to the gender-specific treatment of female bodies as visible in many young adult dystopias. In her analysis of the novels *Wither*, *Fever*, and *Sever* by Lauren DeStefano, Schäfer-Althaus shows how female empowerment visible in many novels is undercut by the problematic instrumentalization and sexualization of bodies that particularly the female heroes are subjected to. Viewed from this angle, such novels are not progressive but rather traditional in the ways in which they portray the female body as an object to be looked at, used, and also discarded.

With her contribution on "'It's So Weird Being Inside History' – Saci Lloyd's Multimodal Hybrid Narratives *The Carbon Diaries 2015* and *2017*," Alessandra Boller turns our attention to current and future environmental problems in her analysis of two prominent examples of eco-dystopias. Contesting the common prejudice against young adult dystopian fiction as being rather simplistic and less relevant than the genre's classics, Boller shows how Lloyd's novels attempt to engage readers in important social, political, and environmental issues by making them both significant and understandable to young readers. As the novel progresses – and the heroine's situation gradually worsens – issues such as social inequality, poverty, class differences, environmentally (un)sound behavior, and even the inaptitude of the political elite to deal with such problems are linked with more personal problems such as pursuing one's dreams, thinking about one's (professional) future, or first love.

Miriam Gertzen's "'Is This Where We Stand Now, Right Here on the Brink?' Geographical and Social Precarity and Adolescent Agency in the Eco-Dystopias of Julie Bertagna and Saci Lloyd" continues the focus on current eco-dystopias discussing Lloyd's novels and Julie Bertagna's *Exodus*. Using Butler's distinction between precarity and precariousness, Gertzen focuses on both the precarity and precariousness of social and geographical spaces to show how they are intimately linked with questions of power and injustice. Moreover, Gertzen shows how, based on this link, the protagonists can only gain agency through accepting their social, political, and environmental responsibility, which is – for both – exemplified in an intellectual and physical journey to new grounds.

The second part "Didactic Explorations" opens with Maria Eisenmann's overview of "The Potential of Young Adult Dystopian Fiction in the EFL Classroom." Claiming the necessity to open up the traditional canon of literature taught in the EFL classroom, Eisenmann shows how young adult dystopian literature can be part of this development. Using numerous examples, she illustrates how the genre takes up relevant topics and areas such as social responsibility, inter- and transcultural competences, globalization, and matters of environmental concern. Using Veronica Roth's *Divergent* as her example, Eisenmann closes by concretizing her ideas showing in detail in which ways and with which tasks the novel can help in teaching topics and competences central for the EFL classroom.

In her contribution "'The Odds Are Never in Our Favor': Dystopia as Metaphor for Adolescence," Nadine Krüger explores the parallels between adolescence and dystopia. Both are, for instance, characterized as "states of crisis" in which young adults have to negotiate and even fight with parental and governmental authorities for their place in society. Moreover, tensions between individual and collective identities, needs, or desires are pressing in both adolescence and dystopia making issues such as awakening, rebellion, maturation and the like significant. Arguing that these metaphorical connections make young adult dystopias important material for the EFL classroom, she exemplifies the genre's potential for teaching, particularly with regard to global matters, environmental concerns, and inter- and transcultural competences.

Christian Ludwig's contribution "'Freedom Is a Small Price to Pay for Survival' – Selected Images of the Posthuman in Catherine Fisher's *Incarceron* Bilogy and Global Education in the EFL Classroom" investigates the reconstruction of diversity in young adult dystopian fiction. Gender, ethnicity, age, and social class are only some of the identities increasingly experimented with in contemporary fiction. They are also at the forefront of Fisher's *Incarceron* in which one part of society is locked-in the apparent utopia of a computer-generated version of the Middle Ages where everything that is non-era is prohibited, while the rest of humanity is locked-out of 'utopia' and damned to life-long imprisonment. Considering the respective other world as 'utopia,' what both societies have in common is how inhabitants are forced to give up individualism and diversity in favor of unity. This contribution tackles exactly this very issue. While the first part discusses the clash between the two societies' systems, the second part sheds light on how dealing with the novels in the EFL classroom can raise the students' awareness of equity and diversity both as recurring themes in contemporary young adult dystopias and our society.

From the longer genre of the young adult dystopian novel, we turn to the picturebook in the next two contributions. In "From Utopia to Dystopia: David Macaulay's Satiric Picturebook *Baaa* (1985) and Media Literacy," Michael Meyer discusses the importance of a multimodal approach for the competence of literacy that encompasses more than 'just' the written word. Analyzing the relation between words and images in his reading of *Baaa*, Meyer argues that the conceptual framing (of words by images and vice versa) is decisive in the readerly production of meaning. Closing, he shows what focusing on framing would mean for the EFL classroom.

The second contribution to look at the genre of the picturebook is Grit Alter's "Society's Cataclysmic Decline in Picturebooks and Visualizations of Fairy Tales." In her reading of two very different adaptations of the fairy tales *Hansel and Gretel* and *The Girl in Red* as well as the visualization of a well-known children's rhyme *The House That Crack Built*, Alter explores the various ways in which words, images, and generic characteristics interact. Here too, the reading of images vis-à-vis other modes becomes important highlighting both the complexity of meaning-making as well as its significance and possibilities for teaching.

Finally, the contribution "Students Exploring Dystopias in Fiction and Film – A Classroom Practice Report" by Nadine Krüger, Christian Ludwig, and Nicole Maruo-Schröder turns our attention to higher education. Based on a project developed and implemented in two Literary and Cultural Studies seminars at the University of Koblenz-Landau and the University of Education Karlsruhe, the contribution focuses on how involving students in small-scale research projects can increase their engagement in their own learning. While one group of students concentrated on analyzing dystopian worlds in fiction and film, the second group looked at young adult dystopian narratives from an EFL-methodology perspective investigating the potential of young adult dystopias for the English classroom. Examples of some of the resulting poster projects demonstrate how the students explored both the realms of dystopia in contemporary texts and used the opportunity to present their research in the context of a real, academic conference. The volume closes with a selected bibliography providing a point of orientation in the current field of researching and teaching young adult dystopian fiction, particularly for those who are new to the topic.

Finally, the contributors would like to thank all those involved in the realization of the conference "'Tell Freedom, I said Hello': Issues in Contemporary Young Adult Dystopian Fiction" which took place in January 2016 at the University of Koblenz-Landau. Despite the rather gloomy topic, we enjoyed lively and fruitful presentations and discussions including the contributions of our students, particularly the participants of Nadine Krüger's and Nicole Maruo-Schröder's "Dystopia-courses" in the winter term 2015/2016 in Karlsruhe and Koblenz respectively. We would like to particularly thank Gisela Anheier, Benedikt Mediger, and Katharina Maurer for their help with the conference organization. Michelle Bebbon, Max Bähr, Patricia Kappenberger, Arthur Klein, and Robin Lohman helped tirelessly with the preparation of the manuscript, including the bibliographies.

Notes

[1] Ursula K. Heise (2015). "What's the Matter with Dystopia?" *Public Books*. 2 Jan. 2015, n. pag. Web. 3 Apr. 2017 <http://www.publicbooks.org/whats-the-matter-with-dystopia/>.

[2] Balaka Basu, Katherine R. Broad, and Carrie Hintz (2013b). "Introduction." *Contemporary Dystopian Fiction for Young Adults: Brave New Teenagers*. Ed. Basu, Broad and Hintz. New York: Routledge, 1-15, 9.

[3] Here, particularly in the connection between the genre of dystopia and the young adult novel, Mike Cadden's notion of "nexus" is useful – understood as "a core of connections and links" to a variety of genres, traditions, and literary modes (2011, 303). Used in the context of the "novel for young readers," the concept highlights that this genre is characterized by aspects as different as "structurally-defined" vs. "age-based" (implying very different hierarchies and categorizations) as well as issues such as length, literary mode, and narrative pattern (2011, 303, 305). Mike Cadden (2011). "Genre as Nexus: The Novel for Children and Young Adults." *Handbook of Research on Children's and Young Adult Literature*. New York: Routledge, 302-313.

[4] Heise (2015), n.pag.

[5] Fátima Vieira (2010). "The Concept of Utopia." *The Cambridge Companion to Utopian Literature*. Ed. Gregory Claeys. Cambridge: Cambridge University Press, 3-27, 4. Yet, she also points out that "More did not invent utopianism" although he coined the word (2010, 6).

[6] Vieira (2010), 5.

[7] Lyman T. Sargent (1994). "The Three Faces of Utopia." *Utopian Studies* 5.1, 1-37, 9.

[8] Vieira (2010), 6.
[9] Alcena M. Davis Rogan (2009). "Utopian Studies." *The Routledge Companion to Science Fiction.* Ed. Bould et al. Oxon: Routledge, 308-316, 309.
[10] Sargent (1994, 9); Graham J. Murphy (2009b). "Eutopia." *The Routledge Companion to Science Fiction.* Ed. Bould et al. Oxon: Routledge, 478-483, 478.
[11] Sargent (1994), 9.
[12] Edward Bellamy's *Looking Backward, 2000-1887* (1888) would be one example. While the novel inspired a variety of movements that took up its 'socialist' ideas, it also sparked a number of 'anti-utopian' responses in the form of novels. See Jean Pfaelzer (1988). *The Utopian Novel in America 1886-1896: The Politics of Form.* Pittsburgh: The University of Pittsburgh Press; chapt. 2 and 4.
[13] Basu, Broad, and Hintz (2013b), 2.
[14] Sargent (1994), 9.
[15] Graham J. Murphy (2009a). "Dystopia." *The Routledge Companion to Science Fiction.* Ed. Bould et al. Oxon: Routledge, 473-477, 473.
[16] Tom Moylan (2000). *Scraps of Untainted Sky: Science fiction, Utopia, Dystopia.* Boulder: Westview Press, 133; see also Murphy (2009a), 473.
[17] Moylan (2000), 122; Murphy (2009a), 473. Moylan discusses the "anti-utopia" extensively, drawing attention to the fact that here, too, one can distinguish a more conservative view, in which utopia is seen as utterly fruitless and a sign of political naivety, from a newer tradition whose anti-utopian vision aims at criticizing and warning the political left, whose 'utopian' visions of equality and egalitarianism can also easily turn into dystopian political structures (2000, 124f.).
[18] Raffaela Baccolini and Tom Moylan (2003). "Introduction: Dystopia and Histories." *Dark Horizons: Science Fiction and the Dystopian Imagination.* Ed. Baccolini and Moylan. New York: Routledge, 1-11, 2. According to them, the critical utopia developed in the 1970s in the wake of the prevalence of dystopian visions after the two world wars.
[19] Scott Westerfeld (2010). "Breaking Down the System." "The Dark Side of Young Adult Fiction." *New York Times Online*, n.pag. Web. 10 June 2017 <https:// www.nytimes.com/roomfordebate/2010/12/26/the-dark-side-of-young-adult-fiction/breaking-down-the-system>.
[20] Maggie Stiefvater (2010). "Pure Escapism." "The Dark Side of Young Adult Fiction." *New York Times Online*, n.pag. Web. 10 June 2017 <https://www.ny times.com/roomfordebate/2010/12/26/the-dark-side-of-young-adult-fiction/pure-escapism-for-young-adult-readers>. See also the other voices in the discussion on the *New York Times* webpage, "The Dark Side of Young Adult Fiction" (2010). Web. 10 June 2017 <https://www.nytimes.com/roomfordebate/2010/12/26/the-dark-side-of-young-adult-fiction>.

Bibliography

Baccolini, Raffaella, and Tom Moylan (2003). "Introduction: Dystopia and Histories." *Dark Horizons: Science Fiction and the Dystopian Imagination.* Ed. Baccolini and Moylan. New York: Routledge, 1-11.

Basu, Balaka, Katherine R. Broad, and Carrie Hintz (eds.). (2013a). *Contemporary Dystopian Fiction for Young Adults: Brave New Teenagers.* New York: Routledge.

---. (2013b). "Introduction." Basu, Broad, and Hintz (eds.) (2013a), 1-15.

Cadden, Mike (2011). "Genre as Nexus: The Novel for Children and Young Adults." *Handbook of Research on Children's and Young Adult Literature.* New York: Routledge, 302-313.

Day, Sara K., Miranda A. Green-Barteet, and Amy L. Montz (eds.) (2014). *Female Rebellion in Young Adult Dystopian Fiction.* Farnham: Ashgate.

Heise, Ursula K. (2015). "What's the Matter with Dystopia?" *Public Books.* 2 Jan. 2015: n. pag. Web. 3 Apr. 2017 <http://www.publicbooks.org/whats-the-matter-with-dystopia/>.

Hintz, Carrie, and Elaine Ostry (eds.) (2003). *Utopian and Dystopian Writing for Children and Young Adults.* New York: Routledge.

Moylan, Tom (2000). *Scraps of the Untainted Sky: Science Fiction, Utopia, Dystopia.* Bolder: Westview Press.

Murphy, Graham J. (2009a). "Dystopia." *The Routledge Companion to Science Fiction.* Ed. Mark Bould, Andrew M. Butler, Adam Roberts, and Sherryl Vint. Oxon. Routledge, 473-477.

---- (2009b). "Eutopia." *The Routledge Companion to Science Fiction.* Ed. Mark Bould, Andrew M. Butler, Adam Roberts, and Sherryl Vint. Oxon. Routledge, 478-483.

Pfaelzer, Jean (1988). *The Utopian Novel in America 1886-1896: The Politics of Form.* Pittsburgh: The University of Pittsburgh Press.

Rogan, Alcena Madeline Davis (2009). "Utopian Studies." *The Routledge Companion to Science Fiction.* Ed. Mark Bould, Andrew M. Butler, Adam Roberts, and Sherryl Vint. Oxon. Routledge, 308-316.

Sargent, Lyman T. (1994). "The Three Faces of Utopia." *Utopian Studies* 5.1, 1-37.

Stiefvater, Maggie (2010). "Pure Escapism." "The Dark Side of Young Adult Fiction." *New York Times Online.* n.pag. Web. 10 June 2017 <https://www.nytimes.com/roomfordebate/2010/12/26/the-dark-side-of-young-adult-fiction/pure-escapism-for-young-adult-readers>.

"The Dark Side of Young Adult Fiction." *New York Times Online* (2010). Web. 10 June 2017 <https://www.nytimes.com/roomfordebate/2010/12/26/the-dark-side-of-young-adult-fiction>.

Vieira, Fátima (2010). "The Concept of Utopia." *The Cambridge Companion to Utopian Literature*. Ed. Gregory Claeys. Cambridge: Cambridge University Press, 3-27.

Westerfeld, Scott (2010). "Breaking Down the System." "The Dark Side of Young Adult Fiction." *New York Times Online*. n.pag. Web. 10 June 2017 <https://www.nytimes.com/roomfordebate/2010/12/26/the-dark-side-of-young-adult-fiction/breaking-down-the-system>.

Part I
Literary and Cultural Studies Perspectives

Rüdiger Heinze (Braunschweig)

Through a Glass, Darkly: Contemporary Young Adult Dystopias

1. Old Wine in New Bottles?

In recent years, dystopias have seen an astounding revival. Not that dystopias were ever dead; but the popular and sometimes critical success of some examples across multiple media (fiction, film, comics, TV series, computer games, etc.) is unprecedented. Although notable critic Ursula Heise has of late complained that this recent "flourishing" adds nothing new or interesting to the idea of dystopia and goes hand in hand with dystopia "becoming routine and losing its political power"[1], it nonetheless deserves closer scrutiny, especially regarding the particular versions of dystopia, their respective ideological investments, and the repercussions that are propagated. Also, I think that Heise is (mostly) wrong, for reasons I will discuss below.

Interestingly, the bulk of recent dystopias is identified by their authors as well as their recipients as young adult fiction, for example *The Hunger Games* (2008-2010), *Maze Runner* (2009-2016), *Divergent* (2011-2013), *The Giver* (1993-2012), *Under the Never Sky* (2012-2014), *Uglies* (2005-2007), *Delirium* (2011-2013), *Matched* (2010-2012), and so on, thus, conjoining two currently exceptionally influential literary fields: dystopian fiction and young adult fiction.[2] Given its pervasiveness and the potential impact young adult fiction may have – and demonstrably has – on its recipients, young adult dystopias and their ideological underpinnings deserve even more attention.

Rather than focus on one example, this essay sets out to map at least broadly the current field of young adult dystopian novels and the storyworlds they create.[3] My argument is quite simple: Once one looks beyond – without neglecting – the most famous examples, the extant diversity of dystopian storyworlds and their social, political, and economic imaginings are both overwhelming and underappreciated – if recognized at all. If anything, this diversity would seem to work against casual habituation and routine consumption, while the political investments are, more often than not, acerbic, poignant, and succinct, as I hope will become clear. In the following, I will first discuss concepts, terms, and ongoing critical debates and then lay out the main characteristics and trends of contemporary young adult dystopias with regard to plot, content, themes, and form.

2. Concepts, Terms, Premises – And a Caveat

I do not want to add to the existing quibbles about how exactly to define, label, and differentiate utopia, dystopia, anti-utopia, critical utopia, or any of its other (purported) variants. In his introduction to *Dystopia, Science Fiction, Post-Apocalypse* Eckart Voigts fills more than half a page by listing critical labels.[4] Very few of them shed substantial new light on the well-known relative conceptualization of utopia as an imagined society organized according to principles that readers are supposed to appreciate as significantly better than those organizing the author's contemporary society, and of dystopia as the exact opposite: significantly worse.[5] As has been pointed out numerous times, many utopias/ dystopias contain – by accident or design – ambiguous and/ or ambivalent elements that taint their straightforward perfection/ defectiveness. Considering the partial dependence of our understanding of a given utopia/ dystopia on implied authorial intention, historical context past and present, as well as our own conceptions of good and bad social organization, it is no coincidence that from any given viewpoint many dystopias contain utopian elements, and vice versa.[6] Since all of the dystopian fictions discussed in this essay are more or less recent (few of them are older than two decades), we may take it for granted that their relative context is our contemporary world.

I do want to add, however, a criterion that complements this definition by adding a qualitative, abstract principle: the right of exit. The concept of right of exit is taken from political/ social theory/ philosophy. At its most basic, it refers to "a person's withdrawal from a group or group activities (such as traditions and customs, but also from group authority and influence)"[7] and the actual feasibility, condition, and cost of such withdrawal. Most often, exit rights are discussed within the context of liberalism and liberal democratic societies,[8] because it is here that civic, group, and personal rights most obviously conflict; in fact, it is a hallmark feature of liberal societies that they may conflict at all. For my discussion here, I am not so much interested in the underlying debate about liberalism rather than in the idea itself, because the absence of a (realistic) right of exit (at acceptable cost) implies coerced participation, which in turn is a typical feature of dystopias. We may thus specify what kind of dystopia we are dealing with not only by identifying its organizing principles but also by analyzing its exit rights and their viability, conditions, and costs. In young adult dystopias, where a young generation is typically pitted against an older one in control of society and, as part of growing up, needs to (more or less violently) negotiate its current and prospective position within or against that society – in other words: participation or exit –, the issue is even more pronounced. It is fitting, then, that it is teenagers who are forced to participate in the *Hunger Games*; who are subjected to experiment in the mazes of *The Maze Runner*; who undergo the grueling selection process in the *Divergent* series. In young adult dystopias, the issue of exit rights and forced participation becomes an allegory of growing up and coming of age. Accordingly, almost all of these novels posit their protagonists at crucial junctures and moments of choice; and this choice is one of (non)identification and (non)participation.

That being said, defining the *young adult* dystopia – implying the generic existence, and distinctiveness, both of itself and an 'adult' dystopia – turns out to be much trickier; indeed, so much so that some critics maintain that it cannot be defined, first and foremost because delineation by age is necessarily arbitrary.[9] And in part, I agree. Whose age are we talking about: the protagonist's or the readers' age? Where exactly would be the dividing line between children, teenagers, and adults? Even if there is such a dividing line, we may reasonably assume (and in fact know) that it is subject to historical change. In addition, readership surveys suggest that almost all books are read by almost all kinds of people. In other words, young adult fiction is also read by adults, and adult fiction is also read by teenagers.[10]

Nonetheless, just because a categorical, absolute definition and distinctiveness is hard to come by does not mean we cannot gradually, cumulatively, and probabilistically identify typical features of contemporary young adult dystopias based on syntactic (i.e. language use), semantic (i.e. storyworld, narrative), and pragmatic (i.e. audience interpellation and context) aspects. Mike Cadden proposes the useful idea of genre as nexus,[11] which here means that young adult dystopias are a combination of various genres, categories, and features that, depending on the order and hierarchy in which we arrange them, allow for differently weighed definitions and conceptualizations. This matches the assessment of Eckart Voigts that "the field of contemporary dystopian narratives [and by extension young adult dystopias] is marked by generic hybridity".[12] I propose the following features as the most common and most relevant.

Perhaps most important is the age of the protagonist, who is typically between twelve and eighteen years old. With this age bracket comes adolescence and all its attending issues (construction of identity and sense of self and self-worth, responsibility, independence, sexuality, leaving home, discovering the trappings and imperfections of the adult world), which of course then play an important thematic role in the narrative, love being prime among these. Put more bluntly: "the *conditio sine qua non* of young adult dystopias is a character whose age and sex is close to the targeted readership".[13] Usually, we have one focalizer or autodiegetic narrator, even though there are often several crucial characters. We also tend to have one main narrative that is fairly cohesive. In other words, there is little discursive complication.

Without exception and unsurprisingly – young adult dystopias are, after all, dystopias – there is a strong focus on social/ political (less often: economic) organization and, of course, a concretized dystopian predicament (i.e. an immediate conflict/ problem which the protagonist faces). While all dystopias have limited exit rights, the majority of young adult dystopias have extraordinarily costly exit rights (high likelihood of death), which the protagonists nonetheless try to claim. We often find science fictional and, less often, fantastic elements that are part and parcel of the dystopian predicament.

There usually is a limit on the length and complexity of sentences and paragraphs; this goes hand in hand with fewer and shorter expository, non-focalized passages than in classical dystopias. As a result, the storyworld tends to be fleshed out through plot, conflict, action, and the protagonists, rather than through long descriptions. Note that total length is not a criterion – obviously, one might add, considering the number of extant series and the length of their parts, many of which exceed 300 pages.

In a majority of texts, we find a similar macro-narrative that is the almost inevitable correlative of the adolescent protagonist: There is an underlying conflict between young adults and adults[14] that becomes manifest in the dystopian predicament and its concretization (often a ritual or symbolic event/ transformation). Children and young adolescents are the hope of change and humanity, even if in some cases the protagonists are initially part of the system and only gradually grow discontent – a classic feature of dystopias.[15] Most of the time, (some) adults are responsible for the current state of affairs; (some) adolescents bring change, new perspectives, an unwillingness to accept things as they are, while (some) adults want to keep their privileges and resist change. "Privileging adolescent points of view, YA fiction inverts power relations between young and old".[16] However, almost all young adult dystopias feature exceptional adults that help the adolescent protagonists. In other words, most young adult dystopias feature a classical coming of age narrative.[17]

Importantly, young adult dystopias are published and marketed as young adult dystopias, although this does not necessarily determine their reception and readership, as I have pointed out above. As Hintz and Ostry argue, the success of recent young adult dystopias is based on a double-coded address[18] that makes them palatable to both young adults and adults.[19]

Some critics claim that young adult dystopias lean towards the didactic and educative mode;[20] I am not convinced this is true. As imaginings of alternative social/ political/ economic organizations, both utopias and dystopias always make a point, of course: about what could be better and what could be worse. In this respect, we could consider them educative in the sense of enlightening and didactic in the sense of being critical. However, this is equally true of much literature and art that is not written in the mode of utopia/ dystopia, and such a generalized understanding in fact empties the educational and didactic of any specific meaning. Even if it were true, it would not be more distinctive of young adult dystopias than of classical ones.[21]

Clearly, the young adult dystopia shares generic features with classical dystopias and other genres of young adult fiction in general so that its distinctiveness, while recognizable, is one of degree, not exclusiveness.

Caveat: my findings and assessments are based on some several dozen, mostly Anglophone novels, which I have chosen based on their recent publication (within the last two decades), their original language and cultural context (English, Anglophone, European and North American), and their popularity and impact (based on sales, reviews, extant or impending film adaptation, transnational spread, fan and critical appreciation).[22] There are, however, literally hundreds of novels in many different languages. To boost, many novels have been or are in the process of being expanded into transmedial, transnational franchises, with films, comics, computer games, smart phone applications, fanzines, and so on. As a result, the following generalizations I make are based on what I consider the most important and influential novels; exceptions can most likely be found to every single one of them.

3. Dark, and Getting Darker: The Reality of Contemporary Young Adult Dystopias

Despite their diversity, the majority of contemporary young adult dystopias share prevalent characteristics in terms of plot, themes, and storyworld. First of all, the protagonist, significantly more often than not, is female, between fourteen and sixteen years of age, and at a crucial (symbolic, ritualistic, liminal) juncture in her life; a juncture that goes hand in hand with the dystopian aspect of the society she lives in. This is, perhaps, the most crucial departure from classical dystopias. The latter typically feature an adult protagonist who has more or less settled into the dystopian regime and becomes disenchanted. His or her (attempted) exit therefore has little to do with coming of age and negotiating (adolescent) issues of identity. As a result, while young adult dystopias spend more time on personal issues, classical dystopias spend more time on social and political ruminations. This does not mean, however, that young adult dystopias are focused purely on personal issues; rather, social and political issues are transported more indirectly via their impact on personal issues.

There is a love interest, but it is often complicated by a love triangle. Here, too, young adult dystopias clearly differ from classical ones, where love may play a role, but does not occupy center stage. The romantic complications are almost always intertwined with the dystopian predicament and the attempted exercise of the right of exit. Along with love and romance comes, predictably, more or less explicit sexuality (much more of it than in classical dystopias, and much more talked about by the characters), which is appreciated and discussed in fan forums and extended in fan fiction. The near absence of sex in *The Hunger Games* or the *Maze Runner* is rather an exception than the rule.

There is quite a lot of violence in the novels, and it is often very explicit.[23] In *The Hunger Games* novels, for example, the characters suffer long-lasting physical and psychological harm. In the *Maze Runner* novels, the death toll is extraordinary. Likewise, *Incarceron*, *Uglies*, *Among the Hidden*, *Feed*, *Unwind*, and many more feature scenes of gruesome and extended violence. It should be noted that violence is neither new to recent young adult dystopias, nor exclusive to them: young adult fiction in general has a long tradition of expressly addressing themes such as war, suicide, persecution, exploitation, and immediate and personal physical and psychical harm. Surprisingly enough, occasionally, main characters – sometimes even the protagonists – die at the end of the novel or series, e.g. in the *Divergent* series; or they are revealed to be collaborators with the enemy/ adults, e.g. in *Maze Runner*. Where they survive, they are usually permanently charred, hurt, and traumatized.

Regardless of the fate of the protagonist, the ending often is ambivalent, neither clearly hopeful – or utopian – nor clearly hopeless – or dystopian.[24] An interesting and perennial debate smolders beneath this simple observation: should young adult dystopias, because of their targeted audience, provide a glimmer of hope? Many critics and writers (among them prominent figures such as Monica Hughes or Lois Lowry) argue they should. Kay Sambell summarizes the dilemma and debate. Dystopias usually are dark and admonishing in an attempt to shock readers into awareness and action. But a bleak outlook – so the argument runs – may lead young readers to resign rather than activate them. Where the classic adult dystopia is, and can get away with being, without compromise and without hope,[25] the young adult dystopia should provide a more uplifting or at least open ending: "Whereas the 'adult' dystopia's didactic impact relies on the absolute, unswerving nature of its dire warning, the expression of moral meaning in the children's dystopia is often characterized by degrees of hesitation, oscillation, and ambiguity."[26]

While I believe that Sambell makes an important point about dystopia endings in general and provides a convincing vindication of ambiguous endings in particular, the premise of the argument itself is contrafactual. Many adult dystopias actually have ambiguous endings or even exit rights (or at least weak forced participation); *We* and *1984* are, in fact, exceptions. In *Anthem*, the protagonist is able to escape into the woods fairly easily and is not pursued; the same escape route is possible in *Fahrenheit 451* from the beginning; even in *The Handmaid's Tale*, escape is possible. In *Brave New World*, dissenters are not killed; they may leave "civilization" to live in a reservation; at the end, two characters are exiled to remote islands. Granted, the exit rights are not pleasant, but a far remove from the cost and possibility of exit in, say, *The Hunger Games* or *Under the Never Sky*. In *Player Piano*, the cost of exit is a bland and purposeless, but comfortable life. On the other hand, many young adult dystopias are far bleaker than their alleged "adult" counterparts. Neither *Incarceron*, *Genesis*, *Delirium*, nor *Feed* have much to offer in terms of realistic and acceptable exit rights or sustainable hope for a better future; and in this they are typical rather than exceptional.

Furthermore, the setting is often apocalyptic or post-apocalyptic as an explanation for the dystopian state of affairs. Quite often, two realms are opposed, either city/ wilderness, or center/ margins, reality/ virtual reality, and so on. These binary oppositions do not necessarily mean, however, that one of them is marked as dystopian and the other as a possible exit or beacon of hope. As it turns out, all realms are suffused with the dystopian predicament.

While gender is almost always an issue (though almost always within a heteronormative framework, only the content of gender roles is questioned – what girls and boys should be like –, not the traditional structural binary opposition per se), and class and socioeconomic stratification make at least occasional appearances, race, surprisingly enough, often does not play a major role in the storyworld itself or remains invisible. Actually, in the fight for survival, "transracial" cooperation or even transracial identity is common in novels where race is mentioned at all. This does, of course, not mean that race ceases to be of importance for a contextual consideration of young adult dystopias. The majority of their authors is, after all, white.

The dominant themes and concerns are well-known from older young adult dystopias and classical dystopias, e.g. state control and social system (personal freedom vs. social responsibility and communal demands); surveillance; environment; technology, especially biological engineering; body and/ or emotions/ sexuality, and so on.[27] However, they are reworked and updated to reflect upon their contextual present.

For example, the majority of contemporary young adult dystopias involve bodily and mental manipulation by the state, often for surveillance purposes, e.g. removal of memory (*Maze Runner*), control chips (*Uglies*), bodily modification (*Hunger Games*), sensory enhancement (*Under the Never Sky*), and so forth. Unsurprisingly, many of them, being US-American, are skeptical about centralized government and state control and emphasize the importance of family and individual agency; most of them are heteronormative (see above). But they also address and subvert gender roles and thematize social injustice, rigid class systems, and peer pressure to conform – mentally and physiologically.[28]

Ideas and themes range, among others, from[29]

- a society without a cultural and collective memory (*The Giver*);
- lethal mandatory "circus" games for teenagers (*The Hunger Games*);
- gigantic, lethal laboratories (*Maze Runner*);
- a society divided into personality factions (*Divergent*);
- enforced beautification and mind control (*Uglies*);
- love as a disease (*Delirium*);
- a gigantic prison that is its own world and a realm where society is intentionally kept in a "medieval" state (*Incarceron*);
- a realm of virtual reality and sensory enhancement where people do not see the deprivation of their actual physical surrounding (*Under the Never Sky*);
- total and relentless control of overpopulation (*Among the Hidden*);
- a world in which humanity, as it turns out, has become extinct and sentient robots populate the planet (*Genesis*);
- rampant consumerism and networking brain implants (*Feed*);
- a stellar colony where an initiation ritual forces boys to kill someone to become "men" (and its inhabitants are telepathic; *The Knife of Never Letting Go*);
- to an underground city that is run by a machine on the verge of collapse (*The City of Ember*), and many more.

The more texts are considered, the more texts can be found that are in some way or another surprising and unconventional. We should at least take note that even though they might not constitute the majority, some young adult dystopias do display narrative complexity, multi-strand and episodic narratives,[30] multiple narrative perspectives/ protagonists/ focalizers, long expository passages, or heavy-handed political and economic critique.

In terms of form, medium, and context, there are equally interesting developments, not all of them surprising. Most obviously, many novels come in series, encouraging prolonged and continuous engagement (and, one might add, consumption). Along the same line, it is increasingly more likely that initially mono-medial storyworlds (predominantly novels) will be expanded and adapted into other media, film foremost among them. Many of the novels I have mentioned have been opted for filmic adaptation. Once this process begins, the novels are usually turned into multi-medial and transnational franchises, with graphic novels, computer games, apps, audiobooks, and merchandise.[31] As a result of the multi-medial expansion of a storyworld, there are various and low-threshold routes of access into the fictional universes these novels/ series create, for example in the form of mobile apps, free online fan-made movies, comics, and so on. Lastly, most young adult dystopias – regardless of whether they have already been turned into a franchise – entail chat groups, fan fiction, fan-made trailers (that are supposed to increase the likelihood of the novel being turned into a film), and so forth. Many of these unauthorized remediations and spin-offs are non-profit.[32]

Again, similar to their themes and contents, I have found that while contemporary young adult dystopias stand in a long tradition, their current formal, medial, and contextual manifestations and complications are challengingly diverse, innovative, and complex; and they deserve much more attention.

4. Summary and Assessment

Contemporary young adult dystopias do not come out of nowhere. The 'genre' has an extensive and variegated history that goes back at least to the nineteen fifties and sixties – as Hintz and Ostry impressively document in their comprehensive introduction to *Utopian and Dystopian Writing for Children and Young Adults*. It is to be expected, then, that there are both continuities and innovations, apart from generically necessary features such as adolescent protagonists. And indeed, most contemporary young adult dystopias show a number of continuities. With adolescence come, as I have written above, issues of personal and social identity, love, sexuality, and body. What has changed is the explicitness and insistence with which some of these issues – specifically body and sexuality – are discussed, although some texts from the nineteen seventies already are quite explicit. Love triangles are, perhaps, somewhat more common in contemporary texts, as are – as far as I have been able to ascertain – female protagonists. It is, thus, not surprising that there are entire collections of critical essays addressing female rebellion in young adult dystopias.[33] What I find much more surprising is the fact that while the content of gender roles is questioned – there are plenty of mentally and physically strong female characters and weak and needy male characters –, the heteronormative binary structure of male and female is not. In other words, transgender, intersex, or bi- and/ or homosexuality do not play a role.

The conflict between young adults and adults that almost inevitably derives from the focus on adolescence is a historical and contemporary staple, as is the typical narrative that I have sketched above.[34] The same is true for explicit violence and, to a lesser degree, the problematization of class and socioeconomic discrimination. The fact that the neglect of race is a constant at least in US-American texts should be irritating, to put it mildly. Other thematic continuities include technology in general, surveillance, totalitarian regimes, and technologies of bodily modification (which become genetic with the advent of genetic engineering); here, too, what has changed is the frequency and quality rather than the issue itself: More and more storyworlds display transhuman scenarios (posthumanism, on the other hand, is rare).[35]

In his book *Representations of Technology in Science Fiction for Young People* (in which he also includes, albeit by default, young adult dystopias), Noga Applebaum points to an interesting paradox: The sense of hope at the end of texts (which I argue above is an exaggerated, if not nonexistent phenomenon) "is often intertwined with a rejection of technology, and thus undermines itself; hope in children's SF [and young adult dystopias; my addition] is often associated with an idealised, un-technological past, and as such bears no relevance in the face of rapidly technologised childhoods and their savy inhabitants".[36] And indeed, contemporary young adult dystopias, even more than their predecessors, couple technology with surveillance and (often enforced) bodily manipulation, making them technophobic.

What is new is the sheer number of contemporary storyworlds that are post-apocalyptic and show a relentless, often hostile environment (in this they are squarely within a general trend towards post-apocalyptic scenarios in novels, films, comics, and computer games). Often, the apocalypse has been brought about by war, biological engineering, or some other form of human 'tampering'; natural or unexplained causes exist, but are less frequent. While, contrary to what we may think, seriality is not new, though perhaps more common, the various new media that have appeared in the last decades have of course brought new medial forms of young adult dystopian storyworlds: While many of them still begin in a 'classic' medium (novel or film), most of them sooner or later expand via adaptations and transmedial extensions.

Lastly, it is my impression that the endings of contemporary young adult dystopias – while never cheerful – have become even bleaker. This becomes obvious when we consider storyworlds and endings in terms of right of exit. Many of them have neither theoretical nor actual exit rights. Where they do exist, their cost is usually so prohibitive as to make them inviable to any but the most desperate – and yet the protagonists are usually willing to accept the risks of exit whatever the costs. When we look at endings, we will find that most of the time, there are revolutions, resistances, and incipient changes; at the very least, the old order is unlikely to endure. However, this does not mean that we get to see a new, better order. On the contrary, we may assume that the old order cannot endure, but the storyworlds give no evidence that there cannot be a relapse. More often than not, the ending leaves us with death and destruction and a glimmer of hope that is faint indeed. Whether we agree that this is a bad thing, as Frederic Jameson or Ursula Heise would have it[37], is a matter of debate – a debate that cannot, I believe, be resolved. If we consider the discussions in the respective fan forums and chats relevant and meaningful (a question that would need another article), then it would seem that the reactions at least of those readers are not characterized by frustration and resignation but rather by exhortations of responsibility, solidarity, engagement, and change.

In light of the findings presented here, I think that it is hard to exaggerate the potential and relevance of contemporary young adult dystopias: generally, academically, and in the classroom. Not only because they are so popular (we should be interested in storyworlds that reach, via different media, literally many millions of readers, viewers, listeners, and players);

but also because of the cultural and imaginative work they do: as analogies, allegories, extrapolations, defamiliarizations, and speculations – about personal and communal identity, the social, political, and economic fabric and, fundamentally, about what it means to be human – here and now, as well as in the future that starts to tomorrow and is shaped today. Unsurprisingly, I do not think they have lost any of their power. On the contrary, I find the sheer number and diversity of ideas and storyworlds staggering and heartening – a diversity that needs to be taken seriously if we are to grasp the ideological investments they make and the impact they may have on exactly those readers that will actually shape our future.

Notes

[1] Ursula Heise (2015). "What's the matter with dystopia?" *Public Books*. 2 January 2015, n. pag.

[2] As early as 2003, Hintz and Ostry, in the introduction to their landmark *Utopian and Dystopian Writing for Children and Young Adults*, made the prophetic prediction that young adult dystopias were likely to become much more popular in the next years. Carrie Hintz and Elaine Ostry (2003a). "Introduction." *Utopian and Dystopian Writing for Children and Young Adults.* Ed. Carrie Hintz and Elaine Ostry. New York: Routledge, 1-20.

[3] I follow David Herman's definition of storyworlds as "mental models of who did what to and with whom, when, where, why, and in what fashion in the world to which interpreters relocate – or make a deictic shift – as they work to comprehend a narrative" (306, fn10). David Herman (2003). "Regrounding Narratology: The Study of Narratively Organized Systems of Thinking." *What is Narratology? Questions and Answers Regarding the Status of a Theory*. Ed. Tom Kindt and Hans-Harald Müller. Berlin: de Gruyter, 303-332.

[4] Eckart Voigts (2015a). "Introduction: The Dystopian Imagination – An Overview." *Dystopia, Science Fiction, Post-Apocalypse. Classics – New Tendencies – Model Interpretations*. Ed. Eckart Voigts and Alessandra Boller. Trier: WVT, 1-11, 1.

[5] Lyman Tower Sargent (1994). "The Three Faces of Utopianism Revisited." *Utopian Studies* 5.1, 1-37; 9. Susanna Layh (2014). *Finstere neue Welten. Gattungsparadigmatische Transformationen der literarischen Utopie und Dystopie*. Würzburg: Königshausen & Neumann; Fátima Vieira (2010). "The Concept of Utopia." *The Cambridge Companion to Utopian Literature*. Ed. Gregory Claeys. Cambridge: Cambridge University Press, 3-27; Graham Murphy (2009).

"Dystopia." *The Routledge Companion to Science Fiction*. Ed. Mark Bould et al. New York: Routledge, 473-477; Darko Suvin (2003). "Theses on Dystopia 2001." *Dark Horizons: Science Fiction and the Dystopian Imagination*. Ed. Raffaella Baccolini and Tom Moylan. New York and London: Routledge, 187-201.

[6] Layh 31; Raffaella Baccolini and Tom Moylan (2003). *Dark Horizons: Science Fiction and the Dystopian Imagination*. New York: Routledge, 3; Jane Donawerth (2003). "Genre Blending and the Critical Dystopia." *Dark Horizons: Science Fiction and the Dystopian Imagination*. Ed. Raffaella Baccolini and Tom Moylan. London and New York: Routledge, 30.

[7] Dagmar Borchers and Annamari Vitikainen (eds.) (2012). *On Exit. Interdisciplinary Perspectives on the Right of Exit in Liberal Multicultural Societies*. Berlin and London: De Gruyter, 1.

[8] Chandran Kukathas (1992). "Are There Any Cultural Rights?" *Political Theory* 20.1, 105-139; Oonagh Reitman (2005). "On Exit." *Minorities within Minorities: Equality, Rights, and Diversity*. Ed. Avigail Eisenberg and Jeff Spinner-Halev. Cambridge: Cambridge University Press, 189-208; Daniel Weinstock (2005). "Beyond Exit Rights: Reframing the Debate." *Minorities within Minorities: Equality, Rights, and Diversity*. Ed. Avigail Eisenberg and Jeff Spinner-Halev. Cambridge: Cambridge University Press, 227-246.

[9] Deborah Stevenson (2011). "History of Children's and Young Adult Literature." *Handbook of Research on Children's and Young Adult Literature*. Ed. Shelby Wolf et al. New York: Routledge, 179-192, 179-180.

[10] Stevenson (2011), 181.

[11] Mike Cadden (2011). "Genre as Nexus. The Novel for Children and Young Adults." *Handbook of Research on Children's and Young Adult Literature*. Ed. Shelby Wolf et al. New York: Routledge, 302-312, 303.

[12] Voigts (2015a), 6. See also Donawerth (2003), 29-30.

[13] Voigts, Eckart, and Alessandra Boller (2015b). "Young Adult Dystopia: Suzanne Collins' *The Hunger Games Trilogy* (2008-2010)." *Dystopia, Science Fiction, Post-Apocalypse. Classics – New Tendencies – Model Interpretations*. Ed. Eckart Voigts and Alessandra Boller. Trier: WVT, 411-430, 415; italics in the original.

[14] Hintz and Ostry (2003a), 8.

[15] Tom Moylan (2000). *Scraps of the Untainted Sky. Science Fiction, Utopia, Dystopia*. Boulder: Westview Press, xiii.

[16] Richard Gooding (2014). "Our Posthuman Adolescence: Dystopia, Information Technologies, and the Construction of Subjectivity in M.T. Anderson's *Feed*." *Blast, Corrupt, Dismantle, Erase. Contemporary North American Dystopian Literature*. Ed. Brett Josef Grubisic, Gisèle Baxter and Tara Lee. Waterloo, Ontario: Wilfrid Laurier University Press, 111-127, 111.

[17] Hintz and Ostry (2003a), 9.

[18] *Ibid.*, 7.

[19] Some, such as Beckett's *Genesis*, are explicitly addressed to both young adult and adult readers; see Sibylle Machat (2013). *In the Ruins of Civilization. Narrative Structures, World Constructions and Physical Realities in the Post-Apocalyptic Novel*. Trier: WVT, 191.
[20] Voigts and Boller (2015b), 412; Stevenson (2011), 181; Hintz and Ostry (2003), 7; Kay Sambell (2003). "Presenting the Case for Social Change: The Creative Dilemma of Dystopian Writing for Children." *Utopian and Dystopian Writing for Children and Young Adults*. Ed. Carrie Hintz and Elaine Ostry. New York and London: Routledge, 163-178, 163.
[21] Gooding (2014), 111.
[22] My corpus comprises all primary texts listed below; however, not every single one of them is expressly mentioned in the essay.
[23] Contrary to what we might expect considering the visuality of the medium film, it is not the film adaptations that introduce or exacerbate the violence.
[24] As such they are fully within the trend Lyman Tower Sargent identifies for the majority of utopias/ dystopias written since the beginning of the nineteen nineties. Sargent (2004). "Utopian Literature in the United States 1990-2000." *Dreams of Paradise, Visions of Apocalypse: Utopia and Dystopia in American Culture*. Ed. Jaap Verheul. VU University Press: 2004, 207-219, 207-208.
[25] Sambell (2003), 164.
[26] *Ibid*., 164. See also Noga Applebaum (2010). *Representations of Technology in Science Fiction for Young People*. London: Routledge, 11-12.
[27] See Boller and Gertzen in this collection for a discussion of environmental problems, Schäfer-Althaus for the discussion of gender/ sexuality, and Maruo-Schröder for a discussion of the body in young adult dystopian fiction.
[28] At this point, entire essay collections are dedicated to a number of young adult dystopia series on top of individual essays on individual books. See, for example, Courtland Lewis (ed.) (2016). *Divergent and Philosophy. The Factions of Life*. Chicago: Open Court; Mary Pharr and Leisa Clark (eds.) (2012). *Of Bread, Blood and The Hunger Games. Critical Essays on the Suzanne Collins Trilogy*. Jefferson, N.C.: McFarland & Company. Many chapters and essays in these collections address issues of gender; some collections specifically the predominantly female protagonists: Sara Day, Miranda Green-Barteet, and Amy Montz (2014). *Female Rebellion in Young Adult Dystopian Fiction*, London and New York: Routledge.
[29] See also Eisenmann's contribution in the second part of the collection for an overview of topics and issues discussed in recent young adult dystopias.
[30] Cadden (2011), 305.
[31] Cynically enough, one *Hunger Games* app claims to test the user's survival skill.
[32] All of these aspects can be used in the classroom to activate and engage students. Young adult dystopian storyworlds are 'cool', they provide multiple points of entry (app, comic, film, etc.), and most of these entries are affordable and thus non-exclusive.

[33] Day, Green-Barteet, and Montz (2014).
[34] I would disagree with the assessment that Pharr and Clark make in their edited collection on *The Hunger Games* that contemporary young adult dystopias end with a personally and socially wider reaching change than older ones (8). Obvious examples to the contrary would be the *Tripod* series or Monica Hughes' *The Tomorrow City*.
[35] By transhumanism, I mean extensions, modifications, and other intentional changes made to the human body and mind in order 'improve' its capacities; post-humanism, on the other hand, I take to stand in the tradition of the rejection of anthropocentrism. One of the very few prominent examples of the latter would be *Genesis* by Bernard Beckett.
[36] Applebaum (2010), 12.
[37] Frederic Jameson (2004). "The Politics of Utopia." *New Left Review* 25, 46. Heise (2015).

Bibliography

Primary Literature

Anderson, Matthew T. (2002). *Feed.* Somerville: Candlewick Press.
Beckett, Bernard (2006). *Genesis*. London: Quercus.
Carmody, Isobelle (1987). *Obernewtyn*. London: Bloomsbury.
--- (1990). *The Farseekers*. New York: Random House.
--- (1995). *Ashling*. New York: Random House.
--- (1999). *The Keeping Place*. New York: Bluefire.
--- (2008). *The Stone Key*. New York: Random House.
--- (2011). *The Sending*. Melbourne: Penguin Books.
Collins, Suzanne (2008). *The Hunger Games*. London: Scholastic.
--- (2009). *The Hunger Games: Catching Fire*. London: Scholastic.
--- (2010). *The Hunger Games: Mockingjay*. London: Scholastic.
Condie, Ally (2010). *Matched.* New York: Dutton Books.
--- (2011). *Crossed.* New York: Dutton Books.
--- (2012). *Reached.* New York: Dutton Books.
Dashner, James (2009). *The Maze Runner*. New York: Delacorte Press.
--- (2010). *The Scorch Trials*. New York: Delacorte Press.
--- (2011). *The Death Cure*. New York: Delacorte Press.
--- (2012). *The Kill Order*. New York: Delacorte Press.
--- (2016). *The Fever Code*. New York: Delacorte Press.
DeStefano, Lauren (2011). *Wither*. London: HarperVoyager.
--- (2012). *Fever*. New York: Simon & Schuster.
--- (2013). *Sever*. New York: Simon & Schuster.

Fisher, Catherine (2007). *Incarceron*. London: Hodder Children's Books.
--- (2008). *Sapphique*. London: Hodder Children's Books.
Haddix, Margaret Peterson (1998). *Among the Hidden*. New York: Simon & Schuster.
--- (2001). *Among the Impostors*. New York: Simon & Schuster.
--- (2002). *Among the Betrayed*. New York: Simon & Schuster.
--- (2003). *Among the Barons*. New York: Simon & Schuster.
--- (2004). *Among the Brave*. New York: Simon & Schuster.
--- (2005). *Among the Enemy*. New York: Simon & Schuster.
--- (2006). *Among the Free*. New York: Simon & Schuster.
Lloyd, Saci (2008). *The Carbon Diaries 2015*. London: Hodder Children's Books.
--- (2009). *The Carbon Diaries 2017*. London: Hodder Children's Books.
Lowry, Lois (1993). *The Giver*. New York: Houghton Mifflin.
--- (2000). *Gathering Blue*. New York: Houghton Mifflin.
--- (2004). *Messenger*. New York: Houghton Mifflin.
--- (2012). *Son*. New York: Houghton Mifflin.
Lu, Marie (2011). *Legend*. New York: G. P. Putnam's Sons.
--- (2013a). *Prodigy*. New York: G. P. Putnam's Sons.
--- (2013b). *Champion*. New York: G. P. Putnam's Sons.
--- (2013c). *Life before Legend: Stories of the Criminal and the Prodigy*. New York: G. P. Putnam's Sons.
Oliver, Lauren (2011). *Delirium*. New York: Harper.
--- (2012). *Pandemonium*. New York: Harper.
--- (2013). *Requiem*. New York: Harper.
Pullman, Philip (2012). *His Dark Materials: Northern Lights, The Subtle Knife, The Amber Spyglass*. London: Scholastic.
Reeve, Philip (2001). *Mortal Engines*. London: Scholastic.
--- (2003). *Predator's Gold*. London: Scholastic.
--- (2005). *Infernal Devices*. London: Scholastic.
--- (2006). *A Darkling Plain*. London: Scholastic.
--- (2009). *Fever Crumb*. New York: Scholastic.
--- (2010). *A Web of Air*. New York: Scholastic.
--- (2011). *Scrivener's Moon*. London: Scholastic.
Robinson, Kim Stanley (1993). *Red Mars*. New York: Bantam Books.
--- (1994). *Green Mars*. New York: Bantam Books.
--- (1996). *Blue Mars*. New York: Bantam Books.
--- (2004). *Forty Signs of Rain*. London: HarperCollins.
--- (2005). *Fifty Degrees Below*. New York: Bantam Books.
--- (2007). *Sixty Days and Counting*. New York: Bantam Books.
Rossi, Veronica (2012). Under the Never Sky. New York: HarperCollins.
--- (2013). *Through the Ever Night*. New York: HarperCollins.
--- (2014). *Into the Still Blue*. New York: HarperCollins.
Roth, Veronica (2011). *Divergent*. New York: Katherine Tegen Books.

--- (2012). *Insurgent*. New York: Katherine Tegen Books.
--- (2013). *Allegiant*. New York: Katherine Tegen Books.
Shusterman, Neal (2007). *Unwind*. New York: Simon & Schuster.
--- (2012). *UnWholly*. New York: Simon & Schuster.
--- (2013). *UnSouled*. New York: Simon & Schuster.
--- (2014). *UnDivided*. New York: Simon & Schuster.
Westerfeld, Scott (2005a). *Uglies*. New York: Simon Pulse.
--- (2005b). *Pretties*. New York: Simon Pulse.
--- (2006). *Specials*. New York: Simon Pulse.
--- (2007). *Extras*. New York: Simon Pulse.

Secondary Literature

Applebaum, Noga (2010). *Representations of Technology in Science Fiction for Young People*. London and New York: Routledge.

Baccolini, Raffaella and Tom Moylan (2003). *Dark Horizons: Science Fiction and the Dystopian Imagination*. New York: Routledge.

Borchers, Dagmar, and Annamari Vitikainen (eds.) (2012). *On Exit. Interdisciplinary Perspectives on the Right of Exit in Liberal Multicultural Societies*. Berlin and London: De Gruyter.

Cadden, Mike (2011). "Genre as Nexus. The Novel for Children and Young Adults." *Handbook of Research on Children's and Young Adult Literature*. Ed. Shelby Wolf et al. New York: Routledge, 302-312.

Day, Sara, Miranda Green-Barteet, and Amy Montz (eds.) (2014). *Female Rebellion in Young Adult Dystopian Fiction*. London and New York: Routledge.

Donawerth, Jane (2003). "Genre Blending and the Critical Dystopia." *Dark Horizons: Science Fiction and the Dystopian Imagination*. Ed. Raffaella Baccolini and Tom Moylan. London and New York: Routledge, 29-46.

Gooding, Richard (2014). "Our Posthuman Adolescence: Dystopia, Information Technologies, and the Construction of Subjectivity in M.T. Anderson's *Feed*." *Blast, Corrupt, Dismantle, Erase. Contemporary North American Dystopian Literature*. Ed. Brett Josef Grubisic, Gisèle Baxter and Tara Lee. Waterloo, Ontario: Wilfrid Laurier University Press, 111-127.

Heise, Ursula (2015). "What's the Matter with Dystopia?" *Public Books*. 2 Jan. 2015: n. pag. Web. 3 Apr. 2017.

Herman, David (2003). "Regrounding Narratology: The Study of Narratively Organized Systems of Thinking." *What is Narratology? Questions and Answers Regarding the Status of a Theory*. Ed. Tom Kindt and Hans-Harald Müller. Berlin: de Gruyter, 303-332.

Hintz, Carrie, and Elaine Ostry (2003a). "Introduction." *Utopian and Dystopian Writing for Children and Young Adults*. Ed. Carrie Hintz and Elaine Ostry. New York and London: Routledge, 1-20.

--- (eds.) (2003b). *Utopian and Dystopian Writing for Children and Young Adults*. New York and London: Routledge.

Hughes, Monica (2003). "The Struggle between Utopia and Dystopia in Writing for Children and Young Adults." *Utopian and Dystopian Writing for Children and Young Adults*. Ed. Carrie Hintz and Elaine Ostry. New York and London: Routledge, 156-160.

Jameson, Frederic (2004). "The Politics of Utopia." *New Left Review* 25, 35-54.

Kukathas, Chandran (1992). "Are There Any Cultural Rights?" *Political Theory* 20.1, 105-139.

Layh, Susanna (2014). *Finstere neue Welten. Gattungsparadigmatische Transformationen der literarischen Utopie und Dystopie*. Würzburg: Königshausen & Neumann.

Lewis, Courtland (ed.) (2016). *Divergent and Philosophy. The Factions of Life*. Chicago: Open Court.

Machat, Sibylle (2013). *In the Ruins of Civilization. Narrative Structures, World Constructions and Physical Realities in the Post-Apocalyptic Novel*. Trier: WVT.

Murphy, Graham (2009). "Dystopia." *The Routledge Companion to Science Fiction*. Ed. Mark Bould et al. New York: Routledge, 473-477.

Moylan, Tom (2000). *Scraps of the Untainted Sky. Science Fiction, Utopia, Dystopia*. Boulder: Westview Press.

Pharr, Mary, and Leisa Clark (eds.) (2012). *Of Bread, Blood and The Hunger Games. Critical Essays on the Suzanne Collins Trilogy*. Jefferson, N.C.: McFarland & Company.

Reitman, Oonagh (2005). "On exit." *Minorities within Minorities: Equality, Rights, and Diversity*. Ed. Avigail Eisenberg and Jeff Spinner-Halev. Cambridge: Cambridge University Press, 189-208.

Sambell, Kay (2003). "Presenting the Case for Social Change: The Creative Dilemma of Dystopian Writing for Children." *Utopian and Dystopian Writing for Children and Young Adults*. Ed. Carrie Hintz and Elaine Ostry. New York and London: Routledge, 163-178.

Sargent, Lyman Tower (2004). "Utopian Literature in the United States 1990-2000." *Dreams of Paradise, Visions of Apocalypse: Utopia and Dystopia in American Culture*. Ed. Jaap Verheul. Amsterdam: VU University Press, 207-219.

--- (1994). "The Three Faces of Utopianism Revisited." *Utopian Studies* 5.1, 1-37.

Stevenson, Deborah (2011). "History of Children's and Young Adult Literature." *Handbook of Research on Children's and Young Adult Literature*. Ed. Shelby Wolf et al. New York: Routledge, 179-192.

Suvin, Darko (2003). "Theses on Dystopia 2001." *Dark Horizons: Science Fiction and the Dystopian Imagination*. Ed. Raffaella Baccolini and Tom Moylan. New York and London: Routledge, 187-201.

Vieira, Fátima (2010). "The Concept of Utopia." *The Cambridge Companion to Utopian Literature*. Ed. Gregory Claeys. Cambridge: Cambridge University Press, 3-27.

Voigts, Eckart (2015a). "Introduction: The Dystopian Imagination – An Overview." *Dystopia, Science Fiction, Post-Apocalypse. Classics – New Tendencies – Model Interpretations*. Ed. Eckart Voigts and Alessandra Boller. Trier: WVT, 1-11.

---, and Alessandra Boller (2015b). "Young Adult Dystopia: Suzanne Collins' *The Hunger Games Trilogy* (2008-2010)." *Dystopia, Science Fiction, Post-Apocalypse. Classics – New Tendencies – Model Interpretations*. Ed. Eckart Voigts and Alessandra Boller. Trier: WVT, 411-430.

--- (eds.) (2015c). *Dystopia, Science Fiction, Post-Apocalypse. Classics – New Tendencies – Model Interpretations*. Trier: WVT.

Wegner, Phillip (2009). *Life Between Two Deaths, 1989-2001. U.S. Culture in the Long Nineties*. Durham and London: Duke University Press.

Weinstock, Daniel (2005). "Beyond Exit Rights: Reframing the Debate." *Minorities within Minorities: Equality, Rights, and Diversity*. Ed. Avigail Eisenberg and Jeff Spinner-Halev. Cambridge: Cambridge University Press, 227-246.

Nicole Maruo-Schröder (Koblenz)

Technological Progress, Adult Power, and Teenage Bodies in 21st-Century Dystopias

1. Introduction: Young Adult Dystopia in the 21st Century

When I grew up, the world was relatively safe, at least from a literary point of view, or so was my impression. Reading my way through the local library's shelves of (young adult) literature in the 1980s, I remember coming across John Christopher's *Tripods* trilogy (1967-1968), Gudrun Pausewang's *Die Wolke* (1987; *Fall-Out*, 1997), Margaret Atwood's *The Handmaid's Tale* (1985), and Richard Bachmann's/ Stephen King's *The Running Man* (1982). I also worked my way through George Orwell's *Nineteen-Eighty Four* (1948) and Aldous Huxley's *Brave New World* (1932), both of which, however, did not captivate me much at the time. While there were certainly more dystopian novels available, I did not encounter any of them, simply because the genre of young adult dystopian novels did not become popular until a couple of decades later.

Today, the story would have been much different. Both, my local library and bookstore feature a lot of dystopian novels for teenage readers in addition to audiobooks and film adaptations. The number of literary dystopias seems, in fact, almost overwhelming. When I started reading young adult dystopian novels in preparation for this project, I was positively surprised by the quality of most of the books. Some of them are formulaic, maybe written and published too quickly after the enormous success of Suzanne Collins' landmark trilogy *The Hunger Games* (2008-2010) and its eponymous film adaptations. And sometimes, after reading so many of them, it is hard to tell them apart, with main characters merging into each other, plotlines becoming confused, and details fuzzy. Nevertheless, what I encountered when I read these novels was a diverse range of ideas, relevant topics, and timely criticism of a lot of the problems that we are creating today. Many of these novels take up important issues, such as effects of war (Marie Lu, *Legend* (2011); Lauren Oliver, *Delirium* (2011); Lissa Price, *Starters* (2012); Veronica Roth,

Divergent (2011); Dan Wells, *Partials* (2012)), environmental destruction (Julianna Baggott, *Pure* (2012); Paolo Bacigalupi, *Ship Breaker* (2010); Saci Lloyd, *The Carbon Diaries 2015* (2008); Veronica Rossi, *Under the Never Sky* (2012)), unchecked, rampant capitalism (Matthew T. Anderson, *Feed* (2002); Alex London, *Proxy* (2013)) as well as the backside of technological and scientific progress (Karen Sandler, *Tankborn* (2011); Neal Shusterman, *Unwind* (2007); Teri Terry, *Slated* (2012)).[1] Taking up motifs and topoi from older examples of the dystopian genre, they are far from simply being repetitive or formulaic. Rather, they update long-standing issues and traditional patterns, making them relevant and comprehensible for a younger audience.

In this respect, a combination of the genre of dystopia with that of young adult literature is only logical since both are linked by their didactic impetus. As I briefly discuss in the next chapter, young adult dystopian fiction draws on two different literary typologies that complement each other: It combines the story of individual maturation with one of political awakening so that finding one's own place in society goes hand in hand with criticizing that society. The concern with individual issues, the personal, so to speak, is linked to and even becomes the political in significant ways in these novels because of their generic hybridity. I argue that one of the key sites of this connection between the personal and the political is the body. In many young adult dystopian novels, the body is not only the battleground for the discussion of morally and ethically controversial questions; it also becomes, as I hope to show, a catalyst for political enlightenment and subsequent action in complex and relevant, sometimes also problematic ways. This concern with the body ranges from alterations of memory and identity to the creation of artificial bodies, a concern that can be linked to current discussions of the posthuman body. In the following, I focus on the aspects of emotions and body alterations. The first dimension becomes particularly visible in the romance plot of these narratives: As I illustrate with a reading of Lauren Oliver's *Delirium* as well as Karen Sandler's *Tankborn*, the function of the romance goes beyond spicing up the plot for a teenage audience and has, in fact, sociopolitical implications. Secondly, I turn to the aspect of physical changes (deliberate or accidental) of the body. Such bodily alterations are closely connected to the issue of social control as I again show with a reading of two recent dystopian novels, Julianna Baggot's *Pure* and Sandler's *Tankborn*, focusing on the multiple ways in which social distinctions are expressed by and inscribed into bodies. While class status is an important factor in many dystopian novels, race and ethnicity, as I will show, are frequently hidden, either because protagonists are white or their racial or ethnic affiliation is not foregrounded. Since the individual body (as an image for society at large) is often the site of political and social control in an attempt to perpetuate and stabilize customary social structures and hierarchies, I will end by discussing the ways in which this can be linked to the negotiation of principles like freedom, choice, and the notion of being (post)human in 21st century dystopias.

2. The Personal is Political: Individual Maturation, Political Awakening, and the Adolescent Body

Dystopia, as Carrie Hintz and Elaine Ostry so aptly observe, "can act as a powerful metaphor for adolescence" since growing up out of sync with one's environment, particularly the seemingly totalitarian authority of parents and the pressure of hostile high-school peers, can pretty much feel like dystopia.[2] Moreover, both genres, dystopia and young adult literature, have further things in common when one looks at their characteristics.[3] With Lyman T. Sargent, dystopia can be understood as "a non-existent society described in considerable detail and normally located in time and space that the author intended a contemporaneous reader to view as considerably worse than the society in which that reader lived."[4] Young adult literature, in turn, features stories of maturation at whose heart lies, in the words of Maria Nikolajeva, "the examination of power positions, the affirmation or interrogation of the existing order of power."[5] While according to her "the protagonist gradually accepts the adult normativity" upon entering adulthood, children's literature can also be subversive, questioning the norms and ideologies of the adult world and making the youngsters powerful enough to interrogate and change existing social structures.[6] Thus, the dystopian genre's interrogation of current social and political developments fits well to the exploration of the ideological and normative bases of the adult world as it is done in young adult literature. The body, as I will show in the following, is important for both.

Throughout human history and in many different ways, the body has served as a site of social control, which becomes visible in ways as diverse as medieval sumptuary laws or 21st-century health discourses.[7] Just as views of the body can be roughly categorized into naturalistic and constructionist perspectives, which see the body as a product of nature and culture respectively,[8] the discourses with which societies control (deviant) bodies can be categorized accordingly: racist body typification, for instance, draws on views that see the body as grounded (exclusively and unchangingly) in biology whereas discourses that seek to form the body according to health or beauty standards are heavily based on the constructionist perspective.[9] Another important aspect that mirrors the divide between nature and culture is the long-standing body-mind division and the frequent denigration of the natural body as merely an outer shell separate from the thinking self. Linked to this opposition between the body's biological needs and characteristics on the one hand and the workings of the intellect on the other are many of the traditional gendered hierarchies that oppose male (standing for, e.g., culture, rationality) and female (standing for, e.g., nature, emotionality) bodies and intellects.[10] This opposition is – in our Western, traditionally patriarchal society – also reflected in the attempt to subject the female body to a variety of controlling mechanisms and practices. Female sexuality in particular has been almost obsessively controlled, which becomes visible, for instance, in marriage practices or discourses about reproductive rights.[11] However, sexuality is one area in which not only the gender aspect of social control becomes visible: The question of who can or should procreate is, of course, intimately linked to race, ethnicity, class, sexual orientation, and disability and the ways they have been negotiated in social, cultural, political, and medical discourses throughout history.

While sexuality is one of the aspects central to my discussion further down, a number of other practices that seek to 'civilize' and control the body are also important. Michel Foucault's notion of the "docile body," disciplined through modern societal institutions and (self-) surveillance shows how views of the biological body, its functions, and needs are influenced by cultural discourses and vice versa.[12] Similarly, Pierre Bourdieu's notion of the "habitus," which highlights the ways in which our bodies can be formed by our social status and the norms and values relevant for it, suggests that human bodies are more than mere biological matter but are influenced by and expressive of social norms, values, and meanings.[13] Put differently, "all of the ways in which the human body has been altered historically can be seen as markers of human culture, and indeed, of humanity."[14] Thus, as Margo DeMello points out, modifications of the body serve to turn "human bodies [...] into social beings,"[15] and consequently, the manner in and degree to which a body has been culturally marked can be used to distinguish between civilized and uncivilized bodies, a distinction that turns bodily differences (absences and presences of 'cultural marks') into hierarchies of humanness and worth. As especially Foucault's idea of disciplining the body makes clear, such cultural practices of (visible and invisible) body modification do not only serve to create hierarchies between bodies but are also used to prescribe the ways in which individuals see, feel, and use their bodies. In Lisa Blackman's words, "*cultural inscriptions*" invite individuals to automatize and, hence, naturalize a society's norms and values by embodying – internalizing – "thoughts, actions, bodily dispositions and habits."[16]

The blurry boundaries between 'natural' and 'cultural' bodies, which become visible in such body modifications, have been acknowledged by more recent theories of 'embodiment.'[17] Based on phenomenological theories, such approaches emphasize that humans and their experiences are grounded in the materiality of the body, and while this materiality is to a certain extent irreducible, social and cultural influences on the body – as history shows – are important as well in the way they create us as humans. This indivisible link between the biological and socio-cultural side of our bodies is highlighted in quite another way in theories of the "posthuman" as well as in notions such as the "cyborg," which also complicate ideas about what it means to be human.[18] Advances in biotechnology and medicine as well as computer science suggest whole new ways to modify – and experience – bodies. What is more, they blur even further the boundaries between the 'natural' and the 'cultural' in ways that range from bodily experience (e.g., in virtual realities) to the body's very materiality (e.g., in the replacement of body parts).

Not surprisingly, therefore, human bodies play a central role in young adult dystopias. Not only does the genre reflect the body's centrality for our sense of self, which becomes especially clear in adolescents' increased concern with their body and bodily changes. The novels also speculate about the future developments of current attitudes to the human body in ways that reflect the above mentioned "cultural inscriptions" with which our bodies are 'formed.' Almost obsessively, teenage bodies are subjected to (social) control in these novels as they are modified – improved and mutilated – or even produced 'from scratch.' In Rossi's *Under the Never*

Sky, (young) bodies are not just genetically enhanced and thus formed according to desired characteristics and traits; they are also kept 'safe' from the 'real' world by way of an eye-implant that links with the virtual world of the "realms," so that actual (bodily) experience is replaced by virtual experience. Moreover, these enhancements and modifications serve to distinguish 'civilized' from 'savage' bodies, creating a hierarchy in which the inhabitants of "Reverie," an artificially built "pod" that keeps humans safe from the consequences of environmental destruction, see themselves as superior to the unmodified "outsiders," a hierarchical distinction that is, however, undermined in the course of the novel. Another striking example is Westerfeld's *Uglies* series, in which teenagers undergo a variety of surgeries that beautify – and standardize – the body and enhance, among other things, sensory experience and the immune system. Part of the procedure is an alteration of the brain that also makes people more docile. Here, too, the 'civilized' city people see their bodies as markers of culture which distinguish them from the less beautiful, less civilized runaways, people who opted to remain unmodified and live in the wilderness. Less comprehensive, yet no less effective are the alterations in Terry's *Slated*, in which the memories of disobedient teenagers are changed to turn them into new, more obedient variations of their old self. At the same time, the 'slated' person is given a bracelet which monitors certain biological processes and thus, helps to keep her or him 'in check.' Despite sometimes horrific side effects, many of the teenagers in these dystopias desire such body modifications to become part of the community, which shows the pressure to fit in with the ideas, norms, and values of society. Moreover, this also visualizes that the social mechanisms at work here do not simply force people to accord with a society's value system but invite them to do so.

As Foucault has pointed out, docile bodies are not necessarily created by (external) force: Rather, people internalize mechanisms and practices of control and therefore participate (unwittingly) in their own surveillance and control.[19] An extreme example of such disciplining can be found in Ally Condie's novel *Matched* (2011), in which people's lives are so meticulously planned that there is literally no space (or time) for deviation. Citizens are required to adhere to a tight daily schedule of work and leisure time, with even their food (vitamins and calorie intake), their daily exercise, their occupation, and their life partner being chosen for them on the basis of statistics. The fact that such regulations pose as necessities for a healthy and happy lifestyle strengthens the conformity that results from such a tightly controlled life, hiding effectively how they actually serve to keep citizens under control. Discipline and (self-) surveillance result in the perpetuation of social norms and values, implemented in conformist behavior, lifestyle, and preferences.

Yet, other, sometimes less obvious or 'invasive' body practices can also serve as means of control. In Collins' *The Hunger Games* trilogy the Capitol exerts power not just via the distribution of resources (notably food) or forms of punishment (the games). Norms and values are also perpetuated via fashion practices, which visualize the exaggeration and abundance of resources in the Capitol and serve to distinguish its inhabitants from those of the districts, an effective categorization that puts everyone in their assigned place in the social hierarchy. Similarly, clothes function as a form of social control in Roth's *Divergent*, as different ways of dressing distinguish the five factions while inscribing the various desired characteristics and traits visibly onto bodies.

In a similarly pervasive manner, teenage sexuality is regulated in these novels, something that I discuss more extensively with the aspect of romance in the next chapter. In Roth's *Divergent*, couples can only come from the same faction and changing one's faction is only possible at the "Choosing Ceremony," not later. In Lu's *Legend*, Kiera Cass' *The Selection* (2012), and Sandler's *Tankborn*, class status is decisive in the regulation of family structures; in the latter, there are even explicit rules forbidding any contact between people – bodies – belonging to the different castes. In Condie's *Matched* and Oliver's *Delirium*, young people are paired for life by the state.[20] In Wells' *Partials*, all women from the age of sixteen upwards are required to become pregnant as often as possible in order to save humanity from extinction. Lauren DeStefano's novel *Wither* (2011) is even bleaker and more obviously brutal in its regulation of female sexuality, since here women are used solely for the pleasure of (older) men.[21] With their rather obvious control of sexual intercourse, these novels ask who owns (teenage) bodies, a twisted reflection of today's discourses on abortion, surrogate pregnancies, and other reproductive rights.

The question of the possession and commodification of bodies becomes similarly visible in the genre's critical assessment of current techno-scientific developments. The production of 'super-humans' in the form of physiologically enhanced soldiers, e.g. in Westerfeld's *Specials*,

Baggott's *Pure*, or Wells' *Partials*, is one important aspect together with the question of whether these enhanced bodies are still human. The boundary between the natural and the artificial body becomes particularly difficult to maintain regarding such techno-scientific modifications of the (natural) body, a decisive problem in many dystopian novels since this boundary determines a person's access to human rights. The soldiers in *Partials*, for instance, serve as underpaid and expendable labor force while the tankborn in the eponymous novel are more obviously slaves. Other novels highlight the profit that can be gained when bodies are 'dispossessed.' While in *Starters* by Price teenage bodies are rented by old people, the question of ownership and commodification of bodies takes an even more gruesome turn in Shusterman's *Unwind*: In a world in which progress in organ transplantation has made it possible to use every single bit of the human body, parents can now get rid of their unwanted and deviant teenage offspring by having them salvaged for their body parts.

As can be seen from my short sketch, young adult dystopias ponder a wide variety of, sometimes long-standing, current and future problems using the body as a field to play out and visualize consequences and implications of current social problems and debates. Moreover, they also visualize the various functions that bodies have in and for social structures, showing a critical awareness of how practices and ideologies impact lives and, more literally, bodies. In the next subchapter, I discuss the aspect of bodily control in more detail with regard to the often found romance in these novels.

3. Romance as Rebellion in Young Adult Dystopias

While all kinds of emotions are controlled in young adult dystopias, love is probably the most important one as at the center of most of these narratives lies a romance,[22] a relationship between the heroine and a partner.[23] Not only does this romance provide a contrast to the dystopian world depicted, it is also complicated, if not made impossible, by the social norms and regulations at play, which threaten to keep the heroine and her love interest apart. In Rossi's *Under the Never Sky*, for instance, Aria meets Peregrin, a so-called 'savage' who lives outside the boundaries of civilized society, and falls in love with him. Similarly, in Lu's novel *Legend*, a romance develops between the main protagonists June and Day, who are divided not just by their class status but also by the fact that they stand on two different sides of the law. In Roth's *Divergent*, Tris is paired with Four although both (seemingly) come from supposedly incompatible communities. The fact that such romantic relationships develop (successfully) 'against all odds,' amidst the mayhem and complications of dystopia probably makes them even more precious for readers, not least since this mirrors to a certain extent the complications of first relationships and young love that teenage and adolescent audiences face.[24]

Particularly in light of the aspect of (sexual) control discussed above, there is more to the romance than a simple catering to teenage interest. The forbidden love is in many cases a catalyst for revealing the shortcomings of the society the heroine lives in; in this sense, it attains political significance, above all in its function as a boundary transgression and rejection of social control. A case in point is the romance found in Oliver's *Delirium*. The novel is relocated in time, set in a highly regulated society of survivors in Portland, Maine. After the destruction of major parts of the US during a war, survivors moved to the few remaining cities, which are heavily guarded against the uncontrolled regions in between, "the wilds." Love has come to be regarded as a disease called "amor deliria nervosa," which is suppressed and considered dangerous since it can lead to passion, hate, and other potentially negative emotions. At the age of eighteen, as an initiation ceremony into adulthood, everybody has to undergo the "cure," a kind of lobotomy that alters the part of the brain responsible for the feeling of love. Adults are then paired by the government to provide for stable, if dispassionate families. All major aspects of life, such as education or media, are likewise highly controlled: Certain types of music and literature – including, for instance, Emily Dickinson's poetry – are forbidden as they are supposed to trigger and further uncontrollable emotions. Similarly, Shakespeare's *Romeo and Juliet* is now considered to be a cautionary tale about the disastrous consequences of love rather than 'the world's greatest love story.'

Having internalized her society's condemnation of emotions, seventeen year-old Lena is looking forward to her own 'cure' when she meets Alex and falls in love with him. Alex turns out to be one of the so-called "invalids," people who opt to live in the wilds, choosing their freedom and emotions over the highly controlled – if safe – environment provided by the totalitarian government. Society's rejection of and attempt to eradicate love, the threat of an ungovernable, illogical emotion, takes up a traditional motif of fictional dystopias, in which governments use all kinds of methods to control people's emotions and bodies to achieve obedience and conformity.[25] It is not surprising, then, that the experience of love makes Lena see the world with new eyes. She undergoes all the phases of the 'disease' but experiences them in a positive way; in fact, the bodily experience of love gives more facets to her life, and all of a sudden, she takes a decisive interest in her own life. After a kiss with Alex, she observes, "[f]or the first time in my life I've done something for me and by choice and not because somebody told me it was good or bad."[26] Combined with the enjoyment of forbidden literature and music as well as the community of friends, the feeling of love clarifies for Lena what people have to give up in order to be unexcitable and 'safe.' The world becomes 'veiled', not governed by preferences, by things that are liked or loved, but by an indifference that characterizes all relations. Moreover, the relationship changes her (self-)perception. Looking at herself in a mirror she realizes,

> [...] I believe what Alex said. I am beautiful.
> But it's not just me. *Everything* looks beautiful. *The Book of Shhh* says that *deliria* alters your perception, disables your ability to reason clearly, impairs you from making sound judgments. But it does not tell you this: that love will turn the whole world into something greater than itself.[27]

The forbidden love for Alex thus helps the heroine to question the totalitarian structures of society. Knowing Alex, moreover, gives her access to the world of the uncured invalids, to which she escapes at the end to join their fight for freedom.[28]

The society shown in *Delirium* takes a long-standing tradition of Western society to its extreme: The dualistic view of body and mind, nature and culture, emotions and rationality, is both questioned and reinforced. Love – signifying an uncontrollable and 'irrational' emotion that influences our actions decisively – is eliminated as dangerous, and the novel clearly shows the negative aspects of a society that is exclusively governed by rationality and control. Without emotions, preferences (the emotional investment in certain things) disappear as well and with them, the novel claims, not just the freedom of choice but also the ability to decide in a morally or ethically sound way.[29] Suppressing the unruly and passionate emotions that threaten to disturb the careful and balanced social order, people in this novel become less human, more inhumane.

Jobs and partners are assigned, literary and musical taste is prescribed; children are cared for but not loved and the same goes for parents and spouses. Even more importantly, everybody who does not succumb or successfully respond to the cure is locked away or even killed.

This body/ mind split is also reflected in the way space is treated in *Delirium*. People live in the city, a highly controlled and restricted space that is guarded against the dangerous wilderness that lies beyond and onto which people project their fear of what they cannot control, including the capability to love. Nature, so the totalitarian government's argument goes, is random and uncontrollable and therefore dangerous, and it becomes the counterpoint to a highly controlled society in which everything is planned, including human preferences. Incidentally, this disorderly wilderness becomes the space of freedom and individuality, where, in turn, the ills of society can be cured. Thus, the novel does not just question the division between body and mind, nature and culture. As nature comes to be a space of freedom in contrast to the 'evil city,' the division between culture and nature, mind and body is to a certain extent reintroduced. Nature – as in a number of other dystopian novels – becomes romanticized as an antidote to whatever has gone wrong with human civilization, a view that is attractive but not very helpful with regard to the tackling of real-life problems.[30]

Although such a dualistic view of body and mind cannot be found in Karen Sandler's *Tankborn*, it also features a love relationship that – among other things – helps to question totalitarian social structures. The novel depicts a world governed by a strict social hierarchy that ranks humans into groups with different rights and privileges. One basic division is, interestingly enough, based on the way someone was born: Those born from a womb are considered humans (both wealthy "trueborns" and poor, landless "lowborns"), whereas genetically engineered people grown in a 'tank' are considered to be non-human (the so-called "GENs" or "tankborns"). In spite of the fact that the technology of genetic modification in a tank is also used by wealthy people to cure and improve themselves, it is used as a marker of difference that distinguishes between freedom and slavery. Tankborns are used as slaves, whose bodies are genetically modified to prepare them for their later assignment as part of a workforce catering to the trueborns. On her first assignment, the novel's main character Kayla meets Devak, the grandson of her 'owner.' Between the two, a forbidden romance develops, which questions the rules and regulations that usually govern relations between trueborns and GENs:

The latter are despised servants, and physical contact, let alone a relationship between tankborns and trueborns is strictly forbidden. Yet, the feelings the protagonists develop for each other help them to cast doubts on the 'naturalized' distinction society creates between naturally born and tankborn people. Despite the 'rational' misgivings about a relationship to Devak, with which she has been indoctrinated, Kayla feels "protected by the emotions that knotted them together" when they kiss, and her love "felt right, perfect."[31] Kayla's feelings, thus, help her to transgress the rules that regulate social interaction, and she realizes that what society has taught her about herself and her proper place in society is not a God-given truth but an ideology which makes sure that the hierarchical caste system stays in place.[32] Devak's attraction to Kayla, in turn, enables him to empathize with her situation so that he feels the inhumanity and injustice of a system that he has taken for granted all his life.

Romance, as these examples illustrate, should not just be seen as a plot device that improves the genre's marketability. As the personal and the political become intertwined in these novels, romance attains a political dimension. In their decision to commit to a relationship that is not sanctioned and even considered illegal by society, these young women also decide to question and rebel against the laws, norms, and values by which their society is governed. "[S]exual awakening," as Sara K. Day observes, can function "as impetus for social resistance" and helps to trigger the heroines' transgression into unsanctioned territory.[33] Moreover, it is the body's capacity to feel that turns people into ethical and moral beings, opposing the inhumanity of social structures based exclusively on rationality and (pseudo-) scientific rules and regulations.

4. (Im)Perfect Bodies: Body Distinctions and the Visibility of Difference

In addition to the emotional and sexual dimension of the body, there are other ways in which the body functions as a site of control in dystopian literature. One of the most obvious aspects is the socially constructed difference between individual bodies. Such a marking of bodies is often closely related to scientific and technological progress in these novels, a timely speculation on the direction today's problems of social and racial stratifications might take. Under the guise of necessity and convenience, ranging from health and improvement to issues of beauty, perfection, or pleasure, teenage bodies are modified – controlled – in many young adult dystopian novels. Here, biological and cultural constructions of the body merge as cultural ideas are inscribed into the biological 'material' of the body without almost any technological (or ethical) limitations. Such fantasies of improvement are – more or less ambiguously – played with so that these novels feature super-healthy citizens (*Matched*, *Uglies*), people with advanced skill-sets (*Under the Never Sky*, *Pure*, *Ship Breaker*), or, simply, perfect – and perfectly functional – super-humans (*Partials*). Still, such enhanced bodies come at a price as most novels point out, thus providing an apt visualization of Foucault's idea of the willingly docile body that submits and responds to social forms of discipline. In Westerfeld's *Uglies*, for instance, cultural ideals (regarding beauty and health) are literally carved onto teenage bodies; yet, the surgical procedures, which render these bodies beautiful and healthy, also make them more "pretty-minded," obedient and uncritical.

Moreover, the enhancement of bodies is also shown to serve as a marker of distinction in these novels, which can work in two ways: While in some novels, bodily modifications are a privilege of the rich and well-to-do (e.g. *Starters* or *Proxy*), i.e. a sign of social distinction that marks the improved bodies as superior, in others, such body modifications serve to create a servant 'underclass,' often also visibly marked as different (e.g. *Partials*).[34] Unsurprisingly, accidental body modifications, often side-effects of environmental problems, are similarly a mark of the socially weak who lack the resources to protect or care for their bodies adequately (e.g. *Pure*).

Although the dystopian genre's focus on problems of social divisions is not surprising – after all, dystopias are extrapolations of current problems and issues – the ways in which these divisions are rendered is. Dystopian worlds are very 'white,' at least on first glance, and the majority of the novels seem to suggest that race and ethnicity will not play a role in the future – and future conflicts – of Western society. How bodies are divided and controlled is mostly based on economic status, which is, however, in most novels not visibly linked to race and ethnicity. This can be regarded as a continuation of the long-standing tradition of representing minorities; as Mary Couzelis convincingly shows, African Americans are either rendered as helpmates of white heroes or ignored altogether.[35] With few exceptions, there are hardly any dystopian novels that feature heroes or heroines of color, and while many of them have all-white casts, a number of them depict secondary characters whose ethnicity is marked as 'non-white.' Thus, in Roth's *Divergent*, Tris' friend Christina is African American, and in James Dashner's *The Maze Runner*, Thomas' friend Alby, the Gladers' leader, is "dark-skinned."[36] Famously, Rue, Katniss's co-contestant from district 11 in *The Hunger Games*, "has bright dark eyes and satiny brown skin and eyes."[37] However, what these characters have in common is that they serve as contrasts and helpers to the main protagonists rather than as heroes in their own right.

While most literary dystopias seem to continue the problem of taking 'white' people as the norm and rendering everyone else invisible, some protagonists are, as a closer look reveals, not necessarily white. In such cases, race or ethnicity is simply not explicitly remarked upon or, rather, it does not play a role in the conflicts depicted. *Legend*'s June, for instance, is "Native, maybe, or Caucasian" with dark eyes and straight black hair whereas her love interest Day features blue eyes and white-blond hair with his face being a "mix of Anglo and Asian."[38] However, distinctions between different social strata of society are not made by skin color but are a matter of access to resources, which is, to my knowledge, nowhere linked to ethnic affiliation in the novel; rather, the description of these features serves to highlight the attractiveness of the protagonists more than anything else. Similarly, the main characters in Bacigalupi's *Ship Breaker* are decidedly non-white, London's main character Syd in *Proxy* is dark-skinned, Baggott's heroine Pressia from *Pure* is half-Japanese, and the fourth installment of Westerfeld's *Uglies*-series, *Extras*, shifts its focus from Tally Youngblood to Aya Fuse, a Japanese girl. Yet, even with such more ethnically and racially diverse heroes and heroines, current problems of racism and racial discrimination are hardly examined in a critical manner.

Tankborn (2012) is a notable exception since it is one of the few novels that take up the issue of race and racism explicitly.[39] Here, "a rich medium brown" is the skin color of status with both darker and lighter colors designating a lower status, a difference in physical features that is supported by clothing style, color, and material as well as little earrings that help identify someone's status.[40] While it uses the wide-spread link between skin color and status, it turns the tables on the West's long-standing assumption that being 'white' is the most prestigious skin color.[41] *Tankborn*'s society is governed by a rigid caste system that strictly regulates the privileges of the different social groups as well as the contact between them. Although skin color is important, the novel also clearly constructs it as an unreliable marker – high-status people (the "true-borns"), usually but not always a "rich medium brown," supplement their status with accessories (clothes and jewelry) to avoid social confusion. Moreover, the most basic social distinction rests not on the body itself but on the way it was 'produced': Those who were grown in a tank and genetically engineered are defined as non-humans who are produced as a slave labor force. Quite in tune with racist colonial practices of bodily mutilations that sought to make 'otherness' unmistakably visible, the tankborn's status is inscribed into the body by a facial tattoo. This tattoo also serves as an 'interface' with which information can be up- or down-loaded into the GEN's brain, which features an additional part, the "annexed brain," that can process data like a computer. Therefore, the tattoo does not simply serve to make visible – and thus detectable – the randomly constructed difference between 'human' and 'slave;' it is a facial marker that also functions as a literal means of control to keep the GEN population in line. It is an appropriate metaphor for the ways in which racist ideologies and how they are caught up in representations of bodies as 'different' serve as means of control and discrimination. Thus, *Tank-born* concerns itself with current ideologies of race, difference, and social status in its critical examination of the mechanisms and practices that invest bodily differences with social meaning. Moreover, it extends this discussion, drawing up a vision of the future in which such ideologies intertwine with science and technology in dangerous ways. In contemplating who is considered human and why, the novel also takes up today's issues and problems surrounding technologies with which humans can be genetically modified and differentiated.

Despite exceptions such as *Tankborn*, it is interesting that in the majority of dystopian novels, in which all our current problems flourish and bloom, issues of race, ethnicity, and the social distinctions that are attached to them simply disappear. I take this less as (naïve) optimism than as a problematic bias continuing the tradition of rendering concerns with and problems of race and racism invisible.[42] Moreover, the mechanisms and practices with which social hierarchies between the privileged and the poor are constructed and regulated in these dystopian societies are very much related to today's racial hierarchies and discriminatory practices. Thus, while race is not explicitly mentioned and tends to remain hidden, its mechanisms are not absent from current dystopian worlds – to the contrary. Here, too, societies are stratified into different groups on the basis of the body's – more or less visible – physical characteristics, which are frequently used to assume different abilities and justify the creation of hierarchies. Moreover, I would argue, race and class are conflated in the merging of the physical, visible dimension of the body with its economic status. The ways in which bodies are marked regulate access to resources and vice versa, as the lack of resources leaves traces on people's bodies.[43] Thus, social divisions become visibly and often permanently inscribed into the body in ways that exaggerate and go beyond what Bourdieu calls a person's habitus. These novels are less concerned with how lifestyle and education, for instance, are inscribed on the body (in often relatively subtle ways), than with artificial interventions into the body in order to mark it as different, either aesthetically (e.g., making it more beautiful) or functionally (improving its abilities). At the same time, many of these novels highlight how socio-economic status is linked to practices of body maintenance such as health care, which also leave traces on the body.[44]

In addition to bodies that are deliberately altered and 'improved' and have been visibly marked by cultural ideas of beauty, health, desired skills, and even leisure time activities, some of the novels feature bodies that have been accidentally altered.[45] A case in point is Baggott's *Pure*, in which humans have survived a nuclear bomb that has not only killed the majority of people but also deformed everybody who was not lucky enough to be inside the protective dome when it went off. The heat and force of the explosion has fused many people with objects they were holding or standing near to. Since outside the dome the world has turned into a post-apocalyptic one, with no medical supplies, food, or other resources, such deformities cannot be undone. Thus, main protagonist Pressia is permanently linked with the doll she was holding during the explosion when she was a little girl. The visible deformity of surviving the war becomes an ostracism in the novel, a justification for the healthy, unmarked people in the dome – the "pures" – not to mingle with the outsiders, the "wretches." While such a distinction between 'pure' and 'impure' bodies is reminiscent of racist ideologies obsessed with racial purity and the categorization and separation of bodies, it also corresponds to ways in which healthy and disabled bodies are distinguished. As discourses about disability show, the 'healthy' and 'perfect' body is often used as standard against which 'unhealthy' bodies are judged and considered as deviant or abnormal.[46] In the novel, 'abnormal' bodies are considered as impure, a representational strategy that suggests bodily deformations to be a defect, even a disease that can spread if one comes into close contact. The human body serves as a marker of difference both visualizing and enforcing the division between people inside and outside the dome, a division that also regulates people's access to resources. Even more interestingly, Baggott adds a religious context, in which the division between the healthy and the deformed, the insiders and the outsiders is constructed and represented as a divine intervention. The prophesied reunion of people from inside and outside the dome is constructed as a 'paradise' for which the "wretched" have to wait patiently since access to it is regulated by the "pure."

In their treatment of (teenage) bodies, young adult dystopian novels reflect thoughtfully on how norms, values, and ideologies can be implemented, perpetuated, and made visible via cultural inscriptions on the body. This includes standards of health and fitness, ideals of beauty as well as desired characteristics, skills, behavior, and even emotions, all of which are – the novels suggest convincingly – intricately intertwined with social distinctions based on class and – often less obviously – ethnicity or race. Bodies, in this sense, have more than individual significance but become carriers of general social meanings that reflect the (dystopian) society's character, most obviously in the visualization of difference.

5. Conclusion: Dystopian Futures in the 21st Century

As my discussion illustrated, dystopian novels for young readers manage to highlight a range of important topics and issues, catering to the concerns and interests of their young audience while also examining issues that their authors see as problematic developments in our current societies. The generic hybridity of these texts allows for a linking of the personal with the political – the individual maturation of the young heroine goes hand in hand with her political awakening: Rebellion against limitations concerning her as an individual turns into a rebellion against the limiting social and political structures imposed by the dystopian society. The importance that the body has for young people in the process of growing up attains therefore an additional dimension: It becomes a key site for the struggle against authority in these dystopian novels. This struggle for control (over individual bodies) has a number of aspects of which I discussed two in more detail: the control of emotions, particularly love and sexual desire as they become visible in the romance plot, and physical modifications of the body. While the romance in these novels can serve as a catalyst, triggering the heroine's political awakening, body modifications often function as visualizations of social control, for example in the form of social distinctions and their inscriptions on individual bodies, something that takes up current discourses on race, ethnicity, and class.

Another aspect prominent in current dystopian novels is the disciplining of teenage bodies. The ways in which alterations of the body – deliberate and accidental – are used as regulatory mechanisms exemplify theories of how (individual, national) bodies can be controlled and, what is more, show the interlinking between coercive power and people's voluntary or unwitting participation in such regulations. While some of the novels fantasize about the almost endless possibilities of such alterations (especially in terms of health, skills, and beauty), most of them never lose their critical edge, illustrating quite clearly the costs – in terms of social inequality or ethical dilemmas, for instance – that might be attached to 'perfect' bodies. Thus, the dream of perfection finds its correspondence in the nightmarish aspects of bodies that are used, commodified, and sold. Additionally, as current medical and technoscientific developments already suggest, the striving for perfection and enhancement brings the increasing convergence of the natural and the artificial into sharp relief, complicating definitions of 'the human.' Illustrating the emergence of the posthuman, dystopian bodies also problematize what it means to be human in more general terms, emphasizing both the idea of human rights and the notion of 'humanity' – being human(e) – which are at stake here. This aspect ranges from the question of which bodies are eligible to enjoy human rights (poor bodies, sick bodies, (semi-)artificial bodies?) to what exactly makes us human and humane in the first place (the way we were 'created', the way we feel, the way we behave or think?).

In addition to such economic and ethical aspects, which are intertwined with issues of class and poverty, the body and its modification can also signify politically: Replacing individuality, diversity, and choice, the (perfected and perfectly controlled) body also signals sameness and conformity. As I argued with regard to the aspect of love, thinking about the body can also serve to reflect on what it means to have a choice, to be human and free: not just the privilege of making (free) choices but also the duty and ability to justify them in a morally and ethically sound way. Moreover, the body also serves to highlight concerns about identity and self-awareness, aspects that are important – as I sketched in the second part of my essay – with regard to the question of who we are. As they are particularly geared toward a younger readership, these dystopian novels provide ample opportunity to discuss and analyze the concerns of the individual (identity, self-awareness, growing-up) in the context of the question of who we want to be and how we want to live in a world of tomorrow.

Notes

[1] Although many of the novels are part of a series, I refer only to the first installment unless otherwise noted.

[2] Carrie Hintz and Elaine Ostry (2003). "Introduction." *Utopian and Dystopian Writing for Children and Young Adults.* Ed. Hintz and Ostry. New York: Routledge, 1-20, 9. See also Bryan Gillis and Joanna Simpson (2015). "Sex and Romance in Dystopian Young Adult Fiction." *Sexual Content in Young Adult Literature.* Lanham: Rowman & Littlefield, 75-100, 76. See Nadine Krüger's contribution here, who discusses dystopia as metaphor for adolescence.

[3] See Alessandra Boller's contribution in this collection, who looks at the overlap of the genres of (eco-) dystopia, the *Bildungsroman*, and the diary.

[4] Lyman T. Sargent (1994). "The Three Faces of Utopianism Revisited." *Utopian Studies* 5.1, 1-137, 9. According to Alcena Madeline Davis Rogan, the critical utopia and the dystopia are sometimes distinguished, sometimes conflated, and she suggests to provisionally "define dystopias as critical utopias that contain the *least* promise for the change or growth of the posited future or parallel space" (Rogan (2009). "Utopian Studies." *The Routledge Companion to Science Fiction.* Ed. Mark Bould et al. New York: Routledge, 308-316, 313). However, I will use the term 'dystopia' here despite the fact that hope is one of the central elements in dystopian fiction for young adults (Sara K. Day, Miranda A. Green-Barteet, and Amy L. Montz (2014). "Introduction: From 'New Woman' to 'Future Girl': The Roots and the Rise of the Female Protagonist in Contemporary Young Adult Dystopias." *Female Rebellion in Young Adult Dystopias.* Ed. Day, Green-Barteet, and Montz. Farnham: Ashgate, 1-14, 10).

[5] Maria Nikolajeva (2010). "Introduction: Why Does Pippi Sleep with her Feet on the Pillow?" *Power, Voice, and Subjectivity in Literature for Young Readers*. New York: Routledge, 1-11, 7.
[6] *Ibid.*, 7, 10.
[7] In the following, I base my discussion mainly on Chris Shilling's *The Body & Social Theory* (2012), particularly the introduction and chapters 4-5. There are, of course, many aspects of the (controlled) body but I concentrate on those that are relevant for my analysis of the dystopian novels later on. Shilling (2012). *The Body & Social Theory.* 3rd Ed. Los Angeles: SAGE.
[8] Shilling (2012), xii.
[9] Of course, there is also considerable overlap between the two.
[10] Such a hierarchization of cultured bodies vs. natural, inferior ones can also be seen with regard to race and ethnicity, i.e. in contexts of colonialism and its aftermath, where the native, 'non-white' body is frequently defined as 'uncivilized,' in need of cultural control. Class (the working-class body) and age (children's bodies) are further categories in which bodies become hierarchized.
[11] See also the contribution by Sarah Schäfer-Althaus and her discussion of Lauren DeStefano's *Wither* in this collection.
[12] Foucault (1995 [1975]), *Discipline & Punish: The Birth of the Prison.* Transl. Alan Sheridan. 2nd Ed. New York: Vintage Books, 135.
[13] Bourdieu (1984 [1979]), *Distinction: A Social Critique of the Judgement of Taste.* Transl. Richard Nice. Cambridge: Harvard University Press, 6, 101.
[14] Margo DeMello (2011). "Modification: Blurring the Divide: Human and Animal Body Modifications." *A Companion to the Anthropology of the Body and Embodiment.* Ed. Frances E. Mascia-Lees. Oxford: Wiley-Blackwell, 338-352, 339.
[15] DeMello (2011), 338; see also 344.
[16] Lisa Blackman (2008). *The Body: The Key Concepts.* Oxford: Berg, 16, emphasis in the original.
[17] For an overview see Shilling (2012), Introduction; chapt. 5-7.
[18] See Donna Haraway (2001 [1985]) "A Cyborg Manifesto: Science, Technology and Socialist-Feminism in the Late Twentieth Century." *The Cybercultures Reader.* Ed. David Bell and Barbara M. Kennedy. London: Routledge, 291-324; and Katherine Hayles (1999), *How We Became Posthuman: Virtual Bodies in Cybernetics, Literature, and Informatics.* Chicago: The University of Chicago Press.
[19] Foucault (1995 [1975]), "Docile Bodies" and "Panopticism."
[20] Such an artificial pairing of couples and families can also be found in older dystopian novels: In Lois Lowry's *The Giver* families (including children) are put together by society to achieve stability, and in Margaret Atwood's *The Handmaid's Tale*, infertile couples who belong to the political elite are assigned fertile women for surrogate pregnancies. In Huxley's *Brave New World* promiscuous sex is encouraged while its procreating function is prohibited since all humans are artificially created and then conditioned according to their social status.

[21] See Schäfer-Althaus' contribution in this collection.
[22] Although many of the older dystopian novels (e.g. Atwood's *Handmaid's Tale*) also feature relationships, romance in young adult dystopian novels seems to have a more vital role, sparking rebellion in ways that cannot be found in the older novels. Moreover, love is not the only emotion that societies try to control in this genre. In Lowry's *The Giver* as well as in Terry's *Slated* memories are controlled (i.e. erased) in order to suppress negative emotions such as sadness or aggressions. In Westerfeld's *Uglies*, desire and emotions are carefully regulated by drugs, whereas society in Condie's *Matched* tries to control them by tight behavioral regulations and the limitation (or elimination) of choices. Well's *Partials*, finally, features artificial humans who (supposedly) operate without emotions and thus, form the perfect labor force.
[23] While the genre also features a number of male heroes (e.g. Dashner's *Maze Runner*, Shusterman's *Unwind*, or Paolo Bacigalupi's *Ship Breaker* (2010)), the majority of them is female. Moreover, probably owing to the primary target group of female readers, love and relationships feature much more prominently in novels with female heroes.
[24] Gillis and Simpson provide an overview of the different ways in which sex and love relationships play a role in young adult dystopian literature. They also point out certain similarities between parental and governmental control of teenage sexuality in real-life (e.g. sex education) and in these novels, pointing out recent trends of sexual abstinence visible in both the US and dystopian young adult literature. (2015), 79, 83-85.
[25] Huxley's *Brave New World* and Atwood's *The Handmaid's Tale* come to mind readily. See also Gillis and Simpson (2015), 76.
[26] Lauren Oliver (2011), *Delirium.* New York, Speak, 239.
[27] *Ibid.*, 261-262, emphasis in the original.
[28] With regard to gender stereotypes, this is a somewhat problematic point: The fact that Lena (just like many of the other heroines in this genre) is enabled to rebel only because of her love interest undermines the (new) agency that so many of them display in this genre. See also Sara K. Day (2014), "Docile Bodies, Dangerous Bodies: Sexual Awakening and Social Resistance in Young Adult Dystopian Novels." *Female Rebellion in Young Adult Dystopian Fiction.* Ed. Day and Montz. Farnham: Ashgate, 74-92.
[29] See, for instance, Lowry's *The Giver*, in which the justification for suppressing emotions is to eliminate wrong choices and thus, irregular behavior; yet this results in a rational and conformist society that euthanizes babies who cry too much and old people once they stop being useful.
[30] In Dashner's final part of the *Maze Runner*-trilogy, *The Death Cure* (2011), Thomas and other survivors end up in an enclave of nature, separated from the rest of civilization for protection. In Rossi's *Under the Never Sky* the motif of the romanticization of the 'savage' is especially obvious in the character of Peregrine;

in the third part, the survivors end up on an island far away from the ruins of civilization (*Into the Still Blue* (2014)).

[31] Karen Sandler (2011). *Tankborn.* New York: Tu Books, 267, 289.

[32] Religion is used to indoctrinate tankborns, who pray to the "Infinite" in gratitude for their "sket," the skill-set with which they were created. They have also been taught that physical contact to trueborn people will have disastrous consequences, a racist regulation against the mixing of (different) bodies, which is also questioned – and proved wrong – because of Kayla's and Devak's mutual attraction.

[33] Day (2014), 75. Her point is similar to mine in reading the heroine's relationship as a trigger for her rebellion. However, she reads the romance more specifically in the context of Western culture's long-standing view of (young) women's sexuality as dangerous and thus in need of control. Accordingly, in her view current young adult dystopian literature "raise[s] questions about the ongoing treatment of the adolescent woman's emerging sexuality as dangerous" (75). Day also points to the more problematic aspects of such a link between romance and rebellion as it becomes visible in some of these novels.

[34] Sometimes the distinctions are not so clear, though: In *Tankborn*, modifications serve to create a servant underclass, yet the ruling class uses the same technology to care for and improve their own bodies.

[35] Mary J. Couzelis (2013). "The Future Is Pale: Race in Contemporary Young Adult Dystopian Novels" *Contemporary Dystopian Fiction for Young Adults: Brave new Teenagers*. Ed. Balaka Basu, Katherine R. Broad, and Carrie Hintz. New York: Routledge, 131-144. See also Jeffrey S. Kaplan (2012), who detects a growing diversification in young adult literature's themes and characters, including multicultural literature (22), a diversification, however, that has not quite reached young adult dystopian fiction ("The Changing Face of Young Adult Literature: What Teachers and Researchers Need to Know to Enhance Their Practice and Inquiry." *Teaching Young Adult Literature Today: Insights, Considerations, and Perspectives for the Classroom Teacher.* Ed. Judith A. Hayn and Jeffrey S. Kaplan. Lanham: Rowman & Littlefield. 19-40).

[36] Roth (2011), 51; Dashner (2009), 6.

[37] Collins (2008), 120. The way district 11 is described (its agricultural character, the public whippings etc.) is reminiscent of slavery. See also Couzelis' reading (2013, 138-141). To be fair, Katniss describes her own people – the miners in district 12 – as having "straight black hair, olive skin" (9), which might indicate that they are of mixed descent rather than 'white.'

[38] Lu (2011), 112, 125.

[39] Sherri L. Smith's novel *Orleans* (2013) is likewise an exception in that its heroine Fen is African American. See also Marotta (2016), who reads both novels as neo-slave narratives that examine Afrofuturism and female leadership ("Sherri L. Smith's *Orleans* and Karen Sandler's *Tankborn*: The Female Leader, the Neo-

Slave Narrative, and Twenty-First Century Young Adult Afrofuturism." *Journal of Science Fiction* 1.2 (May 2016), 56-70).
[40] Sandler (2011), 7.
[41] The color distinctions made in the novel are also reminiscent of today's colorism that is prevalent in many ethnicities while the social structure recalls the Indian caste system. However, there are other aspects in the novel that are quite problematic. The main protagonist Kayla, for instance, has the additional skill set of being exceptionally strong. This has been achieved by introducing animal-DNA into her genetic set-up, an element that echoes nineteenth-century racist ideas that considered African American slaves as 'animals.' For a more extended discussion see Marotta (2016), 65.
[42] Similar things could be said about the ways in which these novels reinforce heteronormativity, particularly in their focus on romance. Most characters in these novels are heterosexual, with very few exceptions, such as Syd, the main character in *Proxy*.
[43] I understand class here as defined by someone's (relatively stable) access to resources over time. See Robert Perrucci and Earl Wysong (2008). "Class in America." *The New Class Society: Goodbye American Dream?* 3rd Ed. Lanham: Rowman & Littlefield, 1-43.
[44] Blackman (2008), particularly chapter 3 "Bodies and Difference."
[45] Sometimes, both deliberate and accidental changes go hand in hand. In Rossi's *Under the Never Sky*, the technologically enhanced lifestyle of the residents in "Reverie" – among other things their increasingly virtual life – leads to a mental defect, a degeneration of the human brain. Similarly, the soldiers treated hormonally in *Pure* are also affected by unwanted side effects.
[46] A number of other aspects in the novel play with this distinction between healthy and deformed bodies. The "mothers," who have literally fused with stereotypically feminine aspects of their (pre-catastrophe) identity, e.g. their children and their jewelry, and who wear these 'deformations' proudly as a marker of their identity, can be seen as a complex visualization of (and comment on) stereotypical representations of gendered bodies that link appearance with ability (see Hemphill (2015), 24-25). Other bodies are more problematic: The "Dusts," "Beasts," or the "Groupies," people who have become fused with the earth, animals, or groups of other people, are, for instance, depicted as less than human. Kara E. Hemphill (2015). "Gender and the Popular Heroines (and Heroes) of the Young Adult Dystopia." *Honors Research Projects.* Paper 132.

Bibliography

Primary Literature

Anderson, Matthew T. (2004 [2002]). *Feed.* Cambridge, MA: Candlewick Press.
Atwood, Margaret (1986). *The Handmaid's Tale.* Boston: Houghton Mifflin.
Bacigalupi, Paolo (2011 [2010]). *Ship Breaker.* London: Atom.
Baggott, Julianna (2012). *Pure.* London: Headline Publishing Group.
Cass, Kiera. (2013 [2012]). *The Election.* New York: HarperTeen.
Collins, Suzanne (2009 [2008]). *The Hunger Games.* London: Scholastic.
Condie, Ally (2011). *Matched.* New York: Speak.
Dashner, James (2009). *The Maze Runner.* New York: Delacorte Press.
--- (2011). *The Death Cure.* New York: Delacorte Press.
DeStefano, Lauren (2011). *Wither.* New York: Simon & Schuster BFYR.
Lloyd, Sacci (2008). *The Carbon Diaries 2015.* London: Hodder Children's Books.
London, Alex (2013). *Proxy.* New York: Speak.
Lowry, Lois (2014 [1993]). *The Giver.* New York: Harper Collins.
Lu, Marie (2011). *Legend.* New York: Speak.
Oliver, Lauren (2012 [2011]). *Delirium.* New York: Harper.
Price, Lissa (2012). *Starters.* New York: Delacorte Press.
Rossi, Veronica (2012). *Under the Never Sky.* New York: Harper.
--- (2014). *Into the Still Blue.* New York: Harper.
Roth, Veronica (2013 [2011]). *Divergent.* New York: Katherine Tegen Books.
Sandler, Karen (2011). *Tankborn.* New York: Tu Books.
Shusterman, Neal (2009 [2007]). *Unwind.* New York: Simon & Schuster.
Smith, Sherri L. (2013): *Orleans.* New York: Speak.
Terry, Teri (2013 [2012]). *Slated.* New York: Speak.
Wells, Dan (2013 [2012]). *Partials.* New York: Balzer + Bray.
Westerfeld, Scott (2005). *Uglies.* New York: Simon Puls.
--- (2006) *Specials.* New York: Simon Puls.

Secondary Literature:

Blackman, Lisa (2008). *The Body: The Key Concepts.* Oxford: Berg.
Bourdieu, Pierre (1984 [1979]). *Distinction: A Social Critique of the Judgement of Taste.* Transl. Richard Nice. Cambridge: Harvard University Press.
Couzelis, Mary J. (2013). "The Future is Pale: Race in Contemporary Young Adult Dystopian Novels." *Dystopian Fiction for Young Adults: Brave New Teenagers.* Ed. Balaka Basu, Katherine R. Broad, and Carrie Hintz. New York: Routledge, 131-144.

Day, Sara K. (2014). "Docile Bodies, Dangerous Bodies: Sexual Awakening and Social Resistance in Young Adult Dystopian Novels." *Female Rebellion in Young Adult Dystopian Fiction.* Ed. Day, Miranda A. Green-Barteet, and Amy L. Montz. Farnham: Ashgate, 74-92.

---, Miranda A. Green-Barteet, and Amy L. Montz (2014). "Introduction: From 'New Woman' to 'Future Girl': The Roots and the Rise of the Female Protagonist in Contemporary Young Adult Dystopias." *Female Rebellion in Young Adult Dystopias.* Ed. Day, Green-Barteet, and Montz. Farnham: Ashgate, 1-14.

DeMello, Margo (2011). "Modification: Blurring the Divide: Human and Animal Body Moficiations." *A Companion to the Anthropology of the Body and Embodiment.* Ed. Frances E. Mascia-Lees. Oxford: Wiley-Blackwell, 338-352.

Foucault, Michel (1995 [1975]). *Discipline & Punish: The Birth of the Prison.* Transl. Alan Sheridan. 2nd Ed. New York: Vintage Books.

Gillis, Bryan, and Joanna Simpson (2015). "Sex and Romance in Dystopian Young Adult Fiction." *Sexual Content in Young Adult Literature.* Lanham: Rowman & Littlefield, 75-100.

Haraway, Donna (2001 [1985]). "A Cyborg Manifesto: Science, Technology and Socialist-Feminism in the Late Twentieth Century." *The Cybercultures Reader.* Ed. David Bell and Barbara M. Kennedy. London: Routledge, 291-324.

Hayles, N. Katherine (1999). *How We Became Posthuman: Virtual Bodies in Cybernetics, Literature, and Informatics.* Chicago: The University of Chicago Press.

Hemphill, Kara E. (2015). "Gender and the Popular Heroines (and Heroes) of the Young Adult Dystopia." Honors Research Projects. Paper 132. Web. 22 Aug. 2018 <http://ideaexchange.uakron.edu/honors_research_projects/132>.

Hintz, Carrie, and Elaine Ostry (2003). "Introduction." *Utopian and Dystopian Writing for Children and Young Adults.* Ed. Hintz and Ostry, New York: Routledge, 1-20.

Kaplan, Jeffrey S. (2012). "The Changing Face of Young Adult Literature: What Teachers and Researchers Need to Know to Enhance Their Practice and Inquiry." *Teaching Young Adult Literature Today: Insights, Considerations, and Perspectives for the Classroom Teacher.* Ed. Judith A. Hayn and Jeffrey S. Kaplan. Lanham: Rowman & Littlefield. 19-40.

Marotta, Melanie (2016). "Sherri L. Smith's *Orleans* and Karen Sandler's *Tankborn*: The Female Leader, the Neo-Slave Narrative, and Twenty-first Century Young Adult Afrofuturism." *Journal of Science Fiction* 1.2 (May 2016), 56-70.

Murphy, Graham J. (2009). "Dystopia." *The Routledge Companion to Science Fiction.* Ed. Mark Bould et al. London: Routledge, 473-477.

Nikolajeva, Maria (2010). "Introduction: Why Does Pippi Sleep with Her Feet on the Pillow?" *Power, Voice, and Subjectivity in Literature for Young Readers.* New York: Routledge, 1-11.

Perrucci, Robert, and Earl Wysong (2008). "Class in America." *The New Class Society: Goodbye American Dream?* 3rd Ed. Lanham: Rowman & Littlefield. 1-43.

Rogan, Alcena Madeline Davis (2009). "Utopian Studies." *The Routledge Companion to Science Fiction.* Ed. Mark Bould et al. New York: Routledge, 308-316.

Sargent, Lyman T. (1994). "The Three Faces of Utopianism Revisited." *Utopian Studies* 5.1, 1-37.

Shilling, Chris (2012). *The Body & Social Theory.* 3rd Ed. Los Angeles: SAGE.

Sarah Schäfer-Althaus (Koblenz)

Withering Bodies: Objectifying the Female Adolescent Body in Lauren DeStefano's *Chemical Garden* Trilogy

> There are so many of us, so many girls. The world wants us for our wombs or it does not want us at all.
>
> Rhine[1]

1. Introduction

Ever since the publication of Margaret Atwood's pioneering work *The Handmaid's Tale* in 1985, the number of female protagonists in young-adult dystopias has increased steadily, from Katniss in Suzanne Collins's *The Hunger Games* trilogy (2008-2010) to Rachel in Teri Hall's *The Line* (2010); from Juliette in Tahereh Mafi's debut *Shatter Me* (2011) to Nina in Julia Karr's *XVI* (2010) to Lauren DeStefano's heroine Rhine in the *Chemical Garden* series (2011-2013), to name only a few. As Sonja Fritz notes in her article "Girl Power and Girl Activism," female protagonists "have taken center stage in YA[2] dystopias as girls who resist the forces of their broken and corrupt societies to create their own identities, shape their own destinies, and transform the worlds in which they live," and as such they have evolved into the "key agents in the resistance of dystopian governments and the rebuilding of a new world."[3] Thereby, in the tradition of classic dystopian fiction such as George Orwell's *1984* (1949) or Aldous Huxley's *Brave New World* (1932), contemporary authors of young-adult dystopias "address larger social and cultural movements and concerns"[4] and create and skillfully integrate, as Ursula Heise reflects, "well-established views of the present" into their contemporary visions of future postapocalyptic societies to illustrate the "ultimate fragility of current socioeconomic systems."[5]

However, as this essay argues, even if these novels address the zeitgeist, and protagonists such as Katniss in *The Hunger Games* can be considered the prototype of the "defiant teenage girl,"[6] successfully rebelling against the dystopian regime she is born into, it cannot be left unnoticed that numerous female protagonists are placed in settings in which women are not only used as political instruments and celebrated as agents of change but are frequently objectified, reduced to their bodies' sexual and procreative means. While "social control of femininity is not new information for anyone who works within the realm of feminist, gender and queer studies,"[7] it is nevertheless surprising that contemporary authors, most of them being women themselves, use their fiction to reinforce traditional cultural expectations of maleness and femaleness, dominance and submission, thereby acknowledging the "universal male right to the appropriation of women's bodies"[8] while at the same time supporting traditional heterosexual gender constructions and emphasizing stereotypical markers of girl-/womanhood.

In this respect, girls in contemporary young-adult dystopian fiction are repeatedly categorized by means of traditional social expectations of femininity. They face stereotypical gendered norms and socializations, such as heterosexual love triangles, and are often scripted into worlds in which, in spite of the apocalyptic wasteland and flawed societies, a girl's unflawed beauty as well as her bodily enhancement are of utmost importance and can decide her life or death. Fashion, dresses, makeup, and beauty competitions are "all items girls are supposed to want, whether in our contemporary societies or in these fictional futures"[9] in order to be pleasing to and compete for possible boyfriends and husbands, and yet, "the belief that girls are automatically heterosexual not only in their sexual relationships but also in their posturing [...] is another misconception these dystopian societies base their relationships on."[10]

Moreover, the objectification of girls and women is twofold, as beyond these superficial, material markers and practices of femininity, which "put a veneer of normalcy on the dystopia and allow the protagonists to feel as if their lives have not changed since the new regime,"[11] the true intention of the totalitarian system unfolds: the objectification of the heroines' adolescent bodies as well as the control of their sexual awakening and desire within skillfully constructed patriarchal systems. In these systems of control, girls and their bodies are treated as possessions and investments,[12] discounted of their bodily self-agency and particularly of their reproductive rights with the effect that the objectification and inferiority of women is, comparable to classic dystopian fiction, based on bodily difference.

In 1985, Offred, the protagonist of Atwood's *The Handmaid's Tale* – itself, as Amy Montz argues, "the quintessential story of women's competition among themselves in a vast dystopian future that discounts women's rights to their own bodies"[13] – reflects in one of the key scenes of the novel:

> Each month I watch for blood, fearfully, for when it comes it means failure. I have failed once again to fulfil the expectations of others, which have become my own. I used to think of my body as an instrument, of pleasure, or a means of transportation, or an implement for the accomplishment of my will. I could use it to run, push buttons, of one sort or another, make things happen. [...] Now, the flesh arranges itself differently. I'm a cloud, congealed around a central object, the shape of a pear, which is hard and more real than I am and glows red within its translucent wrapping.[14]

Almost thirty years later, Rhine, the protagonist of DeStefano's *Chemical Garden* series, describes the moment of her kidnapping in the opening scene of the trilogy's first installment, *Wither*, after which she is sold into polygamous marriage:

> Our hips are measured to determine strength, our lips pried apart so the men can judge our health by our teeth [...] Will I become a murdered reject? Sold into prostitution? These things have happened. There's only one other option. I could become a bride. I've seen them on television, reluctant yet beautiful teenage brides on the arm of a wealthy man who is approaching the lethal age of twenty-five. [...] Girls who don't pass their inspection are shipped to a brothel in the scarlet districts. Some we have found murdered on the sides of roads, rotting, staring into the searing sun [...]. Some girls disappear forever, and all their families can do is wonder. (*Wither*, 2-3)

Even though written thirty years apart, both passages indicate that the dystopian female body as presented in Atwood's pioneering work as well as in modern dystopias is still a docile one, robbed of liberty, self-agency and self-determination, disturbingly selected, examined, categorized, used, consummated, and impregnated, oftentimes by aging men, exploited for medical experiments, and disposed of if no longer needed.

In these dystopian societies, in which death lurks around each corner, in which women tend to die early, in which sterility and fertility are constantly contrasted, and in which tattoos can stigmatize girls as sexual objects, it seems as if conception rituals, forced (polygamous) marriages, female trafficking and chemical treatments on women either ensure the fragile future of a dying nation or function as a form of dystopian birth control. Whereas most, if not all, heroines of recent dystopian futures are younger than Atwood's protagonist was in the nineteen-eighties – girls in DeStefano's *Chemical Garden* are abducted as young as thirteen, for example (*Wither*, 2) – recent publications nevertheless indulge in the "ongoing treatment of the adolescent woman's emerging sexuality"[15] and reduce girls' and women's bodies to objects reigned by patriarchy. Their sexual awakening, procreation and carnal desire in any form, if not surveilled and monitored, is presented as simultaneously desirable and dangerous, decorous and disruptive for the system they live in. The adolescent (female) body in dystopian futures still needs to be "controlled by implicit or explicit rules and regulations" and is "expected to conform to specific physical requirements"[16] – if not, it is considered a failure, as cancerous as the society it was born into, and it is replaced and disposed. As Rhine desperately notes in the series' second installment, *Fever*: "There are so many of us, so many girls. The world wants us for our wombs or it does not want us at all" (39).

This essay intends to trace the persisting (sexual) objectification of young women and their bodies in DeStefano's *Chemical Garden* trilogy. "Reminiscent of some of the more horrific moments of Atwood's *The Handmaid's Tale*,"[17] the novels deal with a withering American society in which the effort to genetically engineer a flawless and cancer-free society has gone wrong. Even though genetically perfected and producing only a few "malformed babies" (*Fever*, 55), a deadly virus reduces the life expectancy of girls to twenty, of boys to twenty-five.[18] While geneticists are desperately looking for an antidote to restore the human race, attractive girls, like the novel's sixteen-year-old protagonist, Rhine, are kidnapped and sold into polygamous marriages with wealthy men to bear more children in an illusionary, sugary world full of surveillance in which nothing is as it seems and in which the clock of death approaching ticks inexorably. The others are sold into prostitution, used for medical and chemical experiments, or murdered. Trapped in her golden cage of marriage together with her two sister-wives, Jenna and Cecily, and "distracted with stereotypical markers of girlhood – dresses, boys, shiny things – as a means of deterring individual agency and resistance against the oppressive totalitarian control of a governmental system,"[19] Rhine manages to run away with her servant and lover, Gabriel. Outside, however, she "finds a world even more disturbing than the one she left behind"[20] – a shattering world full of illusions, ignorance and limited choices – at least for girls and their bodies.

Next to its focus on the persisting objectification of women and their bodies, the following discussion intends to explore the overall development of the adolescent woman's body. According to Sara Day, "[o]nly by overcoming cultural conditioning regarding sexuality [...] can girls gain the agency required to become women, leaders, and heroes."[21] Therefore, in order to trigger social resistance and rebellion against the totalitarian system, it is of the utmost significance that girls and women "recognize and, more importantly, freely act upon desires that are simultaneously coded as welcome and dangerous."[22] Only if these girls "come to their own realization to rebel – and most often they are rebelling against the beauty standards and expectations of girlhood, of their parents, their society, and of course their dystopian governments,"[23] as Montz adds, only then they can truly develop into key agents of change, who ultimately "experienc[e] their bodies in new and empowering ways."[24] Even though I agree with Day and Montz in general, their arguments are, however, at risk given the high amount of sexual violence, physical abuse, and disturbing images of dying young girls sold into prostitution that DeStefano grows in her chemical garden.

2. Setting the Scene: Constructing the (Female) Body

To establish the relationship between the adolescent girls' bodies and their (sexual) objectification, it is necessary to provide a brief theoretical framework of female bodies as traditional locations for the execution and negotiation of power. Generally, "the human body is always treated as an image of society."[25] Therefore, it needs to be understood as a performative construct, which operates within a distinct cultural, corporeal framework of gender and power. In this respect, the "adolescent woman's body has long been the site of contradictory cultural expectations and demands, occupying the space between childhood and womanhood, between innocence and experience, between purity and fertility," and as such it "unsettles the ostensibly clear boundaries that dictate [...] gender roles."[26] Consequently, bodies can arguably function as powerful instruments able to "alter, criticize and even destabilize existing social hierarchies"[27] – an idea deeply rooted in history. As Michel Foucault argues in *Discipline and Punish*, the body has always been regarded as an "object and target of power," which can be "manipulated, shaped [and] trained."[28] In this sense, the body is continuously in an "act of becoming," according to Mikhail Bakthin, "never finished, never completed." [29] While its possibility to perform and to adapt to social systems and circumstances can intrinsically trigger and strengthen the body's power, it is at the same time constantly at risk of being extrinsically manipulated and abused. This turns the body into "an object over which struggles between its 'inhabitant' and others/ exploiters"[30] are frequently negotiated. In particular in the closed, totalitarian societies depicted in dystopian young-adult fiction, the creation and preservation of the body's manipulative state, or what Foucault has termed "docile bodies," is thereby the key to a functioning and successful system of control in which the body "obeys, responds, becomes skillful and increases its forces" while at the same time being "subjected, used, transformed and improved."[31] In this interplay between the body's docility and resistance, it is especially the female body that is traditionally constructed as "docile" and submissive and thus established as inferior to maleness and masculinity. Interestingly, several contemporary authors of young-adult fiction still support this unquestionably archaic "hierarchical gender doctrine designating men as 'head' and woman as 'body,'"[32] which was employed in medieval times to legitimize men's ownership over their wives and female servants[33] and used to reduce women socially and culturally to fallible objects in need of male guidance. Therefore, the female body has arguably continued to be a "location for anti-social desire."[34] This "idea," Bryan Turner continues, is "not a physiological fact but a cultural construct which has significant political implications,"[35] and "in response to the tension located in and projected onto the adolescent woman's body," as Day argues,

> Western culture has largely taken to portrayals of young women as simultaneously desirable and dangerous presenting them as creatures whose sexuality must be controlled by implicit and explicit rules and regulations.[36]

Consequently, the control and conditioning of the female adolescent body in general as well as its sexual awakening, carnal desires, and reproductive means in particular become an expression of social, public control,[37] monitored to document the success and the failure of the controlled. Even with the parental influence removed, the systemic surveillance of teenagers in these novels by

> those seeking to control, eliminate, or impose meanings on bodies and the bodies themselves, understood as active agents impelled by their own willed and unconscious determinations [,...] is nothing less than the intersection of physical bodies, [and] applied technologies of surveillance.[38]

Hence, girls in Hall's *The Line* are given birth control implants, women in Caragh O'Brien's novel *Prized* (2011) are expected to marry and produce ten children each, and teenagers reaching their sixteenth birthday in Karr's *XVI* have their age in Roman letters visibly tattooed on their wrists – which strongly reminds one of Hester Prynne in *The Scarlet Letter* (1850) – in order to announce to the world that they are now sex-teens and as such old enough to consent to sexual intercourse. In similar fashion, Rhine and her sister-wives are surveilled with the help of an implanted tracker in their legs (*Fever*, 329-330).

Surveillance is thus "an integral part of dystopian societies,"[39] and as the examples show, the surveillance and objectification of teenage girls and their bodies is inexorably linked, establishing the female body in contemporary dystopian fiction as "passive and reproductive"[40] – at least at first. Especially "[a]dolescent girls are constructed as a particularly powerless and vulnerable social group"[41] with limited choices and restricted self- and sexual agency. It is therefore not surprising that girls growing up in the dystopian world of DeStefano's *Chemical Garden* are also facing limited options, or as Montz convincingly argues, "the *illusion* of choice," as "taking away actual choice and limiting it" remains the "foundation of life in a dystopian society."[42]

3. Objectifying the Female Body in Lauren DeStefano's *Chemical Garden* Trilogy

In the *Chemical Garden* trilogy's withering society, in which aging to advanced years is impossible for new generations and life expectancy is limited for both men and women, adolescent girls between thirteen and twenty have only three "illusionary choices": to be murdered, married or sold into prostitution. And yet, these options are "entirely dependent at first on situations and circumstances beyond their control."[43] Kidnapped, lined up and inspected by the Gatherers, men in grey coats responsible for abducting girls for marriages and chemical experiments, Rhine notes, "I know girls disappear, but any number of things could come after that. Will I become a murdered reject? Sold into prostitution? These things have happened. There's only one other option. I could become a bride" (*Wither*, 2).

The selection process at the beginning of *Wither* resembles a slave market, and the girls' fates, in Darwinian terms, depend on their beauty, age, fertility, and health status; such a "survival of the fittest" is enforced at times with the utmost brutality: "Our hips are measured to determine strength, our lips pried apart so men can judge our health by our teeth. [...] We are one nameless thing sharing this strange hell. I do not want to stand out" (*Wither*, 2). However, "in many young adult dystopian tales regarding the traffic of girls, standing out becomes a mantra to be picked up according to circumstances,"[44] and in the end, it is Rhine's heterochromia, and as such her nonconformity to beauty standards, which saves her life. In contrast, those girls who do not pass their inspection are eradicated at once: "I hear something inside the van where the remaining girls were herded," Rhine remembers. "It's the first of what I know will be a dozen more gun-shots" (*Wither*, 4). Thus, in the opening scenes of DeStefano's debut, young girls experience (sexual) objectification through an exclusively male gaze as well as through men's visual and physical inspection of their bodies, which "equates a woman's worth with her bodily appearance and sexual functions."[45]

Once selected as brides, Rhine and the two other girls are extensively cleansed, polished and medically examined. Even though Rhine remarks that it is "awkward being naked in front of these strangers" (*Wither*, 20), she obeys and willingly allows others to gaze at her body, to treat it as a separate entity apart from her personality. As a result, she lets herself be distracted by fashion, nail polish, extensive makeup sessions and long bubble baths (*Wither*, 16-18) – all symbols characteristically tied to girlhood and untroubled teenage years – unknowing that the constant visual and physical inspections of her body, its intensive beautification as well as the competitive enhancement of its feminine features are forms of (sexual) objectification and surveillance of the adolescent female body. Moreover, in Rhine's dystopian gilded cage, these "girlish trappings of femininity,"[46] which are used as "illusions of normalcy,"[47] are presented as a sugary cover of the totalitarian system's true intention: to prepare her body for her soon-to-be husband (*Wither*, 23, 29).

The cleansing and re-dressing of her body is arguably constructed as a *rite de passage*, "a ritualized change in status or identity which involves a negation of existing features towards an affirmation of another order and another hierarchy." [48] Rhine's *rites de passage* from childhood to adulthood and hence from a free teenager to an entrapped wife are ultimately completed with the marriage ceremony to Linden Ashby. The wedding sanctions her bodily objectification, legitimizes her sexual accessibility, and therefore fully assimilates her into a society which, in the tradition of *The Handmaid's Tale*, justifies the control of women's reproductive rights, thus depriving teenagers of their rights to an individual sexual awakening.

As Barbara Fredrickson and Tomi-Ann Roberts argue, "the common thread running through all forms of sexual objectification is the experience of being treated *as a body* (or collection of body parts) valued predominantly for its use to (or consumption by) others."[49] In this respect, Rhine's new status as a consumable body is underlined visibly by the dress she changes into after the wedding ceremony: "Every curve of my body protrudes through the velvet material – my breasts, hipbones, even the ghost of ribs" (*Wither*, 48). Justifying this objecttification, her "domestic," Deirdre, explains, "It's a symbol that you are no longer a child. [...] That you are ready for your husband to come to you at any time" (*Wither*, 48). That sexual intercourse is part of the deal, and in DeStefano's dystopian society predominately constructed as a necessity and a mechanical act rather than inspired by love, mutual consent, and desire, is taken for granted by the controlling forces as well as by the controlled. Thus, it is not surprising that Rhine dispassionately informs herself of the wedding night procedures: "So how does this wedding night work? Does he choose us in a lineup? Drug us with sleeping gas? Pool the three of us into one bed?" to which Deirdre patiently replies, "Oh, the House Governor won't consummate his brides tonight" (*Wither*, 52-53).

As the examples show, the female body is robbed of its self-agency as well as its sexual agency. It is presented as a tool, an instrument or "a mechanical device," whose "functioning according to causal laws and the laws of nature"[50] is not only surveilled and controlled but also conditioned by a totalitarian regime. It is a system in which the female body is turned into a "possession, a property of a subject, [...] disassociated from carnality."[51] Moreover, in this archaic value system of traditional gender role socialization, in which young girls and their bodies are defined as passive, inferior and dependent, Rhine dangerously begins to adopt and internalize this dystopian "cultural milieu of objectification" [52] and "begin[s] to self-objectify by treating [herself] as an object to be looked at"[53] and to be consumed. "We are a culture obsessed with beauty and youth,"[54] Montz remarks. Consequently, "it is no accident, then, that our young adult novels would see this obsession become an extreme portrayed and even required in the presented dystopian society."[55] Sexual objectification is therefore nothing new to "any adolescent reading these novels," she continues, but how bodily perfection and (sexual) objectification "ultimately affects young women is where the concerns really should lie."[56] Accordingly, the presence of adolescent sexuality and (sexual) objectification in contemporary dystopian fiction for young adults "must be understood within the larger," ever-present "social discourses about reproductive control, including birth control, abortion, and abstinence discourses that render young women responsible for sexual decision-making while ignoring the experiences of desire,"[57] as Day concludes.

However, as Rhine's abduction and installment as a teenage bride have shown, in dystopian regimes female adolescents' self-responsibility for "sexual decision-making" is denied and (sexual) desire is not only ignored but frequently nonexistent or dangerously distorted. This is particularly visible in the *Carnival d'Amour* – the place in the trilogy's second installment, *Fever*, in which death and decay, sexuality and sexual violence, as well as child prostitution and human trafficking all come together. Even though entrapped, Rhine as a teenage bride can nevertheless enjoy the comfort and privilege of an upper-class lifestyle and is cared for and treated with respect by servants, doctors, and her husband, Linden, who is in no rush to consummate their marriage. The young prostitutes Rhine encounters after her escape from Ashby mansion in Madame's scarlet district, however, function as a raw and uncensored and somehow disturbingly real example of the extremes that sexual objectification and bodily exploitation for girls can result in.

These girls, which the system has categorized as second-quality "material," are not only trapped in a place in which their bodies are controlled, but they are also excessively trained and conditioned in "the art of seduction" (*Fever*, 51) to be repeatedly sold. They are reduced to mere objects of pleasure to satisfy the pedophilic desire of "First Generation" men – men who still age because they were born before the virus appeared. In order to avoid rebellion and resistance, the girls are "completely alienated from their nature,"[58] constantly drugged and robbed of their self-agency and dignity with no indicators of their individuality remaining, since their true identities and names have been replaced by a color-coded social hierarchy in the tradition of Huxley's *Brave New World.* As Rhine observes, "[t]he girls are all the same, like I am looking into a house of mirrors. Long bony limbs hunched against each other, and lipstick smeared mouths full of rotted teeth. And for some girls its not lipstick – its blood" (*Fever*, 37) – the first sign of death approaching. "And farther down is the entryway to another tent that is veiled off by silk scarves trailing sickly sweet perfume and something else. Decay and sweat," she continues. "It was a smell that haunted my dreams. [They] are rotting from the inside out" (*Fever*, 37).

The carnival, itself a location traditionally associated with pleasure and joyful amusement, is thus presented as a dangerous coexisting mirror image of Ashby mansion, in which the anticipated death of the girls at the age of twenty is the only limit imposed on their sexual objectification and exploitation. Until then, however, even girls who are already dying, who are feverishly spitting blood and slowly suffocating, are "chosen by men unwilling to pay more and they're never in the back room for long. Men take them hurriedly, sometimes standing up, against trees, or even in the tent with all the others there to see" (*Fever*, 54-55). Hence, the scarlet district is constructed as a place in which not only desire, love and lovemaking are illusions often sustained through drug-induced sedation (*Fever*, 59-61) but in which the male gaze and the sexual objectification of girls and their bodies is presented as a collectively shared and collectively 'enjoyed' experience. Thus, with the inclusion of the carnival DeStefano creates a truly disturbing, sickening picture of sexual objectification, and with its multiple forms of threatening sexuality and physical abuse on more than a hundred pages, the *Chemical Garden* trilogy makes one wonder whether dystopias like this, to come back to Day's argument from the beginning, do offer truly innovative possibilities for young women to experience "their bodies in new and empowering ways."[59]

4. Conclusion(s)

"It's terrifying to be a girl in this world," Rhine remarks, a girl "who realizes that it [the world] hates her, and who hates it in return" (*Wither*, 57) – the realization of living in an "enclosed, confined society" which is responsible for the "creation of docile bodies"[60] often marks the first step of the female adolescents' resistance and rebellion. In particular "bodies in this perspective," as Mariam Fraser and Monica Greco explain, "are theoretically conspicuous for their capacity to exceed, escape, defy or threaten social order,"[61] which is the reason they require continuous "training or disciplining as a precondition of social life" in the first place. As Day, Green-Barteet and Montz argue, "adolescent women in such dystopian novels both recognize their liminal situations and, over time, use their in-between positions as a means for resistance and rebellion against the social order that seeks to control them."[62] Thus, the enclosed space, which on the one hand secures the docility of the protagonists, simultaneously poses an immediate danger to the stability of the carefully constructed social system the docile woman is trapped in. As long as the "energy of the body is controlled, disciplined, and developed," the "controlling power's goal of order and regulation"[63] is maintained, but the moment the protagonists awake from their sedated state and no longer let themselves and their bodies be used as targets and objects consumed by others, their bodies are gradually established as "space[s] of empowerment and resistance."[64]

Even though Rhine's rebellion is not as defiant and pugnacious as Katniss's in *The Hunger Games*, she does nevertheless show subtle signs of resistance, aligned with "average teenage behaviours such as breaking rules, keeping secrets [and] mistrusting authorities."[65] In addition, she bluntly negates Linden's sexual advances (*Wither*, 118), which ultimately creates a stronger bond between her and her husband than the physical connection he has with her sister brides. In the end, the refusal to share her body rewards her with a number of privileges and the status of "First Wife," which eventually helps her to escape the illusory world of Ashby manor. Moreover, even her liaison with Gabriel "becomes a form of rebellion [which she] can effect through her own body," O'Brien notes, and even if the "act is private [...] it's still treason, and that makes it all the more powerful."[66] As an effect, "such representations suggest that the agency that begins as a renewed sense of embodiment may eventually lead to the possibility of social resistance"[67] and allow Rhine, in contrast to her sister-wives and the young prostitutes, to mature into an "agent of change," who reclaims her self-agency and slowly regains control over her body. Thus, by "presenting young women as agents of change," novels like the *Chemical Garden* series "draw on the seemingly contradictory impulse of turn-of-the-century Western culture to understand young women as both strong and vulnerable, both passive citizens and potential leaders."[68] As such, Rhine represents a "transitional generation"[69] of young women between present and future, definitely tougher and more rebellious than the handmaids were thirty years ago. "We'll grow until we are braver. We'll grow until our bones ache and our skin wrinkles and our hair goes white, and until our hearts decide, at last, that it's time to stop,"[70] Rhine resolves at the end of the trilogy, "and that gives us hope that things will keep changing, that they can keep getting better"[71] so that girls in the near future will no longer be affected by any forms of (sexual) objectification, that they will no longer be reduced to their wombs only.

Notes

[1] Lauren DeStefano (2013a). *Fever*. London: Harper, 39. Further references to this edition will be included in the text as *Fever* with page numbers in brackets.
[2] The abbreviation "YA" stands for "young adult."
[3] Sonya Sawyer Fritz (2014). "Girl Power and Girl Activism in the Fiction of Suzanne Collins, Scott Westerfeld, and Moira Young." *Female Rebellion in Young Adult Dystopian Fiction*. Ed. Sara Day, Miranda Green-Barteet and Amy Montz. Dorchester: Ashgate, 17-32, 17.
[4] Megan McDonough and Katherine A. Wagner (2014). "Rebellious Natures: The Role of Nature in Young Adult Dystopian Female Protagonists' Awakenings and Agency." *Female Rebellion in Young Adult Dystopian Fiction*. Ed. Sara Day, Miranda Green-Barteet and Amy Montz. Dorchester: Ashgate, 157-170, 157.

[5] Ursula Heise (2015). "What's the Matter with Dystopia." *Public Books*. Web. 21 Feb. 2017. <http://www.publicbooks.org/whats-the-matter-with-dys topia/>.
[6] Fritz (2014), 18.
[7] Amy Montz (2014). "Rebels in Dresses: Distractions of Competitive Girlhood in Young Adult Dystopian Fiction." *Female Rebellion in Young Adult Dystopian Fiction*. Ed. Sara Day, Miranda Green-Barteet and Amy Montz. Dorchester: Ashgate, 107-121, 108.
[8] Elizabeth Grosz (1994). "Volatile Bodies." Bloomington: Indiana University Press. Rpt. in: Mariam Fraser and Monica Greco (eds.) (2005). *The Body: A Reader*. New York: Routledge, 47-51, 50.
[9] Montz (2014), 109.
[10] *Ibid*., 111.
[11] *Ibid*., 109.
[12] Lauren DeStefano (2011). *Wither*. London: Harper, 63. Further references to this edition will be included in the text as *Wither* with page numbers in brackets.
[13] Montz (2014), 118.
[14] Margaret Atwood (1996). *The Handmaid's Tale*. London: Vintage, 83-84.
[15] Sara Day (2014). "Docile Bodies, Dangerous Bodies: Sexual Awakening and Social Resistance in Young Adult Dystopian Novels." *Female Rebellion in Young Adult Dystopian Fiction*. Ed. Sara Day, Miranda Green-Barteet and Amy Montz. Dorchester: Ashgate, 75-94, 75.
[16] *Ibid*., 77.
[17] Montz (2014), 118.
[18] DeStefano notes on her website that there is no particular reason why males live longer than females. "The point is," she notes, "that nobody in this world as of yet understands why the virus does what it does, and why males have a longer life span." DeStefano, Lauren (2008-2014). "Lauren DeStefano-FAQ." Web. 27 February 2017. <http://laurendestefano.com/faq.php>.
[19] Montz (2014), 109.
[20] DeStefano (2013a). *Fever*, back cover.
[21] Day (2014), 75.
[22] *Ibid*., 76.
[23] Montz (2014), 108.
[24] Day (2014), 76.
[25] Mary Douglas (1996). "The Two Bodies." *Natural Symbols: Explorations in Cosmology*. New York: Routledge. Rpt. in: Mariam Fraser and Monica Greco (eds.) (2005). *The Body: A Reader*. New York: Routledge, 78-81, 78.
[26] Day (2014), 77.
[27] Sarah Schäfer-Althaus (2016). *The Gendered Body. Female Sanctity, Gender Hybridity and the Body in Women's Hagiography*. Heidelberg: Winter, 39.
[28] Foucault, Michel (1977). *Discipline and Punish: The Birth of the Prison*. New York: Vintage, 136.

[29] Mikhail Bakhtin (1984). "The Grotesque Image of the Body and Its Sources." *Rabelais and His World*. Trans. Helene Iswoslky. Bloomington: Indiana University Press. Rpt. in: Mariam Fraser and Monica Greco (eds.) (2005). *The Body: A Reader*. New York: Routledge, 92-95, 92.
[30] Grosz (1994/Rpt. 2005), 50.
[31] Foucault, Michel (1977), 136.
[32] Alcuin Blamires (1997). "Paradox in the Medieval Gender Doctrine of Head and Body." *Medieval Theology and the Natural Body*. Ed. Peter Biller and A. J. Minnis. York: York Medieval Press, 13-30, 13.
[33] See, for example, Brown, Peter (1988). *The Body and Society: Men, Women and Sexual Renunciation in Early Christianity*. New York: Columbia University Press, 23; and Le Goff, Jacques, and Nicolas Truong (2007). *Die Geschichte des Körpers im Mittelalter*. Stuttgart: Klett-Cotta, 47.
[34] Bryan Turner (1996). *The Body and Society*. London: Sage, 65. See also Fraser, Mariam, and Monica Greco (eds.) (2005). "Introduction." *The Body: A Reader*. New York, 1-42, 10.
[35] *Ibid.*, 65.
[36] Day (2014), 75.
[37] See Douglas (1996/Rpt. 2005), 78.
[38] Michael J.Shapiro (2005). "Every Move You Make: Bodies, Surveillance, and Media." *Social Text* 23.2, 21-34, 22.
[39] Montz (2014), 108.
[40] Grosz (1994/Rpt. 2005), 50.
[41] Meenakshi Gigi Durham (1999). "Articulating Adolescent Girl's Resistance to Patriarchal Discourse in Popular Media." *Women's Studies in Communication* 22.2, 210-229, 218. See also Montz (2014), 108.
[42] Montz (2014), 109, emphasis in original.
[43] *Ibid.*, 119.
[44] *Ibid.*, 119.
[45] Dawn Szymanski, Lauren Moffitt and Erika Carr (2011). "Sexual Objectification of Women: Advances to Theory and Research." *The Counseling Psychologist* 39.1, 6-38, 6.
[46] Montz (2014), 108.
[47] *Ibid.*, 109.
[48] Schäfer-Althaus (2016), 80. See also Turner, Victor (1969). *The Ritual Process*. Harmondsworth: Penguin, 157-158, 196.
[49] Barbara Fredrickson and Tomi-Ann Roberts (1997). "Objectification Theory. Toward Understanding Women's Lived Experiences and Mental Health Risks." *Psychology of Women Quarterly* 21, 173-206, 174.
[50] Grosz (1994/Rpt. 2005), 48.
[51] *Ibid.*, 50.
[52] Fredrickson and Roberts (1997), 177.

[53] Szymanski, Moffitt and Carr (2011), 8.
[54] Montz (2014), 112.
[55] *Ibid.*, 112.
[56] *Ibid.*, 113.
[57] Day (2014), 84-85.
[58] Maryam Kouhestani (2013). "Disciplining the Body: Power and Language in Margaret Atwood's Dystopian Novel *The Handmaid's Tale*." *Journal of Educational and Social Research* 3.7, 610-613, 611.
[59] Day (2014), 76.
[60] *Ibid.*, 77.
[61] Fraser and Greco (2005), 10.
[62] Sara Day, Miranda Green-Barteet and Amy Montz (2014). "Introduction. From 'New Woman' to 'Future Girl.' The Roots and the Rise of the Female Protagonist in Contemporary Young Adult Dystopias." *Female Rebellion in Young Adult Dystopian Fiction*. Ed. Sara Day, Miranda Green-Barteet and Amy Montz. Dorchester: Ashgate, 1-16, 3-4.
[63] Kouhestani (2013), 611.
[64] Day (2014), 85.
[65] Fritz (2014), 18.
[66] Caragh O'Brien (2011b). "Dystopian Birth Control." *Tor.com*. Web. 21 Feb. 2017. <http://www.tor.com/2011/12/01/dystopian-birth-control/>.
[67] Day (2014), 76.
[68] Day, Green-Barteet, and Montz (2014), 7.
[69] Kouhestani (2013, 611).
[70] DeStefano, Lauren (2013). *Sever*. New York: Simon and Schuster, 371.
[71] DeStefano, Lauren, qtd. in O'Brien (2011a), n.pag.

Bibliography

Primary Literature

Atwood, Margaret (1996). *The Handmaid's Tale*. London: Vintage.
Collins, Suzanne (2008-2010). *The Hunger Games*. New York: Scholastic.
DeStefano, Lauren (2011). *Wither*. London: Harper.
--- (2013a). *Fever*. London: Harper.
--- (2013b). *Sever*. New York: Simon and Schuster.
Hall, Teri (2011). *The Line*. New York: Puffin.
Hawthorne, Nathaniel (2016 [1850]). *The Scarlet Letter*. London: Penguin.
Huxley, Aldous (2004 [1932]). *Brave New World*. London: Vintage.
Karr, Julia (2011). *XVI*. New York: Penguin.
Mafi, Tahereh (2011). *Shatter Me*. New York: Harper.

O'Brien, Caragh (2011a). *Prized*. London: Simon and Schuster.

Orwell, George (1961 [1949]). *1984*. New York: Signet Classics.

Secondary Literature

Bakhtin, Mikhail (1984). "The Grotesque Image of the Body and Its Source." *Rabelais and His World*. Trans. Helene Iswoslky. Bloomington: Indiana University Press. Rpt. in: Mariam Fraser and Monica Greco (eds.) (2005). *The Body: A Reader*. New York: Routledge, 92-95.

Blamires, Alcuin (1997). "Paradox in the Medieval Gender Doctrine of Head and Body." *Medieval Theology and the Natural Body*. Ed. Peter Biller and A. J. Minnis. York: York Medieval Press, 13-30.

Brown, Peter (1988). *The Body and Society: Men, Women and Sexual Renunciation in Early Christianity*. New York: Columbia University Press.

Day, Sara (2014). "Docile Bodies, Dangerous Bodies: Sexual Awakening and Social Resistance in Young Adult Dystopian Novels." *Female Rebellion in Young Adult Dystopian Fiction*. Ed. Sara Day, Miranda Green-Barteet, and Amy Montz. Dorchester: Ashgate, 75-94.

---, Miranda Green-Barteet, and Amy Montz (2014). "Introduction. From 'New Woman' to 'Future Girl.' The Roots and the Rise of the Female Protagonist in Contemporary Young Adult Dystopias." *Female Rebellion in Young Adult Dystopian Fiction*. Ed. Sara Day, Miranda Green-Barteet and Amy Montz. Dorchester: Ashgate, 1-16.

DeStefano, Lauren (2008-2014). "Lauren DeStefano-FAQ." Web. 27 February 2017 <http://laurendestefano.com/faq.php>.

Douglas, Mary (1996). "The Two Bodies." *Natural Symbols: Explorations in Cosmology*. New York: Routledge. Rpt. in: Mariam Fraser and Monica Greco (eds.) (2005). *The Body: A Reader*. New York: Routledge, 78-81.

Durham, Meenakshi Gigi (1999). "Articulating Adolescent Girl's Resistance to Patriarchal Discourse in Popular Media." *Women's Studies in Communication* 22.2, 210-229.

Foucault, Michel (1977). *Discipline and Punish: The Birth of the Prison*. New York: Vintage.

Fraser, Mariam, and Monica Greco (eds.) (2005). *The Body: A Reader*. New York: Routledge.

--- (2005). "Introduction." *The Body: A Reader*. Ed. Mariam Fraser and Monica Greco. New York: Routledge, 1-42.

Fredrickson, Barbara, and Tomi-Ann Roberts (1997). "Objectification Theory. Toward Understanding Women's Lived Experiences and Mental Health Risks." *Psychology of Women Quarterly* 21, 173-206.

Fritz, Sonya Sawyer (2014). "Girl Power and Girl Activism in the Fiction of Suzanne Collins, Scott Westerfeld, and Moira Young." *Female Rebellion in Young Adult Dystopian Fiction*. Ed. Sara Day, Miranda Green-Barteet and Amy Montz. Dorchester: Ashgate, 17-32.

Grosz, Elizabeth (1994). "Volatile Bodies." Bloomington: Indiana University Press. Rpt. in: Mariam Fraser and Monica Greco (eds.) (2005). *The Body: A Reader*. New York: Routledge, 47-51.

Heise, Ursula (2015). "What's the Matter with Dystopia." *Public Books*. Web. 21 Feb. 2017 <http://www.publicbooks.org/whats-the-matter-with-dystopia/>.

Kouhestani, Maryam (2013). "Disciplining the Body: Power and Language in Margaret Atwood's Dystopian Novel *The Handmaid's Tale*." *Journal of Educational and Social Research* 3.7, 610-613.

Le Goff, Jacques, and Nicolas Truong (2007). *Die Geschichte des Körpers im Mittelalter*. Stuttgart: Klett-Cotta.

McDonough, Megan, and Katherine A. Wagner (2014). "Rebellious Natures: The Role of Nature in Young Adult Dystopian Female Protagonists' Awakenings and Agency." *Female Rebellion in Young Adult Dystopian Fiction*. Ed. Sara Day, Miranda Green-Barteet and Amy Montz. Dorchester: Ashgate, 157-170.

Montz, Amy (2014). "Rebels in Dresses: Distractions of Competitive Girlhood in Young Adult Dystopian Fiction." *Female Rebellion in Young Adult Dystopian Fiction*. Ed. Sara Day, Miranda Green-Barteet, and Amy Montz. Dorchester: Ashgate, 107-121.

O'Brien, Caragh (2011b). "Dystopian Birth Control." *Tor.com*. Web. 21 Feb. 2017 <http://www.tor.com/2011/12/01/dystopian-birth-control/>.

Schäfer-Althaus, Sarah (2016). *The Gendered Body. Female Sanctity, Gender Hybridity and the Body in Women's Hagiography*. Heidelberg: Winter.

Shapiro, Michael J. (2005). "Every Move You Make: Bodies, Surveillance, and Media." *Social Text* 23.2, 21-34.

Szymanski, Dawn, Lauren Moffitt and Erika Carr (2011). "Sexual Objectification of Women: Advances to Theory and Research." *The Counseling Psychologist* 39.1, 6-38.

Turner, Bryan (1996). *The Body and Society*. London: Sage.

Turner, Victor (1969). *The Ritual Process*. Harmondsworth: Penguin.

Alessandra Boller (Marburg)

"It's So Weird Being Inside History" Saci Lloyd's Multimodal Hybrid Narratives *The Carbon Diaries 2015* and *2017*

1. Introduction

Dystopian fiction seems to bear new relevance in today's turbulent times.[1] Interestingly, while both canonical novels and recent texts incorporating fresh motifs have received a great deal of attention by adult readers and scholars alike, their young adult counterparts have not been attributed the same attention, especially by academia. This is striking since a variety of culturally and politically highly relevant narratives appealing to different audiences and representing new trends in storytelling can be found in this genre.[2]

One example of young adult dystopia in particular has eerily extrapolated contemporary tendencies while simultaneously presenting an innovative approach to a new, multimodal form of the novel: British author Saci Lloyd's *The Carbon Diaries 2015* (2008) and its sequel *The Carbon Diaries 2017* (2010) belong to the eco-dystopian subgenre now prominent in the young adult sector (Susan Beth Pfeffer's *The Last Survivors* series is another example). In these narratives, the notion of the 'bad place' ties in with global ecological catastrophes and environmental issues which are intertwined with threats to contemporary society and individual lives. At the same time, Lloyd stays close to the readers' reality in terms of both the topics of (teenage) life as well as the inclusion of different modes in the narrative as her novels come in the form of a diary allegedly written by the protagonist Laura Brown, who also adds newspaper clippings as well as lists she makes and photos she takes.

On the whole, these two novels challenge and counter a common reservation held against young adult (dystopian) fiction, which is often accused of being simplistic and less relevant than its adult counterpart. This negative evaluation is based on a number of aspects: Firstly, young adult dystopian fiction is often considered to be just a rehashing of well-established motifs known from other genres. Laura Miller, commenting on Suzanne Collins' *Hunger Games* trilogy, states that "[p]ublishers have signed up dozens of similar titles in the past year or two, and, as with any thriving genre, themes and motifs get swapped around from other genres and forms."[3] She also states that many of these narratives "don't even attempt to abide by the strictures of science fiction" because they "follow a logic more archetypal than rational."[4] Besides, some critics have identified the frequent and problematic reinforcement of hetero-normativity and patriarchal structures which surface as crucial motifs in various young adult dystopias. Focusing on new, rebellious female protagonists, Day, Green-Barteet and Montz explain that many narratives essentially still reproduce the established world order:

> [e]ven as these young women actively resist and rebel, then, they also tend to accept that they cannot change every aspect of their societies' controlling frameworks, particularly as these relate to romance and sexuality.[5]

Author John Green also ponders on these reservations and discusses the derogative connotation of the term 'genre fiction' in his article "Does YA Mean Anything Anymore? Genre in a Digitized World." He suggests understanding genre as a "conversation that benefits from many voices,"[6] thereby opposing the often dismissive attitude towards young adult (dystopian) fiction based on the label 'genre fiction.'

Lloyd's novels prove that young adult dystopia can be much more than a conglomerate of worn-out motifs: *The Carbon Diaries*, with their extrapolation and projection of contemporary tendencies only seven years into the future, are highly relevant and manage to make (not only) younger readers ponder political, social, and environmental problems by discussing them in a manner all readers can relate to. The conversation established between the motifs of dystopian fiction[7] and the classic motifs of the *bildungsroman* accounts for both the topicality and the identificatory potential the novels and their characters offer to readers. Moreover, the genre combination and the multimodality of Lloyd's novels further contribute to establishing a seemingly natural connection between issues such as first love, identity construction, problems at school, personal fulfillment as well as environmental and political issues. Without being overtly didactic, the narratives draw on common experiences and worries of young readers, who, like Laura, eventually realise that the personal becomes political[8] and that one's life is not only shaped by the local community but also by global events. This becomes evident when political decisions invade and clearly determine the life of the protagonist, an insight which is also linked to "environmental and ecological topics [which] are becoming increasingly popular in dystopian young adult fiction, and their treatment more critical, complex, and provocative"[9] .

Thus, the central aim of this article is to explore how the multimodal scrapbook format of *The Carbon Diaries* and the conversation established between dystopian fiction and *bildungsroman* motifs tie in with notions of awakening and empowerment. Both the format and the generic hybridity of the novels do not only mirror Laura's development but also invite readers to reflect on their own connections to public political discourse. I begin by discussing the effects of the generic overlap and multimodality before elaborating on the significance of the narratives' pace in the context of political awakening in a global world. The combination of these techniques creates a space for new perspectives and constitutes a notable approach to pressing problems such as global warming, making the two novels relevant comments on current issues and problems and enabling teenage readers to re-evaluate their place in the world and the need to become politically or socially involved.

2. *The Carbon Diaries 2015* and *2017*: The Effects of Multimodality and Generic Hybridity

Laura Brown starts writing her diaries at the age of sixteen in 2015, the first year of carbon rationing in the United Kingdom. The diaries classify as multimodal scrap books since they, in addition to Laura's written descriptions, also incorporate photos, text messages, emails, drawings, exams and newspaper articles, for instance.[10] In line with other multimodal narratives, *The Carbon Diaries* "combine various types of signs"[11] and therefore appear as a mixture of a personal diary and a documentation of changing living conditions and reality in the UK, particularly in London. This aspect of alleged documentation also points to the narratives' topicality and underlines the feeling of reality and authenticity.[12]

The Carbon Diaries thus go beyond the mere language-based narrative, thereby allowing readers to "intuitively draw upon their real-world experiences, including the use of various sensory channels; different types of signs [...] and different symbolic languages."[13] Even though the diary form clearly relies on a first-person narration, the inclusion of collected items, and thus of both visual and verbal elements, offers further viewpoints as well as approaches to the new society depicted here. This multi-perspective element adds to the political and environmental scope of the narrative as the next section will show by discussing three examples from the novels.

2.1 Multimodality

The multimodality of the novels is established right from the start as both novels do not open with an entry written by implied author Laura on January 1st, but instead show what seems to be part of a newspaper page. Wolfgang Hallet explains that

> [s]ince the 1990s an ever-growing number of novels have not merely consisted of verbal text but have also incorporated a wide range of visual representations and modes such as (the reproduction of) photographs, hand-drawn sketches, maps and diagrams, and all sorts of other graphic and symbolic elements in the narrative discourse. Apart from such conspicuous visual elements, other generic and mostly typographically distinct modes [...] and many other generic forms can be identified in an increasing number of novels."[14]

The Carbon Diaries use many of these modes which are regarded as "semiotic resources" "drawn into processes of meaning making and communication"[15]. In line with that, the newspaper clippings are far more than just additional images.

In both cases, these clippings consist of a textual element, which centres on carbon cards, and a visual element, a diagram which also features a map. Besides, they reveal the (scope of the) environmental issues the respective diary will focus on. In the first novel, this fictitious non-fiction newspaper element announces that the UK will enter "Carbon Rationing" as of January 8th, 2015. One of the headlines reads "What does it mean?" and readers are placed on the same level[16] as the UK citizens since both groups need to be told what carbon rationing is and means: The UK will be the first country in the EU to engage in rationing, there will be a "compulsory carbon card for all citizens" and everyone will have a "200 point limit per month."[17] Further, the article underlines that this date has historical relevance since carbon rationing begins exactly 63 years after rationing started in the UK during World War II. Thus, this first page of the novel not only reveals the narrative's scrapbook format, but also alludes to the precarious situation by mentioning the war.

The accompanying image on the right-hand side of the page is captioned "The Great Storm Dec 12th 2 [a part of the page is missing] Damage Analysis." The image shows the UK and Ireland and reveals to what extent agriculture and infrastructure have been affected by the storm. By placing the article on carbon rationing and the damage analysis in close proximity, the newspaper clipping directly establishes a connection between natural disaster and the need to change one's lifestyle[18]. Thus, in addition to introducing the topic of the novel, it also alludes to interconnections between personal life and global issues and points out that the novel will focus on the local level. This is further underlined by the fact that the damage analysis is restricted to the UK and Ireland even though the map also depicts other parts of Western Europe.

The first page of *The Carbon Diaries 2017* is structured in the same manner but now the focus and the scope are more global than local, as the headlines overtly state: "Carbon Rationing Card to Go Global" and "The Global Water Crisis: Is 2017 the Year of the First Water War?" Additionally, the map shows the whole world and thus points out that environmental issues have intensified in the year which passed between the two novels. This first page also foreshadows the global scope of the following novel. During the course of both narratives, Laura often describes the local effects of global events such as natural disasters, but she also denies that she has to change her lifestyle and behaviour. The reader, however, can see that the entanglement of personal local life and global environmental issues is a fact in the story-world. This is a result of the multimodality of the text since "the multimodal novel directs the reader to explore the book page and interrelate its different semiotic elements."[19] This "performative side"[20] directly invites the reader to ponder their own world and situation. This invitation is also linked to the principle of extrapolation, which is the foundation of both utopian and dystopian fiction. Here, extrapolation becomes particularly obvious with regard to global warming and its effects. Due to the novels' setting in the very near future, they could be read as a "direct extension of our present day lives"[21] when they were first published.[22] Thus, readers might think about the possibility of implementations such as carbon rationing in their own societies and what impact these could have on their lives. The invitation to self-evaluation continues throughout the whole novel, as the next subchapter on eco-dystopia and the (features of the) *bildungsroman* will show.

Like other multimodal narratives, Lloyd's novels "use images and text as separate but ontologically equal modes of access to the storyworld."[23] This insight applies to the newspaper clippings introducing the novels' topics and to many further elements which relieve the language channel from tasks such as characterization.[24] Laura's entry on January first shows how her microcosm of family life is affected by carbon rationing, and it also characterises the family members when she inserts a table her father asked the others to complete: "New Year's wish list. He typed out answers into his laptop. Ever since he got made Head of Travel and Tourism at Greenham College he zaps everything into Excel and files it as evidence" (*2015*, 5). This short text describes Laura's father and points to the notion of documentation. Further, the entry eventually features this "evidence" when the printed version of the list becomes part of Laura's diary. Her father has rather modest wishes ("one hour of quiet time in study in the afternoon"), her mother wants to keep the car and focus on her own "Inner Growth" and Laura's sister rejects everything about carbon rationing and just wants "[h]er life back." Laura's table column directly identifies her key concerns: her band *dirty angels*, unchanged features of her former life ("24/7 access to e-pod") and her neighbour Ravi, whom she is in love with (this last aspect is only added when Laura puts the list into her diary) (*2015*, 5). The family members' different wishes already allude to future intra-familial conflicts, which seem to begin even before the first day of carbon rationing and intensify when they realise they cannot continue living (and consuming) as before.

These examples show that "the introduction of nonverbal symbolic forms"[25] (such as clippings, drawings and lists) stresses *what* the novels communicate and influences *how* they communicate it. As Hallet explains with regard to a different multimodal novel, some nonverbal elements offer "the reader access to dimensions of the fictional world that cannot be rendered in verbal form."[26] Besides, they are "artifacts that are produced and located in the fictional world of the novel,"[27] meaning that novels can take on "the character of the scrapbook, which is, simultaneously, a part of the storyworld that it sets up narratively."[28] This also holds true for *The Carbon Diaries* since Laura seems to take the items she puts into her diary from a world external to it, from an extra-literary reality that seems to exist outside of the diary.

When reading becomes a "multi-literate act,"[29] the notion of credibility and the identificatory potential of the alleged diaries are stressed. This technique makes Laura and the dystopian world feel more real and easier to relate to, eventually making the environmental issues depicted appear more pressing. This effect can be traced back to the readers' ability to relate to the semiotic signifiers Laura uses as these are also a part of their lives. Hallet stresses that when the reader is enabled to "study a whole range of artifacts produced or collected by a character from the fictional world," this character is "'naturalized' as a cultural agent who, like the reader, engages in a large variety of modes of signification and communication."[30] He concludes that through multimodal narration, the reader's non-textual experiences, expression and communication can be approximated with "the same process in the fictional world."[31] This is also due to the fact that people's everyday lives are multimodal – their communication is not restricted to language but includes other multimodal experiences and communication means.[32]

The notion of identificatory potential is further extended by the generic markers employed. Alexa Weik von Mossner claims that Lloyd's novels are coming-of-age stories which "come to us in the guise of a critical eco-dystopia."[33] While the connection she establishes between the two genres is inarguably correct, her claim wrongly creates a genre hierarchy. Instead, it seems worthwhile to read the novels as hybrid fiction which gainfully draws on various genres. In this regard, I do not want to focus on what Weik von Mossner calls "genre-related limitations"[34] but rather rely on Green's more positive evaluation of genre. The following section of this article will show how the conversation established between various plot patterns and motifs furthers the effect of Laura's personal and political awakening and, in extension, how it contributes to providing identificatory potential to the readership.

2.2 The Eco-Dystopian *Bildungsroman*

Despite their innovative multimodality and the early allusion to various social, political and environmental changes and crises, the diaries still follow common patterns of young adult fiction:

> The narrative techniques often place us close to the action, with first-person narration, engaging dialogue, or even diary entries imparting accessible messages that may have the potential to motivate a generation on the cusp of adulthood.[35]

Since Laura relates her very personal experience and tries to chronicle her life, particularly with regard to her insecure and developing stance towards politics, the narratives contain the potential to motivate adolescent readers to reflect on their own lives and attitudes.

In this regard, the novels are also self-reflective,[36] and Laura often ponders on the circumstances of writing her entries. Once, she writes: "I can't believe I'm writing about *politics* in my diary. It used to be all about Ravi and Thanzila and shit at school. I'm so getting old before my time."[37] The short quotation exemplifies the mocking and often witty tone of her journal, but it also reveals the development of the diary and its writer. Even though Laura just planned to write about her very specific private problems, she soon chronicles the increasing surveillance and the rise of totalitarianism which are accompanied by a growing distrust in the police and the media (see *2017*, 66). Hence, well-known patterns and motifs from classic adult dystopias become visible and are intertwined with her more personal concerns.

The threat of an environmental disaster of apocalyptic extent (and its impact on human life) has become a "major preoccupation of the dystopian imagination."[38] This motif has also found its way into young adult dystopia, as not only *The Carbon Diaries* show by pointing out that a dystopian society can emerge due to environmental disasters. From the beginning of carbon rationing, riots and protest movements increasingly become a part of quotidian life, and the government seems incompetent and incapable of controlling the situation at first and eventually becomes a danger to society.

The novels portray various effects and forms of climate change. For instance, there are droughts, floods, heat waves and water riots in Andalusia, forest fires in France, and old people freeze to death or die from extreme heat all over Europe (*2015*, 97, 103). Catastrophes hit societies all around the world in different ways and to different extents, which becomes evident when Laura receives emails from her cousin in the USA in 2015 and when she experiences the reasons and effects of a migrant crisis in 2017. The scenario blends in with eco-dystopian fiction which generally discusses the relation between mankind and ecological disaster[39]. While humanity becomes able to increasingly alter the biosphere, it still cannot stand beyond or outside this material world[40]. In line with other eco-dystopian novels, *The Carbon Diaries* stress that mankind has already destroyed the environment to a large extent[41]. Laura repeatedly blames her parents' generation but simultaneously, though often unconsciously, demands to be allowed to make the same mistakes. Her political awaking is thus also linked to the need to realise that her generation has to rethink its relationship to and its responsibility for the environment instead of wanting the former generation to fix everything so that young people can continue living like their parents.

All these issues just mentioned (environmental disaster, totalitarianism, personal problems revolving around boyfriends and family members) already reveal the interconnection between young adult (eco-) dystopia and the *bildungsroman* which many scholars do not seem to be at ease with[42]. For example, they emphasise that the *bildungsroman* tradition tends to impose limitations on the plot, a trend that romantic elements often additionally reinforce by strengthening the status quo of heteronormativity and by limiting (female) characters' agency. Although such elements can impose limitations to a certain extent, the reconfiguration of *bildungsroman* and (eco-) dystopian motifs in connection to the diary and scrapbook format and to Laura's realization of her need to become engaged in a global society also reveals possible gains.

In both novels, passages on rationing and its impact on the microcosmic (Laura's direct surroundings) and the macrocosmic (Europe) level alternate rapidly with Laura's very personal issues[43] such as being in love with Ravi or, later on, being torn between her boyfriend Adi and the new band member Sam. Furthermore, environmental disasters such as a hurricane which hits the United States east coast underline the rapid development of (eco-)dystopia and also emphasise that now everyone is affected by global changes (*2015*, 86, 87). For Laura personally, the development of dystopia and the realization that she will also be affected go hand in hand with her forced loss of innocence and naivety. Even before the beginning of carbon rationing, Laura and her neighbour Kieran regard the upcoming period as the beginning of a new era. The chaos they witness while walking through London is the expression of a society's insecurity which feels robbed of the firm foundation of old normalities: "The roads were full of crazy people and there was smoke and explosions and screaming and singing and fights and madness everywhere" (*2015*, 9).

This rapid alternation between personal and public or political issues is also connected to the conversation between dystopia and the *bildungsroman.* The *bildungsroman* tradition, which lays emphasis on development, might appear contradictory to classic dystopias such as *1984* and *Brave New World* which create a very bleak scenario because the protagonists cannot overcome the apparently static dystopian system. Here, an advantage of the connection between young adult dystopia and the *bildungsroman* is rendered visible: a young adult dystopia often contains a spark of hope.[44] This insight is relevant for *The Carbon Diaries* since the complete absence of hope would invite neither Laura nor the reader to become politically active and to embrace empowerment.

In young adult dystopias adolescent characters are often designed as round, and thus developing, characters. This also becomes evident in *The Carbon Diaries* when a new generation and mindset emerges from inactivity. These characters symbolise the possibility of change and hope and serve as an "antidote to corrupt adulthood."[45] This can also be traced back to common *bildungsroman* motifs such as the construction of identity or the process of becoming responsible and self-dependent. Furthermore, the *bildungsroman* often features motifs such as first love and leaving home, emotional development, moral education, a critical focus on innocence,[46] an active shaping of the protagonist,[47] the ability to critically assess education and value systems[48] and a widening range of experience. All these motifs point to a character's increasing agency and the ability to challenge static systems and routines.

Although Laura's own awakening from passivity is hesitant, her development towards agency along with the portrayal of her peers' empowerment point to a new generation not willing to commit the old mistakes again. In the dark world of Lloyd's novels, the loss of "habitual lifestyle" is painful but "new solidarities, new value systems, and new modes of agency, all propelled by the hope that a different and in some regards ecotopian society will be possible," can emerge.[49]

Although young adult fiction is often attacked for 'recycling' old motifs, these motifs do not appear worn out to younger readers who encounter these "fundamental narrative structures for the first time."[50] As Green states when talking about the development of generic conventions, almost all novels "are novels based on novels based on novels. [...] But they change in the retelling. Novels change to stay relevant."[51] Moreover, through its hybridity, young adult literature can breathe "new life into old forms."[52] When young adult dystopias "recapitulate the conventions of the classic *Bildungsroman*, using political strife, environmental disaster, or other forms of turmoil as the catalyst for achieving adulthood,"[53] this often culminates in the depiction of a fall from innocence, (forced) empowerment and ensuing agency after a critical assessment of one's individual position. These steps of awakening and development are essential in order to overcome dystopia and become especially prominent in Lloyd's *Carbon Diaries* in the context of personal development.

These observations also tie in with the fact that private and political issues are inseparably intertwined in Laura's life. The generic hybridity accounts for the identificatory potential by interlinking the dystopian portrayal of ecological disaster with experiences shared by Laura and the readers. For instance, political awakening can be regarded as related to sexual awakening. Laura's increasingly complicated relationships to Adi and Sam are crucial for her evaluation of her own position in this new society. Since the two young men take different approaches to society and become involved in different manners, Laura also evaluates her relationships to them in political terms. The reader's realisation of shared experience is then even intensified by the diaries' multimodality which provides additional viewpoints and makes the novels appear more authentic and embedded in the readers' reality.

The next chapter explores further interrelations between Laura's awakening and empowerment with regard to her writing of a diary which chronicles her realisation that global events demand local (and thus also individual people's) activity. It will explain how Laura deals with both the local and global impact of the changes she is confronted with. Quoting critic Kay Sambell, Weik von Mossner writes that the "expression of moral meaning in children's dystopia is often characterized by degrees of hesitation, oscillation, and ambiguity."[54] This degree of hesitation is central to the protagonists' awakening and ensuing empowerment (and the acceptance thereof) in a society marked by environmental disaster and the threat of totalitarian regimes. Laura's hesitant and slow road to agency and to a global identity as well as the mediation and comprehensibility of her reluctant empowerment are crucial factors for helping readers to ponder their own attitude and potential to bring about a change.

3. Global Disaster and Local Impact: Laura's Awakening and Empowerment

Since Laura longs for personal fulfillment, carbon rationing signifies first of all a personal crisis for her. Her 2015 diary foregrounds her microcosm of family problems, her band *dirty angels*, and her final realization that she is in love with her best friend and band member Adi. The larger social issues are, nevertheless, always kept within view: "I called Adi who said I have to go to college tomorrow and act like I don't know him [Ravi] cos being mean works with boys. No traffic moving in London. No fuel. So quiet" (*2015*, 47).

Although Laura tries to stay away from politics in order to focus on her (love) life and the band, she is finally forced to realise that in the "world risk society,"[55] the distance or distinction between safe people and victims collapses.[56] Since the novels connect global environmental problems to Laura's preoccupation with 'typical' teenage problems, they eventually point out that "[l]ocal spaces are shaped and local identities are created by globalized contact as well as by local circumstances."[57] Hence, the idea of globalization, the "interconnectedness of the global and local levels,"[58] becomes increasingly prominent throughout the two novels. Laura's reluctant re-evaluation of her former opinions and (political) attitudes on both local and global levels often surfaces in the context of global environmental disaster which has an obvious impact on local life.

Laura's loss of innocence and naivety is gradually rendered more visible. February 2015 can be regarded as both a caesura and a point of departure: Laura and Adi are trapped in the London underground due to a power cut and although they escape from panic and riot unharmed, she sees London differently the day after:

> 30,000 passengers trapped till midnight, 8 million euros' worth of damage in the city, 2 buildings burnt down, 4 separate riots, looters fired on with gas and water cannons, 6 people dead, 260 injured, 800 arrests [...]. I can't

> believe how naïve I was before. I'm so down. Our first test and we failed it so bad. (*2015*, 25)

Despite these insights and in spite of being a member of a political punk band, Laura still does not want to change her life and become involved in activism and politics. Although she is well-informed and interested in what is happening in the UK as revealed by her collection of articles, she nevertheless initially "remains absorbed by the micro-level personal and family concerns more typical of adolescent life."[59]

Therefore, Laura's process of awakening is gradual and hesitant, marked by frequent relapses into inactivity and denial. In 2017, for example, she reveals her still rather naïve world view while talking to her father:

> 'I hate politics.'
> 'That's because you think it's got nothing to do with you.'
> 'It doesn't. Bunch of grey men.' (*2017*, 96)

This evaluation also ties in with her opinion that "[...] it's all a big fat ego trip, this helping people anyway" (*2017*, 87). Although her parents encourage her to make up her mind and to "look outside [her]self a bit" (*2017*, 87), Laura repeatedly stresses that she is "sick of politics" (*2017*, 43) because she feels that people want to pressure her into a specific kind of action: "I'm being dragged in against my will. I don't even believe in politics" (*2017*, 130). However, when she learns about the success of a demonstration her friends participated in, she at least briefly ponders her inactivity: "Unbelievable! I am amazed. The Government's *backed down*. [...] This is the first time I've ever seen something real happen from protesting: makes me feel a bit guilty for not getting stuck in" (*2017*, 51).

This hesitant development can also easily be traced by focusing on Laura's frequent use of the word 'normal.' She insists on normality and wants her normal life back even though she once briefly notices that she feels sick when she "think[s] about getting back to normal" (*2017*, 159). However, as Weik von Mossner has noticed, 'normality' is an ambiguous signifier and it never stands for the life Laura led before carbon rationing[60] as she cannot look back on a perfectly average life. Even though the definition of normality is about to change when rationing is established and she is told that "[r]adical is becomin' mainstream" (*2015*, 129), Laura tries to back away when her friends become too radical in her opinion.

Eventually, she even breaks up with Adi, who has become associated with THE 2, a radical and dangerous underground resistance movement.

However, although Laura does not want to embrace change, she eventually comes to understand that the people surrounding her are not 'abnormal' but that the situation simply demands change (see *2017*, 130). Her temporary insight that she is selfish and self-centered is especially stressed when she acknowledges "I am the ultimate selfish teenage stereotype" (*2017*, 78). Nevertheless, she continues to claim that she is too young to change anything and thus insists on her 'right to be normal.' "This huge longing to be normal swept over me," she admits, and this ties in with her refusal to assume responsibility (*2015*, 96). Despite some minor insights, Laura repeatedly tries to relapse into inactivity and contradicts her own recent evaluation that people cannot and should not disconnect themselves from larger issues in 2017: "what kind of person turns away from something happening right in front of their eyes?" (*2017*, 151, see also *2017*, 178).

Despite her own attitude, Laura frequently criticises her parents for their pretension to be normal and claims the exclusive right to be desperate and to remain passive as she is overwhelmed by the new situation (*2015*, 149) – Laura demands to spend her adolescence without the need to become responsible and self-reliant. In turn, she demands that the adult generation sort everything out and she extends this demand as she wants other countries to go on rationing, too. Laura becomes very agitated about a European voting on rationing: the people have "'[...] to vote yes!' [...] 'People can't be that stupid'" (*2015*, 144). Later, her response to Europe's decision to start carbon rationing is, again, based on her personal concern: "God, it feels so *good* not to be freaks anymore" (*2015*, 145).

Thus, Laura's development (and narrative) is not linear but a meandering process essential for the possibility of identification with the protagonist. The diary reveals that Laura is caught between duty and responsibility on the one hand and inactivity and the wish for a simple life on the other; an understandable reaction to a fast-changing world. However, given that the circumstances of Laura's life demand action, readers might find her relapses outrageous at times and want her to emerge from her 'bubble' for good. Hence, readers are invited to transfer their reactions to Laura's decisions to their own lives and thus to reflect on their own behaviour and (in)activity.

Besides, Laura's reactions reveal her liminal position: On the one hand, she understands that Western society can be held responsible for global problems and that a change of behaviour is urgently needed. On the other hand, she does not want to suffer from these changes. Although Laura does not trust in the adult generation anymore and calls them "selfish bastards" (*2015*, 120) when she realises that her life will be shaped by this generation's mistakes, she still wants to rely on them. While liminality and Laura's lack of trust are reminiscent of the *bildungsroman*, her lack of activity could eventually point to the bleak prospect of many dystopian scenarios. However, as McDonough and Wagner stress, "[w]ithin much of young adult dystopian fiction there is a causal relationship between a protagonist's awakening and agency. Only after being awakened to the realization that choices need to be made can the protagonist engage in the decision-making process that is agency."[61] Laura often wonders what and who is most important in (her) life; her indecisiveness and frequent relapses into inactivity reveal that she is "on the brink of multiple states"[62] with regard to her age, her position in society, her future prospects and plans.

This liminal state and its possible outcomes are particularly emphasised in *The Carbon Diaries 2017* when the tone becomes harsher and the issues more pressing. Simultaneously, Laura's inactivity slowly gives way to the acceptance of agency which is again linked to the wider geographical scope of the dystopian scenario and the narrative. The environmental problems are essentially the same as in 2015, but Laura, now a student in London, witnesses even more extreme effects in her own and other societies: The government becomes increasingly brutal and the right wing party "United Front" becomes more powerful while Europe starts to engage in water wars and is hit by a refugee crisis. Travelling through Europe, at first with her band and later with friends to bring back the ill Adi from Sicily, Laura experiences the rise of the Front National in France, the dehumanizing conditions in refugee camps, police brutality, a battle over water and eventually her own detainment in a camp.

Hence, Laura's journey across Europe mirrors her own inner journey and her eventual acceptance is triggered by artefacts which again find their way into her multimodal diary. While the newspaper clipping on the novel's first page directly focuses on the disasters brought about by climate change and the global need to react, the bleak atmosphere and dire circumstances depicted also have to be attributed to ensuing political changes since extremism and right wing political parties are on the rise (see *2017*, 18, 96). Besides, readers are provided with further information via newspaper clippings or messages relating other characters' opinions. Thus, readers are invited to make up their own minds and eventually wish Laura would realise what they have already noticed: the personal is political, the global is local, and the descent into dystopia is impossible to ignore. While discussing an example of cli-fi (climate fiction), Weik von Mossner stresses that "situations and individual actions must be understood in the larger context of the ecological, economic, and social conditions that bring them about."[63] Through Laura's experiences, the novel emphasises the need to think outside of the box of one's own community and to empathise with other people as most problems are not only local. It thus stresses the interconnection between environmental issues and political reactions on the one hand, and the need for local action as reaction to global issues on the other.

Laura eventually, though gradually, preoccupies herself with pressing questions including her role in this new world order and aspects relating to political activism. This also becomes visible regarding issues of identity which surface in the lyrics she writes for the *dirty angels* (*2017*, 125). While her lyrics deal with the universal topics of growing up and finding one's place in the world, Laura also starts to acknowledge that she has to shift her attention at least partially towards global issues since environmental problems and the resulting new political situations also affect her life and the lives of the people closest to her.

Laura's final epiphany occurs only in November 2017 when she reads a very positive review of her band's latest concert. Laura puts the review in her diary, thereby enabling the reader to follow her epiphany by reading along, which evokes a feeling of immediacy. The reviewer writes that "They ain't pretending no more" and "No stupid slogans, no faux postures and no shit" (*2017*, 190), which makes Laura feel hypocritical. When she notices that she is getting away with pretending to be a political activist, she feels that she is "not being straight with [herself]" (*2017*, 191). She finally accepts that the political is part of her private life and, in fact, intricately intertwined with doing what she loves. She tells the band member Claire "we've got to get stuck in, otherwise we're just a bunch of fakers onstage" (*2017*, 192). Laura's liminality is stressed once again when she claims that "[i]t was like standing on the very, very edge. One step forward for a whole new reality" (*2017*, 197). At a time when London is on the verge of a civil war, Laura starts to re-evaluate herself, her actions and attitudes and admits that "It's such a strange feeling when you see yourself clear, and all your little tricks are so transparent" (*2017*, 192). This realization even results in Laura's participation in a dangerous demonstration which leads to the fall of the government (see *2017*, 205). Such decisions and actions reveal that Laura needed to come to terms with her political attitude and role on her own instead of being forced or at least talked into a specific kind of action, and the reader is granted the same amount of freedom of thought. Here, the visual representation of an element supposedly external to Laura's diary thus again proves to be crucial for both Laura's development and the reader's identification with her.

Eventually, Laura's political decisions and her new awareness of responsibility are reflected in personal decisions once again. She leaves Sam, with whom she feels like "[a] normal boy, a normal girl" (*2017*, 184), for Adi, who is more politically involved. Still, being independent-minded persons, they will stay together as a couple but go separate ways regarding activism. While Adi will again join THE 2, Laura wants to fight "without guns and bombs" (*2017*, 207). Accepting the new world order and the end of 'normality,' she wants to use her now famous band (she also adds a print-out of the download charts which lists the *dirty angels* on position number one (see *2017*, 208)) to raise her voice. In her last entry, she writes that "A part of my life is over, the part where I tried to fit in, to keep it like it was before. I'm done with that shit" (*2017*, 208). The last sentence of her 2017 diary is very straightforward: "No bombs, no guns, no escape. All I want is a straight-up fight with all the crooked, thieving, lying, two-faced, cheating bastards. That's the only thing that matters to me anymore. Revolution!" (*2017*, 208).

4. Conclusion

In Saci Lloyd's *The Carbon Diaries*, the conversation established between (eco-) dystopia, a genre traditionally associated with bleakness and stasis, and the *bildungsroman* tradition, which pronounces development, effects a reconfiguration of established dystopian motifs and allows for hope to overcome the dystopian state and to establish a society aware of former generations' mistakes and of human responsibility for the environment.

This spark of hope, in turn, becomes the very basis for the novels' potential to motivate readers to become politically active and ponder their position in a global society.

Both the generic hybridity and the multimodal scrapbook format of the narratives support the comprehensibility of Laura's hesitant awakening, meandering development and empowerment. Without being prescriptive or overtly didactic, the novels emphasise that reflection and acknowledgement of the interconnection between one's personal life and political and public reality[64] are the first steps to take on the road to active participation in a global world. Personal decisions, identity construction and finding one's place in the world are taken seriously and stressed as integral to growing up in a global society by *The Carbon Diaries* which thus provide and construct a space for new perspectives.

Moreover, Laura's diary functions as a documentation of her reality. The semiotic resources taken from the 'real' world that her diary seems to be part of not only add a notion of credibility or chronicle her development, but evoke a sense of immediacy since they represent events which have triggered specific actions or epiphanies. Since the reader is enabled to follow Laura's development towards agency via her diary entries and the resources added to it, the "reader's construction of the fictional world [...] imitates the multiplicity of modes that are involved in everyday cognitive processes and is [sic] therefore becomes part of the experienciality of reading narrative texts."[65]

This experienciality is also connected to the many perspectives provided by the multimodal diaries which show that a change of perspective is required in an increasingly complex globalised world in which environmental problems in particular affect all nations and therefore all private lives within these nations. Acknowledging globalisation and realizing that everyone can find his or her own way to effect change leads to Laura's awakening. This, in turn, eventually points to the new possibilities and values of a young generation which might arise from the threat of dystopia.

The negotiation of young people's manifold options and formative influence could be considered one of the most powerful and important aspects of *The Carbon Diaries*. Since readers are enabled to identify with the protagonist, they realise, together with Laura, that inactive persons are also affected by change and turmoil and that not only adults can make a difference. Instead,

> [s]ocial and ecological change […] depends upon personal engagement and hard work [...]. The transformative potential of these novels makes them successful examples of critical eco-dystopian texts, as they warn young adult readers about the future while mobilizing them into action.[66]

Only when Laura realises that political activism does not run contrary to her ideas of self-realisation, but that the personal and the political are in fact intertwined, can her fall from innocence and awakening lead to the acceptance of responsibility and to agency. Laura eventually acknowledges that blaming her parents' generation may be easy, but that closing her eyes does not make her less guilty. Actually, the responsibility for dealing with ecological crisis and "for shaping society in the twenty-first century ultimately rests in the hands of [Laura's] generation."[67] Moreover, her neighbour Arthur even ponders if further generations might regard Laura's generation as heroes (*2015*, 152). However, this look into the future presupposes that mankind will then still be here. Laura thus eventually understands that history is not just a record detached from people's lives: "I can't believe what I'm writing. It's so weird being inside history" (*2017*, 147).

Notes

[1] The political reality in Western society and the apparent feeling of threat has triggered increasing sales of texts such as Orwell's *1984* (1949) and Atwood's *The Handmaid's Tale* (1985). Although portraying very different (political) dystopian visions, both novels seem to hit a nerve again. (see "Margaret Atwood: *The Handmaid's Tale* sales boasted by fear of Trump." 11 Feb. 2017. *The guardian.com*. retrieved 20.3. 2017. Similar articles were published in *The Independent* or the *New York Times*, for example, in February and March 2017.).
[2] See Balaka Basu, Katherine R. Broad, and Carrie Hintz (2015). "Introduction." *Contemporary Dystopian Fiction for Young Adults. Brave New Teenagers*. New York: Routledge, and Eckart Voigts and Alessandra Boller (2015). "Young Adult Dystopia: Suzanne Collins' *The Hunger Games* Trilogy (2008-2011)." *Dystopia, Science Fiction, Post-Apocalypse. Classics – New Tendencies – Model Interpretations*. Ed. Voigts and Boller. Trier: WVT. 411-430.
[3] Laura Miller (2010). "Fresh Hell. What's Behind the Boom in Dystopian Fiction for Young Readers?" *The New Yorker* June 14. n.pag. Retrieved 25 May 2017; see also Voigts and Boller (2015), 412.
[4] Miller (2010), n. pag.

[5] Sara K. Day, Miranda A. Green-Barteet, and Amy L. Montz (2014). "Introduction: From 'New Woman' to 'Future Girl': The Roots and Rise of the Female Protagonist in Contemporary Young Adult Dystopias." Ed. Day, Sara K, Miranda A. Green-Barteet, and Amy L. Montz Female Rebellion in Young Adult Dystopian Fiction. Farnham: Ashgate. 1-14, 4. See also the contribution by Sarah Schäfer-Althaus in this collection.

[6] John Green (2014). "Does YA Mean Anything Anymore? Genre in a Digitized World." *The Horn Book Magazine* (November/ December), 15-25, 22.

[7] Both the well-known and the rather recent motifs of dystopian fiction play a role in this conversation. See Voigts and Boller (2015, 413) for a list of common *bildungsroman* motifs and of the most prominent dystopian motifs now reshaped by young adult dystopia. See also Rüdiger Heinze's article in this collection.

[8] Even though this idea can be traced back to a slogan often used by second-wave feminism (itself based on an essay by Carol Hanisch), it does not only apply to feminist movements. *The Carbon Diaries* also ponder female emancipation and eco-feminism but almost all characters, even those that might be labeled post-feminist, eventually have to understand that private life and politics can hardly be disentangled in an age of environmental and political crisis.

[9] Alexa Weik von Mossner (2015). "Hope in Dark Times: Climate Change and the World Risk Society in Saci Lloyd's *The Carbon Diaries 2015* and *2017*." *Contemporary Dystopian Fiction For Young Adults. Brave New Teenagers*. Ed. Basu, Balaka, Katherine R. Broad, and Carrie Hintz. New York: Routledge, 69-83,71.

[10] Saci Lloyd provides many of the extra-diegetic elements used in both novels on her website *sacylloyd.com* and comments on them, which also makes the novels interesting from the viewpoint of inter- or transmediality.

[11] Marie-Laure Ryan and Jan-Noël Thon (2014). "Storyworlds Across Media. Introduction." *Storyworlds Across Media. Towards a Media-Conscious Narratology*. Ed. Marie-Laure Ryan and Jan-Noël Thon. Lincoln: University of Nebraska Press. 13-27, 13.

[12] While *The Carbon Diaries* use the apparently old-fashioned diary form, they still feature representations of new media (e.g. emails and text messages) and thematise their importance to contemporary culture and communication. See Ryan and Thon (2014, 14) for a discussion of the role media play in social and cultural change.

[13] Hallet (2014), 135.

[14] *Ibid.*, 123.

[15] *Ibid.*, 123f.

[16] This technique of simultaneous learning is employed rather frequently (see also *2015*, 8). However, the reader might understand faster than Laura that the material items the family members are longing for are unattainable and that their life will change drastically.

[17] Saci Lloyd (2008). *The Carbon Diaries 2015*. London: Hodder Children's Books, 4. Further references to this edition will be included in the text.
[18] The environmental problems so prominent in the narrative change Laura's whole life, for example with regard to school (new subjects), family life (her father loses his job and her mother decides to become a member of a feminist group) and interpersonal relationships (especially regarding her friends' different attitudes towards forms of political engagement). Again, these changes are displayed on the textual and the visual level of the novels.
[19] Hallet (2014), 126.
[20] *Ibid.*, 126.
[21] Weik von Mossner (2015), 70.
[22] Since both novels are set only seven years in the future, they are, from a 2017 perspective, not about the future anymore. This close temporal proximity evoked a feeling of urgent need for action when the novels were first published but this might be different for readers who encounter the novels after 2015/2017. Nevertheless, the weather conditions are becoming ever more extreme and climate change has become an even more pressing topic with the Paris Climate Agreement and the election of Donald Trump as President of the United States of America.
[23] Marie-Laure Ryan (2014)."Story/Worlds/Media. Tuning the Instruments of a Media-Conscious Narratology." *Storyworlds Across Media. Towards a Media-Conscious Narratology*. Ed. Marie-Laure Ryan and Jan-Noël Thon. Lincoln: University of Nebraska Press. 29-44, 39.
[24] See Ryan (2014), 40.
[25] Hallet (2014), 124.
[26] *Ibid.*, 125.
[27] *Ibid.*, 126.
[28] *Ibid.*, 125.
[29] *Ibid.*, 135.
[30] *Ibid.*, 132.
[31] *Ibid.*, 132.
[32] See *Ibid.*, 132.
[33] Weik von Mossner (2015, 78). In a more recent article, she puts the novels into the "category of climate change fiction or (…), cli-fi." This relabeling also points to the difficult classification of Lloyd's novels and to their generic hybridity. Alexa Weik von Mossner (2017) "Vulnerable Lives: The affective Dimensions of Risk in Young Adult Cli-Fi." Textual Practice (31:3): 553-566, 554.
[34] Weik von Mossner (2017), 555.
[35] Basu, Broad, and Hintz (2015), 1.
[36] Besides, Laura's writing can be seen as an act of identity formation and "her narrative often tells us more about herself and her world than she realizes" (Weik von Mossner 2015, 80).

[37] Saci Lloyd (2010). *The Carbon Diaries 2017.* London: Hodder Children's Books, 142. Further references to this edition will be included in the text.

[38] Basu, Broad, and Hintz (2015), 3.

[39] The diaries could also be discussed from an eco-critical perspective challenging "established cultural, political and ethical normativities" and engaging in a rigorous investigation and re-examination of (concepts of) nature. Catrin Gersdorf and Sylvia Mayer (2006). "Introduction". *Nature in Literary and Cultural Studies: Transatlantic Conversations on Ecocriticism.* Ed. Catrin Gersdorf and Sylvia Mayer. Amsterdam 2006, 10

[40] Rowland Hughes and Pat Wheeler (2013). "Introduction. Eco-dystopias: Nature and the Dystopian Imagination". *Critical Survey* 25.2, 1-6. 4.

[41] Roman Bartosch argues that the literary potential of fiction is a force that helps address ecological crisis. According to him, the semiotic power of literature lies in a "critical engagement with the practice of reading and writing the world." (Bartosch, Roman. (2012) "Literary Quality and the Ethics of Reading: Some Thoughts on Literary Evolution and the Fiction of Margaret Atwood, Iija Trojanow, and Ian McEwan." *Literature, Ecology, Ethics. Recent Trends in Eco-criticism.* Ed. Timo Müller and Michael Sauter. Heidelberg: Winter, 125). Bar-tosch sees a need to turn to so-called minor genres in order to explore literature's eco-critical potential since according to him, some canonised 'high-brow' forms of literature might not live up to contemporary expectations of literature as a tool of ecocriticism (Bartosch 2012, 117). In this context, young adult fiction and especially a generic hybrid and multimodal novel such as Lloyd's *Carbon Diaries* becomes an ideal space to discuss the interconnection of social, environmental and political issues and their connection to very particular personal lives.

[42] See Miller (2010, n.pag.); see for example Day, Green-Barteet, and Montz (2014), 11; Basu, Broad, and Hintz (2015), 8.

[43] The reciprocal influence of these two levels of Laura's life is also mirrored on the image level, for example when messages Laura receives from her friends thematise a battle over water and promise new songs for the band (see *2017*, 131).

[44] See Day, Green-Barteet, and Montz (2014), 10. Due to the sparks of hope included in *The Carbon Diaries*, they also qualify as critical (eco-) dystopias, as Alexa Weik von Mossner, whose discussion of the novels focuses on the notion of hope, stresses (2015, 70). Critical dystopias, according to Tom Moylan, include utopian elements or at least point to the potential of amelioration and utopia in an otherwise bleak, dystopian setting (see Moylan, Tom (2000). *Scraps of the Untainted Sky. Science Fiction, Utopia, Dystopia.* Boulder, CO).

[45] Kay Sambell. (2004). "Carnivalizing the Future: A New Approach to Theorizing Childhood and Adulthood in Science Fiction for Young Readers." *The Lion and the Unicorn* 28.2, 247-267, 252.

[46] Kenneth Millard (2007). *Coming of Age in Contemporary American Fiction.* Edinburgh: Edinburgh University Press, 2-5.

[47] Susan Ashley Gohlman (1990). *Starting Over. The Task of the Protagonist in the Contemporary Bildungsroman*. New York: Garland Publishing, 3-4.
[48] Ortud Gutjahr (2007). *Einführung in den Bildungsroman*. Darmstadt: Wissenschaftliche Buchgesellschaft, 13.
[49] Weik von Mossner (2015), 70.
[50] Basu, Broad, and Hintz (2015), 6.
[51] Green (2014), 19.
[52] Basu, Broad, and Hintz (2015), 6.
[53] *Ibid.*, 7.
[54] Qtd. in Weik von Mossner (2015), 72.
[55] Following Ulrich Beck, Weik von Mossner defines the world risk society as a "transnational, global community that is connected by shared ecological and economic risks and in which one cannot help but be affected by potential or actual devastation that happens elsewhere" (2015, 70).
[56] *Ibid.*, 70.
[57] Joachim Blatter (2013). "Glocalization." *Encyclopedia Britannica*. Britannica.com. n.pag. Retrieved 31 May 2017.
[58] Blatter (2013), n.pag.
[59] Weik von Mossner (2015), 75.
[60] *Ibid.*, 74-75.
[61] Megan McDonough and Katherine A. Wagner (2014). "Rebellious Natures: The Role of Nature in Young Adult Dystopian Female Protagonists' Awakenings and Agency." *Female Rebellion in Young Adult Dystopian Fiction*. Ed. Sara K Day, Miranda A. Green-Barteet, and Amy L. Montz. Farnham: Ashgate, 157-169, 158.
[62] Day, Green-Barteet, and Montz (2014), 9.
[63] Weik von Mossner (2017), 561.
[64] Since political issues are additionally reflected on the level of Laura's personal (love) life, Lloyd's novels also contradict the overly general claim that romance is restrictive (see Basu, Broad, and Hintz 2015, 9) and female friendships are generally sacrificed (see Ann M.M. Childs (2014). "The Incompatibility of Female Friendships and Rebellion." *Female Rebellion in Young Adult Dystopian Fiction*. Ed. Sara K. Day, Miranda A. Green-Barteet, and Amy L. Montz. Farnham: Ashgate, 187-201, 187).
[65] Hallet (2014), 135.
[66] Weik von Mossner (2015), 70-71.
[67] *Ibid.*, 70-71.

Bibliography

Bartosch, Roman (2012). "Literary Quality and the Ethics of Reading: Some Thoughts on Literary Evolution and the Fiction of Margaret Atwood, Iija Trojanow, and Ian McEwan." *Literature, Ecology, Ethics. Recent Trends in Ecocriticism*. Ed. Timo Müller and Michael Sauter. Heidelberg: Winter, 113-128.

Basu, Balaka, Katherine R. Broad, and Carrie Hintz (2015). "Introduction." *Contemporary Dystopian Fiction for Young Adults. Brave New Teenagers*. Ed. Basu, Broad, and Hintz. New York: Routledge, 1-17.

Blatter, Joachim. (2013). "Glocalization." *Encyclopedia Britannica.* Britannica.com. n.pag. Retrieved 31 May 2017.

Childs, Ann M.M. (2014). "The Incompatibility of Female Friendships and Rebellion." *Female Rebellion in Young Adult Dystopian Fiction*. Ed. Sara K. Day, Miranda A. Green-Barteet and Amy L. Montz. Farnham: Ashgate, 187-201.

Day, Sara K, Miranda A. Green-Barteet, and Amy L. Montz (2014). "Introduction: From 'New Woman' to 'Future Girl': The Roots and Rise of the Female Protagonist in Contemporary Young Adult Dystopias." *Female Rebellion in Young Adult Dystopian Fiction*. Ed. Sara K. Day, Miranda A. Green-Barteet, and Amy L. Montz. Farnham: Ashgate, 1-14.

Feder, Helena (2014). *Ecocriticism and the Idea of Culture: Biology and the Bildungsroman*. Farnham: Ashgate.

Gersdorf, Catrin, and Sylvia Mayer (2006). "Introduction." *Nature in Literary and Cultural Studies: Transatlantic Conversations on Ecocriticism*. Ed. Catrin Gersdorf and Sylvia Mayer. Amsterdam: Rodopi, 9-21.

Green, John. (2014) "Does YA Mean Anything Anymore? Genre in a Digitized World." *The Horn Book Magazine* (November/December), 15-25.

Gohlman, Susan Ashley (1990). *Starting Over. The Task of the Protagonist in the Contemporary Bildungsroman*. New York: Garland Publishing.

Gutjahr, Ortrud (2007). *Einführung in den Bildungsroman*. Darmstadt: Wissenschaftliche Buchgesellschaft.

Hallet, Wolfgang (2014). "The Rise of the Multimodal Novel. Generic Change and Its Narratological Implications." *Storyworlds across Media. Towards a Media-Conscious Narratology*. Ed. Marie-Laure Ryan and Jan-Noël Thon. Lincoln: University of Nebraska Press, 123-138.

Hughes, Rowland, and Pat Wheeler (2013). "Introduction. Eco-dystopias: Nature and the Dystopian Imagination." *Critical Survey* 25.2, 1-6.

Lloyd, Saci (2008). *The Carbon Diaries 2015*. London: Hodder Children's Books.

--- (2010). *The Carbon Diaries 2017*. London: Hodder Children's Books.

"Margaret Atwood: *The Handmaid's Tale* sales boasted by fear of Trump." (11 Feb 2017). *the guardian.com*. n.pag. retrieved 20.3. 2017

McDonough, Megan, and Katherine A. Wagner (2014). "Rebellious Natures: The Role of Nature in Young Adult Dystopian Female Protagonists' Awakenings and Agency." *Female Rebellion in Young Adult Dystopian Fiction*. Ed. Sara K Day, Miranda A. Green-Barteet, and Amy L. Montz. Farnham: Ashgate, 157-169.

Millard, Kenneth (2007). *Coming of Age in Contemporary American Fiction*. Edinburgh: Edinburgh University Press.

Miller, Laura. (2010). "Fresh Hell. What's Behind the Boom in Dystopian Fiction for Young Readers?" *The New Yorker* June 14. n.pag. Retrieved 25 May 2017.

Moylan, Tom (2000). *Scraps of the Untainted Sky. Science Fiction, Utopia, Dystopia*. Boulder, CO: Westview Press.

Ryan, Marie-Laure (2014). "Story/Worlds/ Media. Tuning the Instruments of a Media-Conscious Narratology." *Storyworlds Across Media. Towards a Media-Conscious Narratology*. Ed. Marie-Laure Ryan and Jan-Noël Thon. Lincoln: University of Nebraska Press, 29-44.

---, and Thon, Jan-Noël (2014). "Storyworlds Across Media. Introduction." *Storyworlds Across Media. Towards a Media-Conscious Narratology*. Ed. Ryan and Thon. Lincoln: University of Nebraska Press, 13-27.

Sambell, Kay (2004). "Carnivalizing the Future: A New Approach to Theorizing Childhood and Adulthood in Science Fiction for Young Readers." *The Lion and the Unicorn* 28.2, 247-267.

Voigts, Eckart, and Alessandra Boller (2015). "Young Adult Dystopia: Suzanne Collins' *The Hunger Games* Trilogy." *Dystopia, Science Fiction, Post-Apocalypse. Classics – New Tendencies – Model Interpretations*. Ed. Voigts and Boller. Trier: WVT, 411-430.

Weik von Mossner, Alexa (2015). "Hope in Dark Times: Climate Change and the World Risk Society in Saci Lloyd's The Carbon Diaries 2015 and 2017." *Contemporary Dystopian Fiction For Young Adults. Brave New Teenagers*. Ed. Balaka Basu, Katherine R. Broad, and Carrie Hintz. New York: Routledge, 69-83.

--- (2017). "Vulnerable Lives: The Affective Dimensions of Risk in Young Adult Cli-Fi." *Textual Practice* 31:3, 553-566.

Zapf, Hubert (2006). "The State of Ecocriticism and the Function of Literature as Cultural Ecology." *Nature in Literary and Cultural Studies: Transatlantic Conversations on Ecocriticism*. Ed. Catrin Gersdorf and Sylvia Mayer. Amsterdam: Rodopi, 49-69.

Miriam Gertzen (Bonn)

"Is This Where We Stand Now, Right Here on the Brink?" Geographical and Social Precarity and Adolescent Agency in the Eco-Dystopias of Julie Bertagna and Saci Lloyd

1. Introduction

One of the most pressing contemporary issues that is frequently addressed in recent young adult dystopian novels is the destruction of the environment, which is both often caused by and frequently causes political failure and social injustice. Thus the traditional dystopia, which has been described as a "prophetic vehicle" to voice "ethical and political concern" and to warn us "of terrible sociopolitical tendencies"[1] and, similarly, as "a picture of fear, a picture of a society which we would prefer to avoid, a warning,"[2] merges with elements of (post-) disaster fiction in these novels. Whether addressed only implicitly or being a central part of the plot, such environmental destruction is usually shown to be the result of human action and interference.[3] It is brought about mostly either through climate change, resulting from pollution and the exploitation of earth's resources, or, and perhaps more in line with the tradition of the eco-dystopian genre, as an effect of the use of atomic weapons or other means of mass destruction. In both instances, the novels represent worlds which become increasingly difficult to inhabit because the environment is either severely endangered or has already been largely destroyed. What emerges (or remains) are precarious geographies that have a grave impact on the lives of the people inhabiting them.

Even if eco-dystopian images of the future have dominated "the official 'look' of the future in popular culture"[4] since the 1970s, such narratives have often been "constrained as acts of political imagination" due to their tendency "to invalidate hope for any solutions"[5] to the problems at hand, often expressing fatalism and resignation[6] instead of voicing creative responses to the complex and intertwined issues of political failure, environmental destruction and social injustice. In contrast, the novels to be discussed in this paper "indicate that there is an emerging interest in redescribing and renarrating the future in ways that are energizing and provocative rather than nihilistic and disapproving,"[7] thus seeking to enable adolescent readers to become critical agents in their societies by emphasising the important difference that the protagonists make in order to challenge political failure and alleviate social injustice causing and caused by environmental destruction. The focus of my analysis will be placed on the works of two British authors, Julie Bertagna and Saci Lloyd. Bertagna's novel *Exodus*[8] was first published in 2002 and is the first book in a trilogy, with the other two parts, *Zenith* and *Aurora*, having been published in 2007 and 2011 respectively.[9] The protagonist is a teenage girl, fifteen-year-old Mara, who serves as the main focaliser of a heterodiegetic narrator. The other novels discussed here are Saci Lloyd's *The Carbon Diaries 2015*[10] and *The Carbon Diaries 2017*,[11] which were published in 2008 and 2009 respectively and in which autodiegetic narrator Laura is sixteen and eighteen years old. Both protagonists have to navigate and negotiate environmentally as well as socially precarious spaces on the journeys they undertake. While Bertagna's and Lloyd's novels address questions of geographical and social precarity in similar yet distinct ways, both authors suggest a direct link between their protagonist's acceptance of her social and geographical/ environmental responsibility and her gaining agency.

To discuss the ways in which the novels negotiate geographical and social precarity, I will start with a brief outline of Judith Butler's conceptualisations of 'precariousness' and 'precarity'. As "we need to consider social and spatial factors together in order to conceptualize identities, places and socio-spatial formations,"[12] the link between geographical/ spatial precarity on the one hand and social precarity on the other will be examined, demonstrating that these forms of precarity ultimately point towards questions of power and social (in)justice. Furthermore, I will show how the movement through as well as the interaction and negotiation with different precarious spaces are intertwined with the protagonists' growing recognition and acceptance of their responsibility towards these geographies and those inhabiting them, ultimately engendering their ability to find their agency and voice their subject position. Thus, these novels ask young readers to not only confront various notions of precarity but also to critically reflect on their own negotiation(s) with the world around them.

2. Conceptualisations of Precariousness and Precarity

Judith Butler differentiates between the conditions of 'precariousness' and 'precarity', which she both applies to human life: whereas 'precariousness' is conceptualised as "more or less existential"[13] and as "a feature of all life," since life "can be expunged at will or by accident," 'precarity', for Butler, implies "a more specifically political notion".[14] It is described as "that *politically induced* condition in which certain populations suffer from failing social and economic networks of support and become differentially exposed to injury, violence, and death."[15] 'Precarity' thus can be seen as the human-made "condition of maximised precariousness."[16] As Butler contends, this condition of precarity can be produced, exploited and distributed by those in power "for the purposes of profit and territorial defense"[17] and is thus consciously created. The discrepancy in situation between those in power and those who suffer from precarity especially highlights the aspect of (social) injustice implied in Butler's conceptualization.

While Butler is (mainly) concerned with existential, political and social *human* conditions, Ellen Dengel-Janic links this concept to a spatial dimension by pointing out that human 'precariousness' "is not just connected to social and political life, but also to geography and nature" because the "precarious social position of characters [is] undivided from their perilous and shifting locations in nature."[18] Dengel-Janic's argument certainly applies to the young adult dystopian novels analysed in this paper as they demonstrate that 'precariousness' indeed does apply to "all life", to repeat Butler's words, which implies non-human as much as human life as well as the geographies in which this life occurs. I argue that the notion of 'precarity' can also be applied to an ecological and spatial dimension: In a similar sense that people can be exposed to 'politically induced' violence and death, both the natural and non-natural environment can similarly be exposed to exploitation and destruction, resulting in the creation of geographical precarity. Moreover, both novels emphasise that geographical precarity through environmental destruction is very closely linked to the failure of social, political and economic systems and therefore does not only affect "certain populations" but in fact everyone and is often the cause for further situations of precarity.

3. Precarity as a Manufactured Risk

The Carbon Diaries 2015 begins by protagonist Laura telling the reader about the introduction of a carbon rationing system in the UK with the aim to reduce carbon emissions by 60% (*2015*, 4). The reason for this move by the government is the (fictitious) Great Storm that has hit Britain and the rest of Europe a few years previous to the events narrated in the novel, killing many thousand people. In the future of *Exodus*, it is already too late for such actions. The protagonist Mara's world already has largely drowned, instead of Europe there now is Eurosea, and only a few high points remain above the water level. Mara, her family and friends have to leave their island home in the north of Scotland because it, too, is slowly swallowed by the rising sea levels. This underlines Weik von Mossner's summary of the United Nations' stance on the subject of climate change, according to which "climate change is among the most serious and far-reaching threats to human life on earth."[19] Again, it can be added that this does not apply exclusively to human life. Climate change and its effects thus emerge as one way in which Butler's idea of precarity can be applied not only to human life but also to the environment as it can be regarded as a 'politically induced condition' and certainly human-made. In this context, social theories of risk (as developed in social sciences) are frequently referred to in order to frame narratives like Bertagna's and Lloyd's.[20]

Anthony Giddens, who distinguishes between two types of risks, has argued that environmental issues connected with global warming fall into the category of manufactured risk. In contrast to external risks, which strike mostly unexpectedly but occur "regularly enough [...] to be broadly predictable and [therefore] insurable", manufactured risks are "created by the very progression of human development."[21] Tied to this perception of risk is a shift from "worrying [...] what nature could do to us" to "worrying what we have done to nature."[22] Calculating these risks more or less reliably is no longer possible; at best, people can engage in risk-management in order to mitigate the effects.[23] In this sense, the condition of precarity described by Butler as "politically induced" can be seen as a result of consciously and/ or willfully denied risk-management, which constitutes a failure or unwillingness to act ethically.

Both novels emphasise that the natural catastrophes that threaten the future geographies and the people inhabiting them are clearly the ultimate effect of such manufactured risks as excessive pollution and exploitation of resources. A short prologue in *Exodus* makes human responsibility for the earth's drowning explicit:

> *The people feasted upon their ripe world. Endlessly, they harvested its lands and seas. They grew greedy, ravaging the planet's bounty and miracles. Their waste and destruction spread like a plague [...]. And the people saw, too late, their savage desolation of the world. [...] Imagine the vast, drowned ruin of a world washed clean. Imagine survivors scattered upon lonely peaks, clinging to the tips of skyscrapers, to bridges and treetops. Now retrack to the dawn of the world's drowning. Stand at the fragile moment before the devastation begins, and wonder. Is this where we stand now, right here on the brink?* (*Exodus*, i; emphasis in the text)

As this quotation shows, ecological destruction and resulting disasters are very much a manufactured, that is human-made, risk: People, not least politicians, have failed to act ethically and prevent ecological catastrophe and were thus active agents in the creation of their present condition.

Laura, the protagonist of *The Carbon Diaries 2015,* and the society she lives in certainly find themselves on this brink pictured in the quotation above from *Exodus*. The introduction of carbon rationing can be regarded as one of the ways in which "climate change is busily altering all the norms of modern existence"[24] in Lloyd's two novels. While her parents and sister are initially in denial about this new policy, Laura adapts to the new situation more quickly. In her diary, she chronicles not only her daily life at school and at home, but also extreme weather conditions both in the UK and abroad and the effects these have on her city, London. The city, indeed, becomes an ever more precarious space, a condition that truly affects everyone, not only certain parts of the population. Consequently, the city becomes more and more unfamiliar to its inhabitants, both on a spatial and on a social level. For example, the effects of a power cut, by now frequent across the city, unmask the already underlying fragility of society and the unstable character of existing social (and economic) networks. A simple journey on the underground is abruptly interrupted by a blackout, causing panic amongst the commuters. When Laura and her friend finally reach street level, the situation is no better: looting is going on in the West End, and on the Strand in Covent

Garden the two teenagers run into "a massive standoff" (*2015*, 38) between looters and rioters one the one and the police on the other hand. Although the blackout lasts only for two hours, the effects are severe and are summarised by Laura as follows:

> 30,000 passengers [on the underground] trapped till midnight, 8 million euros' worth of damage in the City, 2 buildings burnt down, 4 separate riots, looters fired on with gas and water cannons, 6 people dead, 260 injured, 800 arrests. (*2015*, 39)

Only one month after the introduction of carbon rationing, Laura's city becomes increasingly unsafe and her society has started to disintegrate. Laura's elderly neighbour, Arthur, aptly pinpoints this problem when he says that "[i]n some ways [the war] was easier – we had a clear enemy – but this time it's almost like we're fighting ourselves" (*2015*, 150), underlining again the human agency involved in bringing about various risk-situations through greed and irresponsibility.

Thus, spatial precarity due to ecological disaster is shown here to be the cause for other manufactured risks (according to Giddens) such as crime, demonstrating that the failure of social and economic systems and ecological destruction are very closely intertwined. As Mara in *Exodus* learns later on in the novel, "when the floods devastated New York and Tokyo [...] there was mass panic. Governments began to collapse everywhere. Economies crashed and everything that held society together started to fall apart" (*Exodus*, 195). Both novels therefore clearly argue for a causal relationship between human-made ecological precarity and social meltdown, the latter of which takes almost extreme forms in the novel *Exodus*.

4. Spatial and Social Precarity in *Exodus*

While Laura, her family and friends have to come to terms with the changing city they have known intimately for years, if not all their lives, in a process that stretches across the years spanned by both *Carbon Diaries* novels, Mara and her community in *Exodus* are faced with an existential threat so imminent that "[s]he cannot look away or dismiss it. She must pay attention" (*Exodus*, 47). Set in the year 2100, *Exodus* in a way extrapolates the events from the *Carbon Diaries* novels and represents a world that has already largely drowned. Thus, out of sheer necessity, Mara is moved to take on the responsibility of finding an alternative place to live already early on in the novel. In contrast to Laura, who initially seems to be simply drifting along with events, Mara immediately takes the initiative to find a solution and change her and her community's precarious situation. From the beginning, she "is an active player in the debate over what to do"[25] and persuades her community to set out together in search of New Mungo, a city built into the sky in a tree-like structure on the drowned ruins of Glasgow and whose existence she has learned of on the remains of the internet. She embarks on her journey in the full awareness that it will be a journey with no return.

However, New Mungo is not what Mara and her fellow islanders have hoped for. Instead of being a welcoming safe haven, the sky city has walled itself in "like a fortress" (*Exodus*, 196), barring access to any new arrivals. The city is represented as comprising different layers that both supersede each other and exist simultaneously. The first level is the 'old' Glasgow, the Glasgow of our, the reader's, present time, drowned to a large extent by the rising sea levels. Of this drowned city, the highest points still remain above water and form little islands, which are populated by people that call themselves 'Treenesters' after the homes they have fashioned for themselves in the surviving trees. The new sky city of New Mungo, finally, towers like an "arrogant monolithic structure"[26] above the Treenesters' islands in the so-called "netherworld" (*Exodus*, 96) and casts them in an almost constant shadow. A wall, built by the rulers of New Mungo, surrounds all levels of the city, and on its outside borders a refugee boat camp has formed, adding a further space to the city. Glasgow thus appears as a palimpsest, its layers representing different degrees of and different sides to precarity. Spatial precarity due to ecological catastrophe is again the common experience in all levels of the city, but the implications on the social and economic level differ greatly depending on the people's situatedness, that is on their positioning either within the seat of power that the sky city represents or outside of it.

Especially the boat refugees but also the Treenesters have to struggle for daily survival and are "differentially exposed to injury, violence, and death"[27] as per Butler's conception of precarity. In contrast to Ostry's interpretation of the netherworld as "[a]n ecological utopia of treed islands" in which, "despite scarcity and danger, the inhabitants [...]

survive in harmony with the limited environment,"[28] I consider it an example of precarity: People have lost, or are about to lose, their home to the sea, something to which the authorities of the sky city consciously add as they willfully exclude both groups inhabiting the other levels of the palimpsest-like city. While the sky city was initially supposed to take in or at least provide help to everyone in need it has instead "barred its doors" (*Exodus*, 196) and only allowed access to the brightest people. The authorities now not only bar access to people in need, but even exploit them as slave labour to expand the sky city (see *Exodus*, 161). The behaviour of the sky city authorities clearly exemplifies the willful production, exploitation, and distribution of precarity as described by Butler. Again, the dimension of social meltdown as an effect of ecological disaster is implied here as the authorities only act in their territorial interest and for their economic gain, similar to the looters in *The Carbon Diaries 2015* but with much graver consequences.

As Mara feels she has led her people from bad to worse on the journey from their drowning island to the refugee boat camp outside New Mungo she also believes that she has to rectify their current situation. As Curtis observes, "[s]he recognizes obvious injustice and sees herself as responsible to help fight against it."[29] Moreover, her strong sense of responsibility starts to encompass an increasing number of people as she cannot bear to think of leaving the other boat refugees behind. Refusing to accept the hopelessness in the boat camp, her will to find a solution drives her to find a way inside the city walls into the netherworld, where she meets the Treenesters. With their situation being almost as precarious as that of the boat refugees on the other side of the wall they are added to the list of those that Mara wants to find a new home for. While Grzegorczyk describes them as "a group of rebels thrown out of the city"[30] they do not actively resist New Mungo's injustice and instead passively wait for a saviour, whom they think they recognise in Mara. However, they also supply her with important knowledge and help her with gathering information that enables her to form a more concrete plan of action. Her journey through the netherworld is essential for her finally gaining access to the sky city of New Mungo, her last stop on her transit through the different levels of former Glasgow. Having come to the city of Glasgow, or rather the structure that has replaced it, as an outsider, Mara manages to function "as a bridge between disparate groups at New Mungo."[31]

While the authorities subject those outside the sky city to exploitation and perishing, they subject the inhabitants inside to constant ideological manipulation. They have successfully isolated the inhabitants by cutting off any communication between the different layers of the city, something of which the inhabitants of New Mungo are completely unaware. Furthermore, they have created a sanitised version or "*synthetic Theme Park*" (*Exodus*, 216; emphasis in the text) of the past. While exposure to such manipulation is not life-threatening to the people of New Mungo, it places them, more or less involuntarily, in a position that is irresponsible and unethical. Whether they are aware of it or not, they are complicit in exposing other people to precarious conditions. By allowing their leaders to carry on unchallenged and by signing over their social and ethical responsibility to them, the inhabitants of the sky city are furthermore complicit in the officials' willful mismanagement of the spatial precarity at hand and their consequent creation of an unjust society. The causal relationship between human-made ecological precarity and social meltdown that both novels suggest is thus extended to include questions of power: Social risks such as the ideological aspect of manipulation and the relinquishing of responsibility are both the result of and facilitate spatial precarity and the abuse of power.

Mara's function as a bridge between the different populations of New Mungo is completed once she manages to get inside the sky city. While she questions her role as "*the big heroine*" as she is "*too scared*" and really only wants "*an ordinary life*" (*Exodus*, 304; emphasis in the text), she nevertheless ultimately accepts this role. She seeks out a friend within the sky city whom she had previously met only virtually on the internet and who seems to be the only person within New Mungo who is dissatisfied with the way in which the city is run. In contrast to Sargisson's claim that the novel "privilege[s] the (exceptional) individual and say[s] nothing about collective action [which] makes for an unsatisfactory politics"[32], Mara and her friend engage in a collaborative effort: she shares her knowledge of the outside world with him and receives not only moral but also vital technical support in return, which enables them to start bringing about change. Thus, social justice can only be achieved when people from all layers of the city work together.

Despite finding love in New Mungo and her friend/ boyfriend feeling the need to remain in the city in order to start a rebellion, Mara resolves to carry out her plan to lead the refugees and Treenesters on yet another journey (the title-giving 'exodus') at the end of the novel. By acknowledging that "[she] can't let them down. [...] [She]'d feel so guilty that [she] abandoned them all [...]" (*Exodus*, 301), she clearly defines her subject position as wanting to

> fight to save what she can of the future that her parents, and her grandparents [...] struggled to give her. [...] The only way she can give any meaning to their lost lives is to keep fighting for her own future, and the future of [...] the Treenesters and the refugees. (*Exodus*, 305)

By representing the protagonist as having "a capacity to speak, to be heard, and to act"[33], the novel, "instead of portraying teenagers as inept and self-obsessed, [...] allows them to grow into political awareness with the ability to act and to work with those of different ages."[34]

5. Precarity and Responsibility in *The Carbon Diaries*

Laura's society in *The Carbon Diaries 2015* is less threatened by ideological manipulation, but as already shown above, the inhabitants of London are still exposed to precarious conditions due to rising ecological and spatial precarity and resulting social problems and injustices. As the year progresses, both the weather conditions and the related changes and incidents in the city that Laura records in her diary become more and more severe. For example, during an unprecedentedly hot and dry summer, water is strictly rationed in the city to the extent that it is switched off in private homes and only available via public standpipes. With these regulations, Laura observes, the city turns into a "[...] police state. There's a 24-hour patrol all over the city – and a hotline for grassing up your neighbours. It's prison for stealing water – what happened to drugs and mugging?" (*2015*, 226). The impression of increased surveillance and draconic punishment is reinforced when, at a demonstration against the turning off of a public standpipe, first the mayor "respond[s] by bringing in the riot police" and the police then shoots "directly into the crowd with live bullets" (*2015*, 226), killing five people. The mayor tries to justify this incident by claiming that he acted for the "[p]rotection of democracy" (*2015*, 226-227), but Laura's comment of "blah, blah. It's a load of bullshit" (*2015*, 227) demonstrates that she and her peers are not as easily manipulated as the people in the sky city of New Mungo in Bertagna's novel.

When the authorities in Laura's London also try to extend their power and begin to expose people in various ways to the risk of not having access to drinking water anymore, the people of London actively fight this development, countering the social meltdown that began earlier in the novel. Faced with the mayor's unethical behaviour of willfully increasing people's precarity and even having some people killed, the inhabitants of the city are reminded of their own responsibility and create new networks of support for each other, which becomes especially visible towards the end of the first novel when the city is threatened to be flooded by a surge tide caused by a massive storm. By accepting their responsibility towards each other and acting as a community the people of London cannot avert ecological disaster and spatial precarity, but they are able to fight the added threat of society breaking apart.

However, despite the fact that towards the end of *The Carbon Diaries 2015* Laura has learned that communal action can change the situation and be effective in resisting irresponsible and greedy politicians, in the beginning of *2017* she reverts to a more passive stance. Although carbon rationing and extreme weather conditions have altered her life substantially, the tipping point has not yet been reached or, indeed, exceeded. Neither, it seems, has the level of what she is willing to tolerate socio-politically as she repeatedly declares herself as "sick of politics" (*2017*, 67) and, much to the annoyance of some of her friends, remains largely "'so ... *passive*'" (2017, 48; emphasis in the text) and has to be coerced into participating in their various activities. In contrast to Mara in *Exodus*, who "consistently denies, challenges and resists passivity"[35] from the very beginning of the novel and thus appears as an example of what Mousseau calls "engaged citizens of the world", Laura here seems to represent the category of "inactive citizens of the West."[36] While Mara's journeys in *Exodus*, apart from occurring out of an existential necessity, can be furthermore regarded as enactments of an already strong personality, the element of the journey in *The Carbon Diaries 2017* is used in a more traditional way "as the construct enabling [the] characters' development."[37]

Therefore, Laura's journey in this novel initially has very different connotations than Mara's journey since it begins as a "European tour" (*2017*, 63) that she undertakes with her band, the *dirty angels*. Constituting a wish come true for her and the other band members, the tour leads them first to France and then on to Italy, retracing the traditional Grand Tour of the long eighteenth century. Like the traditional model, this journey also serves as an educational rite of passage, especially for Laura. However, whereas the traditional Grand Tour was undertaken to experience culture and to become acquainted with continental upper-class society, in the twenty-first century of *The Carbon Diaries 2017* Laura's tour is characterised and determined by various confrontations with social, political and geographical precarity.

The dream of band success turns into a nightmare when social and political unrest erupts in the countries they visit as a consequence of fears and events connected with climate change. Laura and her friends have to flee from France to Italy for political reasons after the Front National has won the general election as a result of fearmongering and insecurity. This turn is due to a rising environmental and thus geographical precarity, which again underlines the close connection between environmental destruction and socio-political instability. In Italy, the combination of extreme conditions due to climate change and resulting socio-political unrest is even more explosive. The country is confronted with a severe drought as well as a refugee crisis because of perilous climate conditions in many African countries, leading to experiences that will finally raise Laura from her passive political stance. After she and her friends have joined a village riot against water theft by the authorities because they felt "*[t]here just wasn't anything else to do*" (*2017*, 280; emphasis in the text), they are detained in a prison camp, awaiting their deportation back to the UK. Here, Laura meets a refugee girl from Ghana, who tells her she has lost her siblings during the crossing to Europe. For the first time Laura becomes fully aware that she still has "[her] choice, [her] home, [her] future – and this girl, nothing. The unfairness. It nearly [makes] [her] choke with shame" (*2017*, 291). Although joining the villagers in their protest had been more or less intuitive, it contributes to Laura's growing political maturation, similar to the confrontation with the girl's horrible experience and her own feelings of shame and guilt. Therefore, both events lead to her acceptance of responsibility not only towards those people close to her, i.e. her family, friends and the band, but rather to anyone she meets who suffers from injustice and the increasing geographical precarity. This feeling is increased by her realisation that, in contrast to some of those she has met on her journey, she still has much to fight for. Ultimately, her experience, especially in Italy, enables her to become active back home as well, where the socio-political situation is no less explosive than on the continent.

When London is faced with "civil war" (*2017*, 370) because of a fight over a planned new citizen tax, Laura decides to actively join the fight together with her friends. Whereas her acceptance of responsibility occurred more or less unconsciously in Italy because "there wasn't anything else to do", she is very aware of the situation this time: "It was like standing on the very, very edge. One step forward for a whole new reality. And then suddenly I felt this surge of excitement and nausea … and I took the step forward into … what? I don't know […]" (*2017*, 377). Moreover, she feels "proud to be out there, to be part of it all" (*2017*, 385) and, one might add, to have taken responsibility for the world she lives in, both socio-politically and environmentally. Thus, in one of her last diary entries, Laura is able to clearly define her subject position when she explains to her boyfriend that, while she accepts that he has to "'go [his] own way [by joining a radical group], […] [she has] got to do the same too'" (*2017*, 397), her way being peaceful resistance via her band's music (see *2017*, 397, 400).

6. Conclusion

All three novels clearly show how the characters' geographical journeys are intertwined with their personal maturation: In experiencing – and sharing – the precarious socio-political conditions that characterize the spaces they journey through, both Laura and Mara develop a sense of responsibility and agency. However, clear differences are also noticeable. On the one hand, Laura's journey is circular, from Britain to the European continent and back, mirroring not only the European Grand Tour as discussed but also the classic quest pattern, which brings the heroine back home in the end as a changed person. On the other hand, Mara's journey can only be linear, constituting a series of displacements with no possibility to return home, which aligns her experience with that of many refugees and migrants who seek to escape from war, famine and general poverty. Nevertheless, Mara's experience of various degrees of geographical and socio-political precarity is to a large extent concentrated on the relatively narrow space of the different levels of former Glasgow,[38] thus relocating the experience of forced migration to the Global North, while Laura's journey comprises an international perspective. The result, however, is similar again: Both protagonists emerge with strong and self-assured subject positions that are inextricably linked to the recognition and acceptance of their responsibility. Whereas Mara is represented as a questioning and resisting character from the beginning, Laura has to develop these aspects. In both cases, such character traits are represented as indispensable for the girls' gaining of agency and thus serve as a positive example for the implied readership. Only by becoming active and critical of the world around them are the protagonists able to find and go 'their own way,' which has to be different both from that of their elders and from that of their boyfriends. Mara grows into the role of leader that she has occupied all along, and Laura resolves to fight the system with those means that make sense to her, finally feeling that she does not "even have to justify it" (*2017*, 397) anymore.

The novels analysed here also correspond in the possibilities they illustrate for countering negative developments that result in precarious social and geographical conditions. Clearly, the solution is not to continue as is and rely on politicians to solve the existing problems. As I have shown in the discussion of the novels, authorities are at best expected to engage in managing the problems as and when they arise, but depending on their (economic and/or territorial) interests, there is no guarantee that such management will be effective, or, in fact, performed at all. The examples given in the novels point to the contrary as governments are shown to abuse their power in several ways. First, they fail to enact effective measures, including legislation, which has led to the ecological catastrophes in the first place. Furthermore, instead of trying their best to limit people's precarious conditions as best they can, the authorities even exploit the situation for their own interests, actively engaging in increasing both ecological and social risks and, ultimately, in creating a thoroughly unjust society. The fact that the authorities consciously create such conditions for the people makes these conditions an example of precarity, which according to Butler represents the human made 'condition of maximized precariousness'. Thus, But the responsibility does not only lie with the authorities. If people, like the inhabitants of New Mungo, relinquish their responsibility and ultimately their agency entirely to the authorities and thus allow them to abuse their power, they are complicit in the creation and continuation of precarious conditions for themselves and for others.

Both Bertagna's and Lloyd's novels therefore have the potential to raise the political consciousness of young readers by asking them to become critically aware and responsible agents in their community and society. Furthermore, these novels can show young people that their voice and their actions can make a difference and thus motivate them to self-confidently develop their own strategies for challenging dominant discourses. Ultimately, the novels encourage their readers to develop a strong subject position from which they are able to positively shape their future as well as that of those around them.

Notes

[1] Raffaella Baccolini and Tom Moylan (2003). "Introduction. Dystopia and Histories." *Dark Horizons. Science Fiction and the Dystopian Imagination.* Ed. Baccolini and Moylan. New York and London: Routledge, 1-12, 2.
[2] Maria Nikolajeva (2012). *Power, Voice and Subjectivity in Literature for Young Readers*. New York and Abingdon: Routledge, 74.
[3] A notable exception among the titles recently published for adolescents in this generic field is Susanne Beth Pfeffer's *Last Survivors* trilogy: *Life as We Knew It* (2006), *The Dead And The Gone* (2008) and *This World We Live In* (2010). In these novels, a meteor hits the moon, thus changing its orbit to the extent that hardly any sunlight can reach the earth anymore and that the weather in general changes considerably. Humanity is thus portrayed as a helpless and innocent victim of forces they have no influence on or control over.
[4] Andrew Ross (1991). *Strange Weather. Culture, Science, and Technology in the Age of Limits*. London: Verso, 144.
[5] Frederick Buell (2003). *From Apocalypse to Way of Life. Environmental Crisis in the American Century*. New York and London: Routledge, 256.
[6] See Richard Kerridge (2002). "Narratives of Resignation. Environmentalism in Recent Fiction." *The Environmental Tradition in English Literature*. Ed. John Parnham. Aldershot: Ashgate Publishing Limited, 87-99, 87.
[7] Kimberley Reynolds (2011). *Children's Literature. A Very Short Introduction*. Oxford: Oxford University Press, 111.
[8] Julie Bertagna (2002). *Exodus*. London: Young Picador. All further references to this edition will be included in the text.
[9] However, these further two novels will not be discussed in this paper.
[10] Saci Lloyd (2008). *The Carbon Diaries 2015*. London: Hodder Children's Books. All further references to this edition will be included in the text.

[11] Saci Lloyd (2009). *The Carbon Diaries 2017*. London: Hodder Children's Books. All further references to this edition will be included in the text.
[12] Clare Bradford and Raffaella Baccolini (2011). "Journeying Subjects. Spatiality and Identity in Children's Texts." *Contemporary Children's Literature and Film. Engaging with Theory*. Ed. Kerry Mallan and Clare Bradford. Basingstoke: Palgrave Macmillan, 36-56, 37.
[13] Judith Butler (2010). *Frames of War. When is Life Grievable?* London and New York: Verso, 3.
[14] *Ibid.*, 3.
[15] *Ibid.*, 3, my emphasis.
[16] *Ibid.*, 26.
[17] *Ibid.*, 32.
[18] Ellen Dengel-Janic (2014). "The Precariousness of Postcolonial Geographies. Amitav Ghosh's *The Shadow Lines* and *The Hungry Tide*." *Narrating "Precariousness". Modes, Media, Ethics*. Ed. Barbara Korte and Frédéric Regard. Heidelberg: Universitätsverlag Winter, 72-84. 71.
[19] Alexa Weik von Mossner (2013). "Hope in Dark Times. Climate Change and World Risk Society in Saci Lloyd's *Carbon Diaries 2015* and *2017*." *Contemporary Dystopian Fiction for Young Adults. Brave New Teenagers*. Ed. Carrie Hintz, Balaka Basu, and Katherine R. Broad. London: Routledge, 69-83, 69.
[20] See Weik von Mossner (2013), 70, as well as Fiona McCulloch (2011). *Children's Literature in Context*. London and New York: Continuum, 129.
[21] Anthony Giddens (1999). "Risk and Responsibility." *The Modern Law Review* 62.1, 1-10, 4.
[22] *Ibid.*, 3
[23] See *Ibid.*, 4-5.
[24] Vanessa Thorpe (2010). "Forget Harry Potter. Saci Lloyd Thrills Teenagers with a Heroine who Battles Climate Change and Extremism." *The Observer*. 17 January. Web. 13 January 2017.
[25] Claire P. Curtis (2013). "Educating Desire, Choosing Justice? Susan Beth Pfeffer's *Last Survivors* Series and Julie Bertagna's *Exodus*." *Contemporary Dystopian Fiction for Young Adults: Brave New Teenagers*. Ed. Carrie Hintz, Balaka Basu, and Katherine R. Broad. London: Routledge, 85-99, 94.
[26] Fiona McCulloch (2007). "A New Home in the World. Scottish Devolution, Nomadic Writing, and Supranational Citizenship in Julie Bertagna's *Exodus* and *Zenith*." *ARIEL: A Review of International English Literature* 38.4, 69-96, 74.
[27] Butler (2010), 3.
[28] Elaine Ostry (2013). "On the Brink: The Role of Young Adult Culture in Environmental Degradation." *Contemporary Dystopian Fiction for Young Adults: Brave New Teenagers*. Ed. Carrie Hintz, Balaka Basu, and Katherine R. Broad. London: Routledge, 101-114, 103.
[29] Curtis (2013), 96.

[30] Blanka Grzegorczyk (2015). *Discourses of Postcolonialism in Contemporary British Children's Literature*. New York and London: Routledge, 80.
[31] Lucy Sargisson (2012). *Fool's Gold? Utopianism in the Twenty-First Century*. Basingstoke and New York: Palgrave Macmillan, 111.
[32] Sargisson (2012), 115.
[33] Curtis (2013), 97.
[34] Reynolds (2011), 111.
[35] Sargisson (2012), 112.
[36] Robert Mousseau (2016). "Connecting Travel Writing, Bildungsroman, and Therapeutic Culture in Dave Eggers's Literature." *The Poetics of Genre in the Contemporary Novel*. Ed. Tim Lanzendörfer. Lanham: Lexington Books, 255-269, 257.
[37] *Ibid.*, 257.
[38] A wider international perspective is incorporated in Bertagna's follow-on titles to *Exodus*, *Zenith* and *Aurora*.

Bibliography

Baccolini, Raffaella, and Tom Moylan (2003). "Introduction. Dystopia and Histories." *Dark Horizons. Science Fiction and the Dystopian Imagination*. Ed. Baccolini and Moylan. New York and London: Routledge, 1-12.

Bertagna, Julie (2002). *Exodus*. London: Young Picador.

Bradford, Clare, and Raffaella Baccolini (2011). "Journeying Subjects. Spatiality and Identity in Children's Texts." *Contemporary Children's Literature and Film. Engaging with Theory*. Ed. Kerry Mallan and Clare Bradford. Basingstoke: Palgrave Macmillan, 36-56.

Buell, Frederick (2003). *From Apocalypse to Way of Life. Environmental Crisis in the American Century*. New York and London: Routledge.

Butler, Judith (2010). *Frames of War. When is Life Grievable?* London and New York: Verso.

Curtis, Claire P. (2013). "Educating Desire, Choosing Justice? Susan Beth Pfeffer's *Last Survivors* Series and Julie Bertagna's *Exodus*." *Contemporary Dystopian Fiction for Young Adults: Brave New Teenagers*. Ed. Carrie Hintz, Balaka Basu, and Katherine R. Broad. London: Routledge, 85-99.

Dengel-Janic, Ellen (2014). "The Precariousness of Postcolonial Geographies. Amitav Ghosh's *The Shadow Lines* and *The Hungry Tide*." *Narrating "Precariousness". Modes, Media, Ethics*. Ed. Barbara Korte and Frédéric Regard. Heidelberg: Universitätsverlag Winter, 72-84.

Giddens, Anthony (1999). "Risk and Responsibility." *The Modern Law Review* 62.1, 1-10.

Grzegorczyk, Blanka (2015). *Discourses of Postcolonialism in Contemporary British Children's Literature*. New York and London: Routledge.

Kerridge, Richard (2002). "Narratives of Resignation. Environmentalism in Recent Fiction." *The Environmental Tradition in English Literature*. Ed. John Parnham. Aldershot: Ashgate Publishing Limited, 87-99.

Lloyd, Saci (2008). *The Carbon Diaries 2015*. London: Hodder Children's Books.

--- (2009). *The Carbon Diaries 2017*. London: Hodder Children's Books.

McCulloch, Fiona (2007). "A New Home in the World. Scottish Devolution, Nomadic Writing, and Supranational Citizenship in Julie Bertagna's *Exodus* and *Zenith*." *ARIEL: A Review of International English Literature* 38.4, 69-96.

--- (2011). *Children's Literature in Context*. London and New York: Continuum.

Mousseau, Robert (2016). "Connecting Travel Writing, Bildungsroman, and Therapeutic Culture in Dave Eggers's Literature." *The Poetics of Genre in the Contemporary Novel*. Ed. Tim Lanzendörfer. Lanham: Lexington Books, 255-269.

Nikolajeva, Maria (2012). *Power, Voice and Subjectivity in Literature for Young Readers*. New York and Abingdon: Routledge.

Ostry, Elaine (2013). "On the Brink: The Role of Young Adult Culture in Environmental Degradation." *Contemporary Dystopian Fiction for Young Adults: Brave New Teenagers*. Ed. Carrie Hintz, Balaka Basu, and Katherine R. Broad. London: Routledge, 101-114.

Reynolds, Kimberley (2011). *Children's Literature. A Very Short Introduction*. Oxford: Oxford University Press.

Ross, Andrew (1991). *Strange Weather. Culture, Science, and Technology in the Age of Limits*. London: Verso.

Sargisson, Lucy (2012). *Fool's Gold? Utopianism in the Twenty-First Century*. Basingstoke and New York: Palgrave Macmillan.

Thorpe, Vanessa (2010). "Forget Harry Potter. Saci Lloyd Thrills Teenagers with a Heroine who Battles Climate Change and Extremism." *The Observer* (17 January). Web. 13 January 2017 <https://www.theguardian.com/books/2010/jan/17/carbon-diaries-saci-lloyd-television>.

Weik von Mossner, Alexa (2013). "Hope in Dark Times. Climate Change and World Risk Society in Saci Lloyd's *Carbon Diaries 2015* and *2017*." *Contemporary Dystopian Fiction for Young Adults. Brave New Teenagers*. Ed. Carrie Hintz, Balaka Basu, and Katherine R. Broad. London: Routledge, 69-83.

Part II
Didactic Explorations

Maria Eisenmann (Würzburg)

The Potential of Young Adult Dystopian Fiction in the EFL Classroom

In the first part of this article, I will discuss the role of literature in the EFL classroom. The second part introduces the importance of opening up the canon with young adult dystopian fiction. Afterwards, the benefits of contemporary dystopias for the EFL classroom are emphasized. In part four the focus will be on the potential that contemporary dystopian fiction has by giving an overview of a wide range of texts which can be used in class. How these recent novels can be employed in EFL teaching contexts will be illustrated in part five by Veronica Roth's novel *Divergent* (2011).

1. The Role of Literature in the EFL Classroom

In addition to teaching language and culture, teaching literature has always been part of the core curriculum of the EFL classroom. In the last two decades, literary texts have taken on a firmly established role for all ages and for all school types. Nowadays a wide range of texts is taught, ranging from rhymes, songs or picturebooks using simplified readers in the primary classroom up to linguistically more demanding authentic texts for advanced students. The reasons why foreign language literature is read "are manifold and include scientific literary analysis such as aesthetic education, genres and types of texts, stimulus to imagination, textual analysis, as well as important components of EFL teaching such as media competence, student motivation and creativity".[1]

Although literature learning in TEFL can look back upon a long history it was not until the turn of the century that young adult fiction was taught in schools. Traditionally, literary learning was strongly focused on canonised texts such as William Golding's *The Lord of the Flies* (1954), Aldous Huxley's *Brave New World* (1931) or J.D. Salinger's *The Catcher in the Rye* (1951). This is currently changing, as curricula are increasingly moving away from a uniform and static canon integrating young adult fiction, which has become a part of many national curricula for (foreign) languages. This was in particular enhanced by the advent of reader response in literary criticism and the communicative approach and communicative possibilities in language pedagogy, which had a high impact on the learner's role.

Consequently, the canon is expanding, which is not only due to the changed nature of language teaching but also because young adult fiction itself has changed considerably in terms of content, style and genres, especially since the 1990s. Young adult fiction has received increasing attention in recent years, not only with regard to the general book market but also to the EFL classroom. There are many subgenres of young adult fiction such as problem novels, LGBTQ, fictions of migration and multicultural novels, historical fiction, adventure fiction, mystery and fantasy, crime and detective novels, ghost and horror stories, post-apocalyptic narratives, science fiction and dystopias covering a wide array of interests and topics while also addressing different genders and age groups.[2]

Imagination and empathy enhance intercultural and transcultural learning because these novels show the many similarities young people have, very often problems specific to adolescents and their crossing the threshold between childhood and adulthood, especially regarding bullying, violence, social norms, friendship, love and gender roles, to name but a few. Dealing with these issues also provides opportunities to foster students' political awareness and critical thinking skills. Usually told from the teen perspective, the stories focus on multifacetted processes of identity construction in transcultural and globalised worlds.

2. Opening up the Canon with Young Adult Dystopian Fiction

The subgenres of dystopian literature and post-apocalyptic narratives in particular are now enjoying a remarkable popularity. This is most probably because they often address topical issues while making them accessible for learners by embedding them in themes which are relevant to the students. Thus, they offer a great potential and an especially good opportunity for teenage readers to identify and empathize with the adolescent characters. A glance at the central school leaving exam in Hesse (here the topic is called *Utopia and Dystopia – Utopie und Dystopie*[3]) or North

Rhine-Westphalia (here the topic area is called *Visions of the Future – Exploring Alternative Worlds*[4]) also show that utopias, dystopias and science fiction are keeping their set place in EFL teaching. Dealing with dystopias one quickly comes across terms such as post-apocalyptic narratives or science fiction because the field of contemporary dystopian narratives is marked by a fundamental generic hybridity which Curtis emphasises as follows: "Postapocalyptic fiction exists at a genre cross-roads between science fiction, horror and utopia/dystopia".[5] Generally, some of the texts are more distinctly science fiction than others, e.g. the films *The Matrix* or *Blade Runner*. Some of them qualify more clearly as dystopian without showing any science fiction elements, e.g. Kazuo Ishiguro's *Never Let Me Go* (2005), which could also be seen as "coming of age horror".[6] Texts such as J.M. Coetzee's *Waiting for the Barbarians* (1980) share dystopian concerns by creating a post-apocalyptic atmosphere but do not share any of the science fiction features. Thus, the boundaries between the different genres have become fluid.

It is difficult to explain what a dystopia is without having a look at its opposite: the utopia. For Lyman Tower Sargent "utopianism is essential for the improvement of human condition," but "if used wrongly, [...] utopianism is dangerous".[7] In his entry on "Dystopias" Brian Stableford argues that the significance of the firm establishment of a dystopian image of the future in literature should not be underestimated: "Literary images of the future are among the most significant expressions of the beliefs and expectations we apply in real life to the organization of our attitudes and actions".[8]

According to Spisak

> Dystopias are characterized as a society that is a counter-utopia, a repressed, controlled, restricted system with multiple social controls put into place via government, military, or a powerful authority figure. Issues of surveillance and invasive technologies are often key, as is a consistent emphasis that this is not a place where you'd want to live.[9]

Thus, in a dystopian society propaganda is used to control the citizens. Information, independent thought, and freedom are restricted, usually a figurehead or concept is worshipped by the citizens of the society and people are under constant surveillance. As a result the dystopian protagonist often feels trapped and is struggling to escape, questions the existing social and political systems, believes or feels that something is terribly wrong with the society in which he/she lives, and helps the audience recognize the negative aspects of the dystopian world through his/her perspective.[10] This can be found in classics of dystopian science fiction novels like Aldous Huxley's *Brave New World* (1932) and George Orwell's *Nineteen Eighty-Four* (1949) as well as in recent ones like David Eggers' *The Circle* (2013) that shares similar storytelling techniques, situations and themes.

But what is it that makes dystopias so attractive and successful, particularly for EFL teaching? And what can we read in the EFL classroom? In 2000 Tom Moylan stated:

> Dystopian narrative is largely the product of the terrors of the twentieth century. A hundred years of exploitation, repression, state violence, war, genocide, disease, famine, depression, debt, and the steady weakening of humanity through the buying and selling of every-day life provided more than enough fertile ground for this fictive underside of the utopian imagination.[11]

Thus, apart from Mary Shelley's *Frankenstein* (1818) and some of H. G. Well's novels in the nineteenth century, which can be viewed both as forerunners of science fiction as well as dystopian fiction, all other texts of the canon were written in the twentieth century. Novels such as Aldous Huxley's *Brave New World* (1932) or Anthony Burgess' *A Clockwork Orange* (1962) as well as Ray Bradbury's *Fahrenheit 451* (1953) are among the first dystopian texts and came to represent the classical, or canonical, form of dystopia. Probably the most well-known example of classic dystopian literature is *1984* by George Orwell, written in 1949. It is an example of a dystopia in which British society, over time, became warped and transformed into an extreme totalitarian state. However, within the following decades, in the 1960s, 1970s and 1980s, the dystopian narrative faded into the literary background and it was not until *1984* that, because of its title, George Orwell's novel renewed the interest in this literary genre.[12]

Margaret Atwood's *A Handmaid's Tale* (1985) can be viewed as a return to the roots of dystopian fiction in its classical sense. It is important to note that Margaret Atwood herself suggests that her novels often reflect her concerns about the world we live in, but particularly the environmental problems of our time and the role of women in society: "I began as a profoundly apolitical writer, but then I began to do what all novelists and some poets do: I began to describe the world around me".[13] *The Handmaid's Tale* has become standard reading in schools and university courses around the world. It has also been a very popular text for teaching purposes, especially within German schools. Among others mentioned above it became part of the literary canon that took their place on the prescribed list of class readers, leaving hardly any room for other texts to be taught. But there is no reason to focus just on these classics because most of the current, revised German curricula do not prescribe texts that have to be read. Literary examples can now be freely chosen and the time is ripe to open up this literary canon, to read and discuss contemporary 21st century texts.

Keeping to the traditional literary canon in the EFL classroom bears the risk that the twentieth century texts tend to prevent access to many topics instead of opening them for the students, because they are so distant to current discourses on society, politics, bioethics or the media. And what is more, the protagonists are not at all interesting for young readers. Our world has changed as have our problems today. While the classical, canonical forms of dystopia were written under the influence of totalitarian or authoritarian governments and the threat of dehumanization by a perfectionist oppressive state machinery (particularly Communism in the Soviet Union and National Socialism in Nazi Germany), learners today are faced with the massive problems caused by a neoliberal society. The problems of the 21st century differ from those of the twentieth century. This is why "narratives of a future societal collapse or crisis have responded to a set of urgent challenges that [...] have increased at the beginning of the 21st century".[14]

In his claim that "dystopias are no longer written these days" Zygmunt Bauman clearly refers to the dystopian texts of the twentieth century.[15] This becomes obvious when he explains that in our "'fluid modern' world of freely choosing individuals" we certainly do "not worry about the sinister Big Brother who would punish those who stepped out of line".[16] He further comments on a "liquid modernity", where "nothing can […] keep its shape for long" and where the responsibilities for success and failure increasingly lie with the single individual.[17]

All of these issues have an enormous impact on EFL teaching. The genre has changed in the course of time and contemporary dystopian fiction has a high potential within the EFL classroom when it comes to promoting critical thinking and challenging students to develop political consciousness, especially for teaching students at higher levels. And this is why it is time to turn away from classical dystopias and explore the immense potential of recent texts if we want to do the dystopian genre justice.

3. The Benefits of Contemporary Dystopias for the EFL Classroom

Burnett and Rollin state that dystopias "depict the worst of all possible societies" and "exaggerate contemporary social trends and in doing so, offer serious social criticisms".[18] However, young adult dystopias have not yet received the academic attention they deserve. In 2003 Carrie Hintz and Elaine Ostry were among the first researchers to consider this genre by predicting its ground-breaking future within literary studies:

> Utopian and dystopian fiction is a productive space to address cultural anxieties and threats as well as to contemplate the ideal; [...] we can expect that this genre will become increasingly popular and provocative. Utopian and dystopian literature talks about the fears, questions, and issues that interest children and young adults.[19]

In the following the focus will be on issues such as learning about social responsibility, gaining inter- and transcultural competences, entering the discourse on global matters and ecodidactics.

3.1 Social Responsibility

Dystopias, therefore, offer the opportunities for readers to ask "big-scale life questions"[20] and since our world is changing right before our eyes year after year, we have to be aware of this. Dystopian fiction mirrors what can go wrong and thus helps students to see how the potentially problematic developments can inspire change and those involved to work together in order to achieve a common goal, e.g. students can learn not only about the abuse of power, but can be enabled to see political structures in order to develop an ethical commitment towards them.

According to Wolk, teaching through inquiry and for social responsibility go hand-in-hand: "classroom inquiry nurtures social responsibility, and living a socially responsible life means to live a life of inquiry".[21] In dystopian novels, students see the moral dilemma that characters have to face and are confronted with what they would do in the characters' situation. With a focus on social responsibility, students can be taught about historical consciousness and current problems such as political conflicts, war, constitutional rights, propaganda, etc. The idea is to create what Wolk calls a "living curriculum", and using dystopian literature to teach students about social responsibility supports a process of inquiry that can only be described as something active and living, which finally leads to "a belief in the common good".[22]

The dichotomy of good and evil is also an essential element, e.g. in Suzanne Collins' *The Hunger Games* (2008), Veronica Roth's *Divergent* (2011) and James Dashner's *The Maze Runner* (2009). The dystopian society and its political system decides what is good and evil. Through the imagined encounter with another society in a world with so many issues that are stacking up, dystopias invite students to critically reflect on questions of political, cultural and social relevance in their own society. Thus, they need to be aware of these issues and have to learn to believe in a way to incite change for the greater good. This finally allows for a change of perspective, and thus helps to promote students' critical thinking in terms of political and social awareness.

3.2 Intercultural and Transcultural Competences

By touching problems that are not bound to a particular nation or culture and dealing with topics of general human concern, these texts go beyond mere interculturality and promote transcultural competences.[23] The ability to take on someone else's point of view is closely connected to the ability to develop empathy, both of which are part of both intercultural and transcultural communicative competence (see Delanoy 2013, Volkmann 2010). Dystopias can thus help students to foster intercultural and transcultural competences because their fictional worlds are very often depictions of real existing places which can be recognised by the recipients. As these texts, however, usually show very negative political, economic and ecological developments, they can be defined as "[…] dark side of utopia – dystopian accounts of places worse than the ones we live in".[24] Many texts have strong connections to the learners' own world because they feature 'real' places, e.g. Panem, the country in which The

Hunger Games is set, is described as having developed "out of the ashes of a place that was once called North America",[25] Chicago, which serves as setting for Veronica Roth's novel Divergent, or Glasgow in Scotland, which partly serves as the setting for Julie Bertagna's Exodus (2002). Usually it is "[...] a non-existent society described in considerable detail and normally located in time and space that the author intended a contemporaneous reader to view as considerably worse than the society in which that reader lived [...]."[26]

The texts all focus on fundamental and existential concerns of human existence such as global and ecological developments, technical innovations as well as the abuse of political power. All of these cross-cultural issues raise the question of the individual's responsibility. "With its capacity to frighten and warn, dystopian writing engages with pressing global concerns: liberty and self-determination, environmental destructtion and looming catastrophe, questions of identity, and the increasingly fragile boundaries between technology and the self".[27] What these narratives offer the reader is not a vision of a possible future, but a fundamental scrutinising of the present.

3.3 Global Matters

We are all confronted with overpopulation and demographic crises, extinction of species, dynamics in biotechnology, climate change, shortage of resources, global injustice and financial crises, ecological disasters, unchecked surveillance of computer data, terrorism, migration and displacement etc. In the last decade on an international level, the pedagogical direction of environmental education has emerged, which in turn is closely connected with ecocriticism and ecodidactics from cultural and literary studies. In the German-speaking world as well, such ecologically oriented (ecocritical) concepts could provide a clear impetus for research, university teaching and school education. New or re-named concepts of global education, global learning and transcultural competence have become indispensable key terms in EFL discourse.[28] However, ecodidactics is not just an exemplary or representative theme selection on global issues. Global education is all about enhancing students' emancipatory, critical-reflexive skills needed in order to raise an awareness for global-local interdependencies.[29] Furthermore, global education is about the students' development of identifying the current planetary threat and actively addressing these dangers in a shared ethics of responsibility.[30] Focusing on global issues thus has become of utmost importance in today's classrooms.

While Huxley, Orwell and even Atwood were writing about the 'victory' of industrialisation and capitalism, we now "live in a world that has to make decisions concerning its future under the conditions of manufactured, self-inflicted insecurity".[31] And while Aldous *Huxley's Brave New World* or Orson Scott Card's *Ender's Game* (1985) deal with ambitious projects of human engineering and the social consequences of eugenics, the issue of genetic engineering has been accepted as a terrible fact in Neal Shusterman's *Unwind* (2007), which concentrates on the ethical and philosophical concerns raised by a society which transplants their children's organs into different recipients. The novel engages with contemporary concerns about artificial human reproduction and mirrors the fact that we now live in a world that

> […] can no longer control the dangers produced by modernity; to be more precise, the belief that modern society can control the dangers that it itself produces is collapsing – not because of its omissions and defeats but because of its triumphs. Climate change, for example, is a product of successful industrialization which systematically disregards its consequences for nature and humanity.[32]

The threats, dangers and risks of modernity, the inequalities and abuses in the field of economy, politics and society, all influence dystopian writing.

3.4 Ecodidactics

Since the 1990s humanities have been contributing to ecocritical debates starting within the field of ecocriticism. International pedagogy has just recently transformed into the direction of environmental education, which has been formed and associated with cultural and literary studies approaches of "'ecocriticism'" or "'ecodidactics'".[33] A transition towards such environmentally oriented ecocritical concepts can also be found in German classroom contexts.

However, the question must be asked to what extent the relatively new ecodidactic approach[34] can be justified in the field of TEFL, and why the objectives of environmental education should be embedded into the disciplines of humanities such as teaching language, literature and culture. The most important impact of humanities most probably consists of enriching ecological discussions by appreciating contradictory scientific doctrines and various opinions, or as Parham puts it:

> This fact, that environmental education is regarded by many of its practitioners as a matter of raising awareness by fostering the 'correct' sympathies, values and imagination, implies that humanities disciplines such as literary and cultural studies have an important contribution to make to an education founded on environmental principles.[35]

Students should be enabled not only to take part in global discourses, but also to reflect on their responsibility as individuals. Consequently, teaching and learning does not mean following the common tenet or preaching to the converted,[36] Students need to be engaged to have an opinion on their own and the classroom should be an opportunity for open, democratic constructive interdisciplinary exchanges of ideas.

Due to the global growth of ecological challenges the field of research has expanded into the area of ecological education.[37] There are diverse and varied definitions and also approaches of ecocriticism, e.g. as "the study of the relationship between literature and the physical environment"[38] or as "[the] study of the relationship between literature and the environment conducted in a spirit of commitment to environmentalist praxis".[39] Environmental responsibility and the call for commitment have acquired great importance also in the context of EFL teaching. One of the major attempts is to make students understand how environmental global issues concern us all, stressing commonalities in order to ensure the survival of humankind in view of global challenges.[40]

Since many of today's dystopian novels portray global ecological degradation and show how these environmental issues have an immense impact on the inner world of their fictional societies, they lend themselves to being taught according to ecodidactic principles.[41] This can be exemplified e.g. in Paolo Bacigalupi's *The Drowned Cities* (2012), which depicts the story of the direct results of global warming and the wasting of resources. It can also be illustrated in Julie Bertagna's novel *Exodus* (2002), in which due to global warming the sea levels have risen so much that most of the world has drowned and even the life on some remaining islands is constantly threatened so that alternative ways of living have to be found.

4. Exploring Alternative Worlds – A Selection of Dystopian Fiction

The fast and constantly increasing number of dystopias does not mean that all contemporary dystopian novels are suitable for teaching purposes. Furthermore, Hintz and Ostry emphasise that regarding the choice of dystopian novels for adolescents "the stakes are high: these writings may be a young person's first encounter with texts that systematically explore collective social organisation".[42]

According to Groenke and Schwerff, twentieth century dystopian fiction can roughly be assigned into two key issues: (1) governmental abuse of power and (2) science and ethics.[43] Quite obviously some of the texts fit into both categories. Although each dystopian text has its own characteristic political concerns as well as aesthetic qualities, they can be categorised according to the threats they depict.[44] In the following some examples of contemporary young adult dystopias will be given, which can be used as class readers and can serve as an orientation for teachers and their learners. Many of the titles have been written as series, trilogies or even quartets but all of the books can stand on their own:

Thematic focus	Examples of literature
Postapocalyptic scenarios with world-changing catastrophes such as plague or World War III, which turn communities into societies marked by secrecy, fear, and control	• Julianna Baggot (2013): *Pure* (trilogy) • Marie Lu (2011): *Legend* (trilogy) • Philip Reeve (2001): *Mortal Engine*s (quadrilogy) • Veronica Rossi (2012): *Under the Never Sky* (trilogy)

Environmental and ecological destruction by global warming, pollution and the wasting of resources	• Paolo Bacigalupi (2012): *The Drowned Cities* • Julie Bertagna (2002): *Exodus* (trilogy) • James Dashner (2009): *Maze Runner* (trilogy) • Saci Lloyd (2009): *The Carbon Diaries 2015* • Saci Lloyd (2015): *It's the End of the World As We Know It* • S.J. Kincaid (2012): *Insignia* • Veronica Rossi (2012): *Under the Never Sky* (trilogy)
Depiction of conformity where uniformity is embraced out of a fear that diversity brings conflict	• Allie Condie (2011): *Matched* (trilogy) • Lois Lowry (1993): *The Giver* • Lauren Oliver (2011): *Delirium* (trilogy) • Veronica Roth (2011): *Divergent* (trilogy) • Scott Westerfeld (2005-2007): *Uglies* (quadrilogy)
Rigid methods of economic, affective and/or technological enslavement and silencing of citizens, e.g. by physical and/ or mental imprisonment	• Jeolle Charbonneau (2013): *The Testing* (trilogy) • Suzanne Collins (2008): *The Hunger Games* (trilogy) • Allie Condie (2011): *Matched* (trilogy) • Dave Eggers (2013): *The Circle* • Kazuo Ishiguro (2005): *Never Let Me Go* • Gemma Mally (2008): *The Declaration* • Marissa Meyer (2012): *Cinder* • Lauren Oliver (2011): *Delirium* (trilogy) • Veronica Roth (2011): *Divergent* (trilogy) • Neal Shusterman (2007): *Unwind* • Scott Westerfeld (2005): *Uglies* (trilogy)

Most of the contemporary young adult dystopian fictions mentioned above follow the traditional models written by Huxley, Orwell, Bradbury and Atwood, but unlike the classics of dystopias they directly address young adult readers and take up aspects of other young adult genres such as problem, adventure or fantasy novels. The design of a dystopian future society can thus serve to criticise current politics as well as address adolescent issues of the young protagonists. At the very heart of the novels there are young adults who not only protest against the regime and search for alternative forms of life but also develop their own identity, while very often taking a stand against their families in the course of finally growing up.

5. Teaching Veronica Roth's Novel *Divergent* – An Example

The theoretical considerations will be illustrated by an example of young adult dystopian fiction. Veronica Roth's novel Divergent (2011) is the first part of the trilogy, which can be read as a stand-alone piece of literature. The predominant issues belong to the field of governmental abuse of power, violence and discriminating social structures within a post-apocalyptic society. Due to its language and topical complexity the novel is appropriate for an advanced EFL classroom.

It is a captivating and fascinating book about Beatrice Prior's dystopian future Chicago world, shortly after a war has just finished. The society, that ironically believes it is still a utopia, is divided into five personality-based factions, each of which is dedicated to the cultivation of a particular virtue and responsible for a specific function: the government is run by Abnegation (the selfless), law by Candor (the honest), security by Dauntless (the brave), social services by Amity (the peaceful), and invention by Erudite (the intelligent). Posing as a practice that secures social stability and functioning, the categorization of people serves, in fact, as a means of control over human nature. On an appointed day of every year, all sixteen-year-olds must select the faction to which they will devote the rest of their lives. But the protagonist and Abnegation member Beatrice Prior (Tris) is not able to find her place in this system. When she takes her personality test, which is supposed to tell her into which faction she belongs, the results are unclear and she is told that she is "Divergent". In fact, those who are divergent are the truly admirable people in the story because they possess manifold virtues which makes them unclassifiable. Hence, it is impossible to group them into one of the five factions. Having been warned that Divergence is an "extremely dangerous" condition which may result in her death Tris rebels against society's conformity mania.[45]

Regardless of which of the reading procedures is selected, the reading process should be accompanied by pre-, while- and post-reading activities, which help to provide appropriate scaffolding. Commonly known pre-reading activities such as predicting the plot from the text's title or book cover, reading the first sentence, or listening to music/sound samples of the film version which are related to the plot, can help to activate previous knowledge and raise reader expectations. In order to prepare students both emotionally as well as in terms of language and content the teacher can ask the students to discuss the formation of teen social circles and how people join and fit in (or not). This can be part of a think-pair-share activity: Students approach the initial (open-ended) question on their own and then discuss their findings with a fellow student before settling on a final answer because choosing a faction in Divergent can be compared to choosing a peer group, e.g. in school. Finally, the teacher collects the different responses, visualizes them (e.g. with the help of a word cloud via wordle.com) and invites all students to take part in a lively class discussion. Not only does this approach raise the level of student motivation, but it is also a good way to obtain insights into what students already know or think about the book, its topics, and publishing background.

As a further step and in order to raise an awareness for the governmental division of society into personality types, teachers can ask their students to take one of the online aptitude tests connected to the novel.[46] Students can discuss not only their results in class but also the term "Divergent" by online research or by consulting a dictionary before they start reading the novel. In order to aid students in their active reading process while-reading activities can be used as guidance when reading inside or outside the classroom. These activities can include structural aids such as filling in character profiles, writing characterisations or chapter summaries. While reading *Divergent* it is essential for students to gain an understanding of the beliefs and values of each faction and how they work. For this, students should fill in a worksheet with the most important, relevant information under each faction:

Faction	Abnegation	Amity	Candor	Dauntless	Erudite
Definition					
Characteristics					
Physical Traits					
Relationship					
Government Type					

For the definition of the faction name students should be encouraged to look up the word in an online dictionary. For characteristics students will have to find out about what the faction members are like, e.g. raucous and rowdy or quiet and stern. The list of the faction's physical traits comprises the members' physical appearance such as hairstyle, jewellery and tattoos or colours and type of clothes they wear. For the relationship part students should list other factions which they are particularly (un)friendly with. Finally, government type means to find out whether there is a set leader of the faction or whether they settle matters by talking it out. This way the novel can be made more accessible and can help students to get into the social structures of this dystopian post-apocalyptic society. To work on the faction profiles the following tasks can be very helpful:

- *While reading the novel choose one of the five factions and take notes by focusing on its characteristics, physical traits, relationship towards other factions and government type.*
- *Find other students in class who have worked on the same faction. Get together in one group, design a poster about your faction, and present it to the class. Compare and discuss your results in class.*

With the adolescent character Tris in the centre of this captivating story the process of identification is facilitated and thus has a high potential for engagement. Many of the reading processes of self-reflection and re-evaluation require a change in perspective to see the world through Tris' eyes. A prerequisite is that students are willing to suspend disbelief, to let themselves be drawn into the world of the story, and to subject themselves to the rules of the world created in Divergent. Students need to understand that Tris' reasons for rebellion are not intrinsic. She is rather forced into a situation that causes an "awakening", a "realization of how ruined the adult world has become", which in turn leads to "a standoff between adolescents and adults that empowers young people to turn against the system as it stands and change the world in ways adults cannot".[47] However, the realisation that the rebellion is indeed up to herself as an individual scares Tris, and Divergence is not an identity she is willing to accept. She feels that she cannot bear so much responsibility, that she is not strong enough to live without a faction, and fitting into one community seems to be the most desirable choice in her world: "To live factionless is not just to live in poverty and discomfort; it is to live divorced from society, separated from the most important thing in life: community".[48] In the context of this quote the question should be discussed whether conformity to a common goal makes a society stronger or weaker. In the text, the conformist society embraces their uniformity out of a fear that diversity will breed conflict. As the novel depicts the struggle between the protagonist Tris and the oppressive government, it attempts to tease out the appropriate balance between personal freedom and social harmony.

With Tris being in the focus of the plot, *Divergent* is also a novel of polarised identities because Tris possesses traits and aptitudes that belong to multiple factions. Thus, she sees herself as having many different selves. For a better understanding of Tris' conflict students could be asked the following questions:

- *If you were Tris which faction would you (not) have chosen? Why/ Why not?*
- *Do you sometimes feel yourself as belonging to something like a faction? Which one(s)?*

At the end of *Divergent* Tris realizes that she actually has many identities which resolve her personality crisis and allow her to find a meaningful, less restrictive form of identity in between defeat and hope. She has no alternative but to accept her Divergence, concluding with her lesson learned: "I have no home, no path, and no certainty. I am no longer Tris, the selfless, or Tris, the brave. I suppose that now, I must become more than either".[49]

After having read the novel teachers should not only ensure students' comprehension of the story, but also concentrate on their personal reaction to the plot. For instance, in re-writing the plot using a different viewpoint or even genre, students can demonstrate not only their understanding of the plot or characters of the story they have read, but also train their literary competences, all of which can be done in the post-reading activities.

Since the world depicted in Divergent is a prime example of a dystopic future society and governmental abuse of power, the students should learn about the features of a dystopia. This can be done by first sensitising the students for the term "utopia":

> *Imagine your own perfect place to live in. Think about a few things that would make this world a perfect one for you. Share your ideas with the class.*

In a first step, students would learn about the term "utopia" and, in a second step, about its opposite – the "dystopia". A follow-up task could be the following:

> *The opposite of a utopia is a dystopia. In the novel Divergent you can find utopian and dystopian aspects. Create a list of both characteristics.*

Here students should come up with elements such as futuristic setting, governmental control, class system, Tris as a heroine who feels that something is wrong etc.

In order to make students reflect on the whole novel, the post-reading activities should be as creative as possible. This goal can be reached by a creative writing task in which the students are asked to design their own faction with the following instructions:

> *Get together in groups and describe a faction of your own design. The faction can be based on anything from a way of thinking, to the way people look, ethnicities, gender, creativity, favourite hobbies, etc. Think of the following faction details: Where is it located? What people are in your faction? What do they look like? How are they chosen? What are your*

faction values? What are your faction duties/tasks? What makes it a good and/or bad faction? What are some potential problems within your faction?

Subsequently students can present their factions in class. The idea behind this task is to make the novel more accessible for students despite the complexity of the genre.

6. Conclusion

When technological societies have gone awry and a strong necessity for social change is visible, it seems that people need utopian and dystopian literature more than ever.[50] Through the imagined encounter with another society it may invite students to critically reflect on questions of political, cultural, and social relevance in their own society, allow for a change of perspective, and thus help to promote students' critical thinking as well as political and social awareness. Thus, dystopias display their critical potential on the one hand and offer their readers experiences which can be of great significance for their personal development and their interaction with society on the other hand. Each of the above-mentioned texts provide a reading of young adult fiction that allows teens to find hope in each character through their rebellion. Not only do the texts mentioned provide hope but they also offer a support platform for discussion and open political debates to teenagers across the world.

Notes

[1] Rüdiger Ahrens (2013). "Teaching Literatures." *Basic Issues in EFL Teaching and Learning.* Ed. Maria Eisenmann and Theresa Summer. Heidelberg: Winter, 181-189, 181.

[2] See Katherine T. Bucher and KaaVonia M. Hinton (2010) *Young Adult Literature. Exploration, Evaluation, and Appreciation.* Boston: Allyn & Bacon; Mechthild Hesse (2009). *Teenage Fiction in the Active English Classroom.* Stuttgart: Klett, 6; Carl M. Tomlinson and Carol Lynch-Brown (2010). *Essentials of Young Adult Literature.* Boston: Pearson.

[3] https://kultusministerium.hessen.de/sites/default/files/media/kcgo-e.pdf

[4] https://www.standardsicherung.schulministerium.nrw.de/cms/zentralabitur-gost /faecher/ getfile.php?file=3388
[5] Claire P. Curtis (2010). *Postapocalyptic Fiction and the Social Contract.* New York: Lexington, 7.
[6] Eckart Voigts (2015). "Introduction. The Dystopian Imagination – An Overview." *Dystopia, Science Fiction, Post-Apocalypse. Classics – New Tendencies – Model Interpretations.* Ed. Voigts and Alessandra Boller. Trier, WVT, 1-11, 6.
[7] Lyman T. Sargent (1994). "The Three Faces of Utopianism Revisited." *Utopian Studies* 5.1, 1-37, 9.
[8] Brian Stableford (2016). "Dystopias." *The Encyclopedia of Science Fiction*, n.pag.
[9] April Spisak (2012). "Dystopian Novel?" *Horn Book Magazine* 88.3, 55-60, 55.
[10] Albert Rau (2010). "Margaret Atwood's *The Handmaid's Tale*: A Dystopian Novel in the EFL Classroom." *Teaching the New English Cultures & Literatures.* Ed. Maria Eisenmann, Nancy Grimm, and Laurenz Volkmann. Heidelberg, Winter, 109-124, 115.
[11] Tom Moylan (2000). *Scraps of the Untainted Sky.* Boulder: Westview Press, xi.
[12] Frauke Matz (2015). "Alternative Worlds – Alternative Texts: Teaching (Young Adult) Dystopian Novels. *Learning with Literature in the EFL Classroom.* Ed. Werner Delanoy, Maria Eisenmann, and Frauke Matz. Frankfurt: Lang, 263-280, 267.
[13] Margaret Atwood (1982). *Second Words: Selected Critical Prose 1960-1982.* Toronto: House of Anansi Press, 15.
[14] Voigts (2015), 2.
[15] Zygmunt Bauman (2012 [2000]). *Liquid Modernity.* Cambridge: Polity Press, 61.
[16] *Ibid.*, 61.
[17] Bauman (2012), 62.
[18] G. Wesley Burnett and Lucy Rollin (2000). "Anti-Leisure in Dystopian Fiction: The Literature of Leisure in the Worst of All Possible Worlds." *Leisure Studies* 19.2, 77-90, 77.
[19] Carrie Hintz and Elaine Ostry (2003). *Utopian and Dystopian Writing for Children and Young Adults*. London: Routledge, 12.
[20] Spisak (2012), 60.
[21] Steven Wolk (2009). "Reading for a Better World: Teaching for Social Responsibility with Young Adult Literature." *Journal of Adolescent & Adult Literacy* 52.8, 664-773, 666.
[22] *Ibid.*, 666.
[23] Matz (2015), 265.
[24] Raffaela Baccolini and Tom Moylan (2003). "Introduction. Dystopia and Histories." *Dark Horizons, Science Fiction and the Dystopian Imagination.* Ed. Baccolini and Moylan. New York: Routledge, 1-12, 1.

[25] Suzanne Collins (2008). *Hunger Games*. London: Scholastic, 21.
[26] Sargent (1994), 9.
[27] Balaka Basu et al. (2013). "Introduction." *Contemporary Dystopian Fiction for Young Adults. Brave New Teenagers*. Ed. Basu et al. New York: Routledge, 1-18, 1.
[28] See, for example, Reinhold Freudenstein (1999). "Global Issues im Englischunterricht." *Praxis des neusprachlichen Unterrichts*. 46.3, 237-249; John Parham (2006). "The Deficiency of Environmental Capital: Why Environmentalism Needs a Reflexive Pedagogy." in Mayer and Wilson (eds.) (2006), 7-22; Sylvia Mayer and Graham Wilson (eds.) (2006). *Ecodidactic Perspectives on English Language, Literatures and Cultures*. Trier: WVT; Laurenz Volkmann (2012). "Ecodidactics als Antwort auf die planetarische Bedrohung? Zum Einsatz von Ecopoetry im Englischunterricht." *Anglophone Literaturdidaktik – Zukunftsperspektiven für den Englischunterricht*. Ed. Julia Hammer et al. Heidelberg: Winter, 393-408.
[29] Volkmann (2012), 394.
[30] Ulrich Beck (2012 [2009]). *World at Risk*. Cambridge: Polity Press.
[31] Beck (2012), 8.
[32] *Ibid.*, 8.
[33] See Parham (2006), Mayer and Wilson (2006).
[34] See, for example, Mayer and Wilson (2006), Volkmann (2012).
[35] Parham (2006), 9.
[36] Volkmann (2012), 396.
[37] Volkmann (2012), 396-397.
[38] Glotfelty qtd. in Volkmann (2012), 396.
[39] Buell qtd. in Volkmann (2012), 396.
[40] See, e.g., Mayer and Wilson (2006).
[41] See also the contributions by Alessandra Boller and Miriam Gertzen in this collection, who both focus on texts that depict the serious consequences of climate change.
[42] Hintz and Ostry (2003), 2.
[43] Susan L. Groenke and Lisa Schwerff (2010). *Teaching Young Adult Literature through Differentiated Instruction*. Urbana: NCTE.
[44] Basu et al. (2013), 3-4.
[45] Veronica Roth (2011). *Divergent*. New York: HarperCollins Publishers, 23.
[46] The flowchart can be found on the following webpage: http://bookclub.wikia.com/wiki/Divergent_Faction_Flowchart
[47] Basu et al. (2013), 7.
[48] Roth (2011), 20.
[49] Roth (2011), 487.
[50] See Hintz and Ostry (2003), ix.

Bibliography

Primary Literature

Atwood, Margaret (1986). *The Handmaid's Tale*. Boston: Houghton Mifflin Company.
Bacigalupi, Paolo (2012). *The Drowned Cities*. London: Atom.
Bertagna, Julie (2008) [2002]. *Exodus. Vol. 1*. New York: Walker.
Bradbury, Ray (1996) [1953]. *Fahrenheit 451*. New York: Random House Publishing Group.
Burgess, Anthony E. (1962). *A Clockwork Orange*. London: Heinemann.
Card, Orson Scott (1985). *Ender's Game*. London: Century.
Coetzee, J. M. (1980). *Waiting for the Barbarians*. London: Secker & Warburg.
Collins, Suzanne (2008). *Hunger Games*. London: Scholastic. (Part 1 of the Hunger Games series)
Dashner, James (2009). *The Maze Runner*. New York: Delacorte.
Eggers, Dave (2013). *The Circle: A Novel*. New York: Alfred A. Knopf.
Golding, William, and Edmund L. Epstein (1954). *Lord of the Flies: A Novel*. New York: Perigee.
Huxley, Aldous (1932). *Brave New World*. New York: Harper Brothers.
Ishiguro, Kazuo (2005). *Never Let Me Go*. New York: Alfred A. Knopf.
Lowry, Lois (1993). *The Giver*. Boston: Houghton Mifflin.
Orwell, George (1949). *Nineteen Eighty-Four*. New York: Harcourt, Brace.
Roth, Veronica (2011). *Divergent*. New York: HarperCollins Publishers.
Salinger, J.D., E. Michael Mitchell, and Lotte Jacobi (1951). *The Catcher in the Rye*. Boston: Little, Brown, and Company.
Shelley, Mary Wollstonecraft (1998 [1818]). *Frankenstein, Or, The Modern Prometheus: The 1818 Text*. New York: Oxford University Press.
Shusterman, Neal (2007). *Unwind*. New York: Simon & Schuster for Young Readers.

Secondary Literature

Ahrens, Rüdiger (2013). "Teaching Literatures." *Basic Issues in EFL Teaching and Learning*. Ed. Maria Eisenmann and Theresa Summer. Heidelberg: Winter, 181-189.
Atwood, Margaret (1982). *Second Words: Selected Critical Prose 1960-1982*. Toronto: House of Anansi Press.
Baccolini, Raffaella, and Tom Moylan (2002). "Introduction. Dystopia and Histories." *Dark Horizons, Science Fiction and the Dystopian Imagination*. Ed. Baccolini and Moylan. New York: Routledge, 1-12.

Basu, Balaka, Katherine R. Broad, and Carrie Hintz (2013). "Introduction." *Contemporary Dystopian Fiction for Young Adults. Brave New Teenagers.* Ed. Basu, Broad, and Hintz. New York: Routledge, 1-18.

Bauman, Zygmunt (2012 [2000]). *Liquid Modernity.* Cambridge: Polity Press.

Beck, Ulrich (2012 [2009]). *World at Risk.* Cambridge: Polity Press.

Bildungsportal des Landes Nordrhein-Westfalen. "Vorgaben zu den unterrichtlichen Voraussetzungen für die schriftlichen Prüfungen im Abitur in der gymnasialen Oberstufe im Jahr 2016." *Bildungsportal des Landes Nordrhein-Westfalen.* Web 24 April 2017. <https://www.standardsicherung.schulministerium.nrw.de/cms/zentralabitur-gost/faecher/getfile.php?file=3388>.

Book Club Wikia. "Divergent/Faction Flowchart." *Book Club Wikia*, 2013. Web 19 April 2017. <http://bookclub.wikia.com/wiki/Divergent/Faction_ Flowchart>.

Bucher, Katherine, and KaaVonia Hinton (2010). *Young Adult Literature. Exploration, Evaluation, and Appreciation.* Boston: Allyn & Bacon.

Burnett, G. Wesley, and Lucy Rollin (2000). "Anti-leisure in Dystopian Fiction: The Literature of Leisure in the Worst of all Possible Worlds." *Leisure Studies* 19.2, 77-90.

Curtis, Claire P. (2010). *Postapocalyptic Fiction and the Social Contract.* New York: Lexington.

Delanoy, Werner (2013). "From 'Inter' to 'Trans'? Or: Quo Vadis Cultural Learning?" *Basic Issues in EFL Teaching and Learning.* Ed. Maria Eisenmann and Theresa Summer. Heidelberg: Winter, 177-189.

Freudenstein, Reinhold (1999). "Global Issues im Englischunterricht." *Praxis des neusprachlichen Unterrichts* 46.3, 237-249.

Groenke, Susan L., and Lisa Schwerff (2010). *Teaching YA Lit through Differentiated Instruction.* Urbana: NCTE.

Hesse, Mechthild (2009). *Teenage Fiction in the Active English Classroom.* Stuttgart: Klett.

Hessisches Kultusministerium. "Kerncurriculum Gymnasiale Oberstufe Englisch." *Hessisches Kultusministerium.* Web 24 April 2017. <https://kultusministerium.hessen.de/sites/default/files/media/kcgo-e.pdf>.

Hintz, Carrie, and Elaine Ostry (2003). *Utopian and Dystopian Writing for Children and Young Adults.* London: Routledge.

Matz, Frauke (2015). "Alternative Worlds – Alternative Texts: Teaching (Young Adult) Dystopian Novels." *Learning with Literature in the EFL Classroom.* Ed. Werner Delanoy, Maria Eisenmann, and Frauke Matz. Frankfurt: Lang, 263-280.

Mayer, Sylvia, and Graham Wilson (eds.) (2006). *Ecodidactic Perspectives on English Language, Literatures and Cultures.* Trier: WVT.

Moylan, Tom (2000). *Scraps of the Untainted Sky.* Boulder: Westview Press.

Parham, John (2006). "The Deficiency of Environmental Capital: Why Environmentalism Needs a Reflexive Pedagogy." In Mayer and Wilson (2006), 7-22.

Rau, Albert (2010): "Margaret Atwood's *The Handmaid's Tale*: A Dystopian Novel in the EFL Classroom." *Teaching the New English Cultures & Literatures*. Ed. Maria Eisenmann, Nancy Grimm, and Laurenz Volkmann. Heidelberg, Winter, 109-124.

Sargent, Lyman Tower (1994). "The Three Faces of Utopianism Revisited." *Utopian Studies* 5.1, 1-37.

Spisak, April (2012). "Dystopian Novel?" *Horn Book Magazine* 88.3, 55-60.

Stableford, Brian (2016). "Dystopias." *The Encyclopedia of Science Fiction*. Web. 19 April 2017 <http://www.sf-encyclopedia.com/entry/ dystopias>.

Tomlinson, Carl M., and Carol Lynch-Brown (2010). *Essentials of Young Adult Literature*. Boston: Pearson.

Voigts, Eckart (2015). "Introduction. The Dystopian Imagination – An Overview." *Dystopia, Science Fiction, Post-Apocalypse. Classics – New Tendencies – Model Interpretations*. Ed. Voigts and Alessandra Boller. Trier, WVT, 1-11.

Volkmann, Laurenz (2010). *Fachdidaktik Englisch: Kultur und Sprache*. Tübingen: Narr.

--- (2012). "Ecodidactics als Antwort auf die planetarische Bedrohung? Zum Einsatz von Ecopoetry im Englischunterricht." *Anglophone Literaturdidaktik – Zukunftsperspektiven für den Englischunterricht*. Ed. Julia Hammer et al. Winter: Heidelberg, 393-408.

Wolk, Steven (2009). "Reading for a Better World: Teaching for Social Responsibility with Young Adult Literature." *Journal of Adolescent & Adult Literacy* 52.8, 664-673.

Nadine Krüger (Würzburg)

"The Odds Are Never in Our Favor": Dystopia as Metaphor for Adolescence

1. Introduction

One reason for dystopian fiction's popularity with adolescent readers may be that, as Hintz and Ostry have argued, the genre can be read as a powerful metaphor for adolescence itself:[1] Both dystopia and adolescence have been conceptualized as liminal, even traumatic 'states of crisis' marked by a limitation of personal freedom and an ensuing struggle with oppressive (adult) authority. Young adults, while trying to find their own place in society, question the morals and value system that society is based on, gradually becoming aware of its flaws and deficiencies. As a result, adolescence is widely believed to entail a conflict with all (adult) authority. In dystopia, a genre expressly concerned with questions of social organization, this conflict takes on new momentum, as the individual adolescent's conflict with the powers governing society frequently becomes the catalyst for the rebellion that aims to overthrow the dystopian state as a whole. On the other hand, the challenges of a society aiming to overcome dystopia may be seen as reflecting adolescent growth.

Young adult dystopian fiction thus speaks to its intended audience in very specific ways, addressing some of the issues and concerns most pressing and challenging to contemporary teenagers while placing them in the wider social and political context of the dystopian society. The parallels between dystopia and adolescence may not only help to further understand and conceptualize young adult dystopian fiction as a genre; they also make it an excellent vehicle to be used in the EFL classroom. In this chapter, the implications of describing adolescence as dystopia will be examined. Since dystopia as a concept is analyzed elsewhere in this volume, it will not be discussed at length here.[2] Thus, after an initial consideration of the term adolescence, the main focus of this chapter will be to show the parallels between the two concepts in more detail, both theoretically and through references to selected textual examples. In the last part, possible ramifications for the classroom will be considered.

2. Constructions of Adolescence

Variously described as a "time of turmoil" marked by conflict and tension, a "subjectivity in crisis"[3], a period of heightened sensitivity and interiority or a "moratorium"[4] during which the adolescent is not yet expected to fully embrace his or her role as a full-fledged member of society, adolescence as a distinct category of development remains elusive. Framed as a period of transition between childhood and adulthood, adolescence is characterized as a liminal, transitory 'in-between' state of becoming which, by its very nature, is bound to end eventually. Consequently, adolescence is predominantly associated with change in various forms: Marked in a biological sense by the onset of puberty and the ensuing physical, hormonal and neural changes, it also entails significant changes in the individual's social, cognitive, and emotional development. As a result of the various processes of development and maturation which shape it, "[a]dolescence has been defined via an uneasy mixture of the biological and the social."[5]

Although it is now generally acknowledged that adolescence, as a separate category clearly distinguishable from other stages of life, is a social construct, the dominant model of adolescence remains the one developed by Stanley Hall in the early twentieth century. Hall describes adolescence in mainly biological terms, attributing the turbulences and conflicts of puberty to hormonal changes.[6] In many ways, he is often considered the founder of the scientific investigation of adolescence as a distinct period of life, even if more recent publications have found some of his observations to be no longer tenable. While Hall's ideas have shaped and informed conceptualizations of adolescence in a number of disciplines, however, the focus here will be on how it has been imagined in social and literary terms.

Due to the difficulties involved in defining the term, one way of approaching adolescence is by way of the metaphorical. According to McLennan, there is a long-standing, albeit often unrecognized tradition of conceptualizing adolescence through the means of metaphor and the figurative.[7] Rather than being considered as "a stage of development experienced differently by individuals (which it is)", McLennan argues that adolescence "is in effect employed metaphorically in academic discussions as a figurative container for the uncontainable."[8] In a similar vein, Meyer Spacks claims that "the term has gradually enlarged its metaphoric reference and become a generalized designation, usually of blame."[9] Essentially – and ambiguously – an "adult idea", adolescence has served as a screen onto which adults have projected their own "fears, hopes, and accurate or distorted memories"[10], not just in academia, but in their everyday interactions with teenagers as well. Thus, rather than allowing adolescents to speak for themselves, both academic discourse and literature have frequently sought to categorize adolescence from an adult perspective. While this is necessary to a certain extent (scientists as well as authors usually being adults), it has led to generalizations or even distortions not always in keeping with individual adolescent experience. As a result, while holding a strange fascination for the adult beholder to whom it is irretrievably lost, "that mysterious, powerful phenomenon we have labelled *adolescence*"[11] is fraught with ambiguity and contradiction, as it is simultaneously loathed and glorified by adult society.

Traditionally, this ambiguity has partly found expression in the idea of a *Sturm und Drang* period characterized by extremes of feeling and conduct, as well as psychological tension and interpersonal conflict.[12] This idea also combines adult notions of adolescent delinquency with the idealized idea of an, often nostalgically remembered or distorted, period of endless possibilities during which one was still free of the burdens and responsibilities of adult life. More recently, this classic imagery has been modified somewhat and is now conceptualized in more contemporary terms as the negotiation between "adjustment [and] turmoil."[13] At least in the field of developmental psychology, this has included a shift in perspective, as conflict and tension are no longer considered universal markers of adolescence. Interestingly enough, however, while individual teenage experience may, in fact, often be much less troublesome than is commonly believed,[14] images of conflict and stress prevail in popular depictions of adolescence.

Perhaps this contradiction is still most adequately expressed in Kristeva's notion of the *abject*. The concept is also employed by McLennan in her discussion of the metaphoric conceptualization of adolescence cited above, as it suitably combines some of the central ideas she identifies: According to her, adolescence has frequently been depicted as "existing on the edges"[15], as marginal, in-between, something both threatened by and threatening the established order. Similarly, abjection – and the adolescent-as-abject – is that which "disturbs identity, system, order. What does not respect borders, positions, rules. The in-between, the ambiguous, the composite."[16] This description of adolescence is indeed fitting for the way that teenagers are represented in the genre discussed here: In contemporary young adult dystopias, the adolescent protagonists are most certainly the ones disturbing the established order of society in many ways, as their questioning of and rebellion against the system frequently become integral parts of the plot.

McLennan also identifies the phenomenon of conceptualizing adolescence in terms of the metaphoric as a specifically American tradition. She argues that the "apparently universal nature of adolescence provided an illusory uniformity at a time when the construction of a united national identity and culture was of paramount importance"[17], a tendency which can be associated with both the post-Civil War era and the period following the end of the Second World War. Moreover, the idea of America as adolescent is closely connected to the narrative of the birth of the nation, which can be seen as a coming-of-age process, a breaking away from European parental authority to develop an independent social and political identity.[18] While focusing on the parallel construction of adolescence and America as a nation as a prominent theme in American literature, McLennan asks whether "a depiction of existence in the world [is] a metaphorical means of describing adolescence, or [...] a description of adolescence provide[s] a metaphorical means of describing the world", concluding that both operate simultaneously.[19] Like many of her observations about the parallels between adolescence and the 'American character', this statement holds equally true for the construction of adolescence as dystopia: In their combination, both concepts inform and shape the other.

Patricia Meyer Spacks, tracing the origins and evolution of *The Adolescent Idea*, notes that "[t]he crucial question [is] not, What is adolescence? but, How has adolescence been perceived, remembered, imagined?"[20] Dystopia, and in particular the latest wave of young adult dystopian writing, may thus provide one of the many responses to that question which have been proposed over the years. While the combination of adolescence and dystopia, like other metaphoric renderings of the concept, cannot claim to provide a universal answer to the question, young adult dystopian fiction does have something to contribute to the discourse Meyer Spacks identifies. It may tell us something about the way society has perceived and constructed its youngsters, as well as the extent to which the dystopian genre has shaped this imagining, and been shaped by the adolescent mode in turn.

3. Adolescence and Dystopia

In the following part, the parallels between adolescence and dystopia will be analyzed in more detail. Based on the theoretical considerations outlined in the first part, the implications of imagining adolescence as dystopia will be discussed and illustrated through references to selected textual examples.

With their tendency to engage with "pressing global concerns", dystopian texts have the "capacity to frighten and warn"[21] their readers "of terrible socio-political tendencies that could, if continued, turn our contemporary world into the iron cages portrayed in the realm of utopia's underside."[22] In addition to offering a form of imaginative escape, young adult dystopias thus also contain a note of, sometimes very explicit, didacticism, a combination which holds enormous potential for the classroom context. However, there is another aspect characteristic of young adult dystopian fiction which makes the genre appealing to its intended readership, and which is perhaps more to the point of the argument developed in this chapter: In addressing issues of social organization and harmony, these texts engage with questions and decisions mirroring the ones young adults face as part of the process of growing up, such as the complex relationship between personal freedom and individuality on the one hand and social harmony and conformity on the other. It is in the negotiation of these questions that the parallels between adolescence and dystopia unfold, mutually influencing each other and shaping the texts in the process.

Perhaps most importantly, both adolescence and dystopia have been perceived and conceptualized as permanent 'states of crisis' marked by conflict and anxiety: At the individual level of the adolescent, this manifests itself in the challenge of mastering the transition from childhood to maturity and the ensuing struggle to find one's own place in society. Frequently, this goes hand in hand with a questioning of or even rebellion against parental authority, which teenagers often experience as oppressive. Still denied full access to and participation in adult society, the adolescent constantly has to negotiate the tension between the desire to belong and the urge to reject what he or she feels excluded from. This process is consistent with the oscillation between "adjustment" and "turmoil" described above.

In a dystopian setting, rather than individual parental figures, society itself becomes the antagonist. It is marked by oppressive government control, surveillance, terror, social inequality, a loss of individual rights and, frequently, a constant threat to the – non-conforming – individual's life. Much more severely than their real-life counterparts, fictional adolescents growing up in a dystopian setting are limited in their personal freedom and possibilities by the oppressive powers that govern and control society in ways much more detrimental to their development. Thus, in addition to the challenges faced by contemporary teenagers, the young adult protagonists of dystopian literature find themselves placed in a hostile environment which they justifiably experience as antagonistic. Consequently, the adolescent conflict with adult authority becomes a conflict with society as a whole. Adolescents growing up under these conditions experience frustration and helplessness at being denied more power and control over their own life and being at the mercy of the oppressive governmental structure. Adolescent anxiety and insecurity about their own position in society thus become mirrors of the terror resulting from life under dystopian conditions; even more so, one amplifies the other.

Similarly, the oscillation between the poles of individuality on the one hand and the desire to belong to a social collective on the other, common enough to adolescent growth, also takes on additional significance in the dystopian society. More specifically, the pressure to conform is enhanced dramatically in a dystopian setting, as it becomes a guiding principle of society. In *The Giver* (1993), for example, the community is built on the principle of *Sameness* – perfect harmony based on the complete conformity of all members of society. Although life in this community seems nigh-utopian at first, Jonas gradually becomes aware of the price humanity has had to pay to achieve this goal. Thus, while the desire to belong and be part of a social group may be a basic human instinct, it often becomes a question of survival in a dystopian setting, as non-conformity can have terrible consequences. In *The Hunger Games* (2008), for instance, Katniss has to embrace her role in the Capitol's games to a certain degree, both inside the arena and outside, to ensure her own survival and that of the people dearest to her while simultaneously struggling to remain true to her own sense of what is right. In *Divergent* (2011), Tris' desire to belong and become accepted as a member of her newly chosen faction, the Dauntless, may mirror the average teenager's efforts to be accepted by her peers; however, the challenges she has to face during the process of initiation take an increasingly dramatic turn as her true status as *divergent* – not conforming to the ideals of any of the five factions which form her society – begins to threaten her life.

Young adults often find themselves faced with questions and decisions mirroring the ones made by society as a whole, while simultaneously having to come to terms with their own role within the wider social order of the (dystopian) society.[23] As part of the process of learning to negotiate their own position within – or sometimes outside – that framework, adolescents often begin to question the very principles that society is based on, interrogating the norms and values represented by their elders. Once again, this tendency is intensified in a setting which severely limits the freedom of its citizens and denies them basic human rights: In many ways, Katniss displays traits of the 'typical' taciturn teenager, shutting out her environment and questioning the actions of the adults around her – her mother, her mentor, Haymitch, or Effie Trinket, the Capitol's representative in charge of the tributes from district 12. However, her critical, brooding perspective takes on additional urgency as it increasingly becomes the voice exposing the injustice and exploitation intrinsic to Panem's society, which culminate in the Capitol's annual demonstration of absolute power in the form of the Hunger Games. Thus, as the adolescent protagonist increasingly questions the dystopian society, she uncovers its flaws and weaknesses in the process, as much to the reader as to herself.

Consequently, as Basu, Broad, and Hintz have argued, many young adult dystopias "feature an awakening, sudden or gradual, to the truth of what has really been going on"[24] and the principles on which the dystopian society is founded, a moment of realization which alters the protagonist's understanding of the world they inhabit. While Katniss may have been aware of much of the Capitol's oppression of the districts from the start, Jonas in *The Giver* experiences a gradual process of awakening to the shortcomings of his community. As a result of his training to become the new *Receiver of Memories*, he begins to realize for the first time that the principle of *Sameness* has deprived the community of memories, colours, feelings, and all sense of individuality. He discovers that adults can lie, and that "release" is simply a euphemism for euthanasia. As a result of this realization, Jonas, like several other protagonists of dystopian novels, "move[s] from apparent contentment into an experience of alienation and resistance."[25] The fact that important life decisions are made for him, an aspect which formerly seemed to ensure the happiness of all citizens of the community, begins to feel unnatural to him, as he becomes aware of the importance of having choices. Similarly, characters like Tally in the *Uglies* series (2005-2007) or Lena in *Delirium* (2011) are initially neither unhappy with the world they inhabit nor their own role in society. It is only once they learn that they have been deceived about things they have always taken for granted that their attitude towards the society they live in changes. Like Jonas, they gradually realize that the choices seemingly offered to them by society are, in fact, very limited and strictly regulated: Although Tally may be allowed to envision different versions of her future self in preparation for the operation making her *Pretty*, in the end, she will have to conform to the beauty standards determined by the authorities. Lena, while given a quasi-choice between different potential partners, is only allowed to make a decision within the limits created for her by others.

This process of realization, in turn, forms an integral element of the plot of many young adult dystopias: From their initial questioning or criticism of society, the protagonists frequently move to open rebellion in order to achieve a change of the social order both in their own and society's general interest. Although she only embraces the role of the Mockingjay very reluctantly, Katniss does concede that "[her] holding out the berries had been the spark" to start the rebellion, even if she herself "had no way to control the fire."[26] Eventually, she does, at least for a time, accept the role the rebels expect her to fill – that of the figurehead and symbol of the rebellion she helped to ignite. Thus, in the struggle for more freedom, choice, and control over their own life, adolescent protagonists not only have to learn to negotiate their own place in society; even if they rarely choose to do so entirely of their own accord, they eventually come to embrace a central role in the rebellion and overthrowing of the oppressive regime and thus help to transform the dystopian world and save its citizens from destruction. In turn, the crisis and "growing pains" of a society aiming to overcome dystopia may be seen as synonymous with adolescent growth itself and the struggles involved in developing agency.[27]

Interestingly, this evokes another comparison: Similar to the totalitarian dystopian state which, in many dystopian novels, is overthrown in the course of the plot, adolescence as a stage of life eventually ends as the teenager 'grows up' and fully embraces a mature, adult role in life. As a matter of fact, in young adult dystopias, both processes often occur simultaneously: As they accept their role in the complexities of political upheaval, the protagonists are forced to grow up, sometimes prematurely, at the same time. Thus, both adolescence and dystopia can equally be characterized by their liminality: They describe precarious, transitory states which are in constant danger of being overthrown. In the case of dystopia, this liminality also manifests itself in connection with questions of genre: Through imagining possible future outcomes of current sociocultural developments, dystopia occupies a liminal position between present and future.[28] Moreover, it also oscillates between the poles of the utopian hope for change and anti-utopian despair that all possibility for a positive transformation of society is lost.[29] In the case of texts written for a younger readership, like the ones discussed here, this negotiation between hope and despair is especially important: "Whereas the [classic] 'adult' dystopia's didactic impact relies on the absolute, unswerving nature of its dire warning"[30], often accomplished through the ultimate failure of the protagonist's resistance against the system, the texts written for young adults usually "hold[…] out hope that the dystopia can be overcome."[31] This is particularly obvious in the series' endings, which rarely see the dystopian state triumph; on the contrary, they often feature at least a partial success on the part of the rebellious adolescent. Whether in the *Hunger Games, Divergent*, or *Uglies* series, even though the protagonists carry the scars of the violence they have suffered, there is a sense that a new beginning and change for the better may (yet) be accomplished in the aftermath of the system's downfall.

Finally, one last point of comparison between dystopia and adolescence is the issue of interiority, which is yet another marker frequently associated with adolescence: a certain tendency to be immersed in self-discovery and, thus, a preoccupation with one's own internal processes which is considered characteristic of many adolescents.[32] Consequently, much young adult literature has centred around the adolescent absorption with the self and, more specifically, the protagonist's own feelings and thoughts. In some ways, young adult dystopian fiction continues this tradition. Once again, however, the dystopian context influences how this structural device is used, as it becomes a central element of many dystopian works. Conspicuously, many of the novels are told by first person narrators. While this in itself is nothing unusual, I would argue that the style of narration is, in fact, inherently shaped by the dystopian condition as such: In a society which controls its citizens through various means of surveillance or even mind control, voicing criticism is dangerous, if not impossible. As a result, the protagonist turns inward, contemplating her misgivings in private rather than out loud. In combination with the protagonist's role as the voice exposing the system's injustice to the reader, the first person point of view seems a natural form to give expression to this interiority. In addition, it also allows the reader to share an insider's perspective and furthers empathy with the protagonist's sufferings caused by the dystopian setting.

Once again, Katniss serves as a good case in point here: While she may be described as a taciturn, brooding anti-heroine on the one hand, her introversion is actually a defense mechanism to cope with the conditions she has grown up in. She turns inward to protect her innermost feelings and thoughts from a hostile environment and, later, in response to the various forms of physical and emotional trauma she experiences. Like many modern-day teenagers, Katniss is silenced by society. Her struggle to (re)claim her voice and the ability to tell her own story forms an important element of the trilogy's plot.[33]

Through these parallels, young adult dystopian fiction may thus speak to its intended readership in very specific ways, allowing adolescents to empathize with the characters despite the extreme conditions these are placed in. In combination with the engaging plots of the novels, these elements may well explain the genre's popularity with teenage readers despite its darkness and often challenging cultural criticism. One aspect in particular may be appealing to adolescents: In contrast to what teenagers experience in their own lives, the adolescent protagonists of dystopian literature are empowered to become agents of social transformation, shaping the future of the society they live in. At an age when teenagers often feel a certain degree of frustration at being denied access to the adult world, reading about fictional characters filling a role denied to them in real life may give them a sense of hope. It may also inspire them to actively work towards social or political change in their own society. This hypothesis will be explored in more detail in the final part of this chapter.

4. Adolescence, Dystopia, and the EFL Classroom

What, then, are the benefits to be derived from including young adult dystopian literature in the EFL context? The reasons for using contemporary young adult dystopias are manifold: First of all, the thrilling adventure plots of the novels, in combination with the parallels between dystopia and adolescence outlined above, may help to motivate students to take on the somewhat daunting task of reading a novel of 200-300 pages in a foreign language. However, while the motivational aspect should by no means be underestimated, this alone may not yet justify the choice of text. There are a number of other reasons to use contemporary dystopias in an EFL context.[34]

Volkmann[35] and Matz[36] in particular have already made the case for young adult dystopias to be included in the EFL classroom because of their contribution to the discussion of so-called *global issues*, which are not tied to a specific place or cultural context, but concern all of us in an increasingly interconnected, globalized world. Interestingly, in addition to topics such as human conflict, globalization, and a sustainable relationship between human beings and the natural world, which are more or less obviously addressed in dystopian texts, these *global issues* also include "central issues of human existence" – such as growing up, for example. [37] The similarities between adolescence and dystopia demonstrated above may thus provide an additional starting point for approaching these texts, allowing for a discussion of some of the questions most pressing to young adults today. When dealing with *The Giver* in class, for example, one could discuss the relative importance of individuality and freedom of choice on the one hand, and conformity and social harmony on the other. Questions such as what students would be willing to give up for a life of perfect harmony and safety are perhaps more pressing today than ever before, as matters of public safety and surveillance are pitted against individual freedom in an increasingly agitated manner.[38]

Furthermore, issues like belonging to a social collective and being accepted as an individual, but also the dangers of peer pressure can be addressed through novels like *Divergent* or *Uglies*. Both Tris and Tally have to learn to position themselves in relation to the conflicts prevalent in their societies, sometimes leaving behind old friends and forming new relationships in the process. Thus, both series put a strong emphasis on the role of friendship, but also on the importance of making choices and standing up for what one believes in. In addition, the *Uglies* series is particularly interesting because of its treatment of issues of physical appearance and the meaning of beauty. These topics frequently cause a lot of anxiety among teenagers, as the pressure to conform to beauty standards promoted through advertisements and the media influences adolescents' self-perception in negative ways. Again, while the protagonists of dystopian literature may find themselves placed in circumstances far more extreme than those of their contemporary audience, these parallels may help adolescents to relate to the characters and thus serve as an additional incentive to include the novels in the EFL classroom.

In addition to inspiring empathy with the protagonists, this leads to another benefit to be derived from using young adult dystopias in an EFL context: Through the encounter with an alternative world, readers are encouraged to consider the issues and questions addressed in the novels from a new, different perspective. Given the possibility to address topics which are relevant to them through the medium of the fictional text, students may be relieved of the pressure of discussing them with direct reference to their own lives. Nonetheless, this can still lead to a critical reflection and reassessment of their own presuppositions and opinions and give them a chance to articulate them. This ability to reconsider one's assumptions and decentre one's own perspective is a central element of inter- and transcultural competences, which form a central objective of the EFL classroom.

This change of perspective can be further promoted through the use of learner-centred, process-oriented approaches which, in combination with reader-response tasks, generally lend themselves to approaching dystopian texts and the questions they address. Discussion and writing activities can be supplemented by creative tasks encouraging the students, for example, to transfer (parts of) the novels to other media and text forms, such as film, advertisements, or graphic novels. The students can be asked to create film posters or trailers, rewrite and perform scenes from a novel in dramatic form, or stage interviews with the characters. The novels can also be complemented and contrasted with non-fictional texts about the issues central to a particular text, such as reality TV (*The Hunger Games*), the pressure to conform (*Divergent*) or beauty standards and cosmetic surgery (*Uglies*), as well as experiences of real-life teenagers, thus making the connection to the students' everyday life even stronger.

Finally, actively engaging in a debate of questions not only relevant to their own lives, but also of wider political, socio-cultural, and ecological significance may encourage students to take action themselves, in their own communities. What Hintz and Ostry say about utopian literature may thus equally hold true for the discussion of dystopian literature:

> Utopian literature encourages young people to view their society with a critical eye, sensitizing or predisposing them to political action. In the long tradition of utopian literature, an imagined encounter with another culture urges readers to reflect on their home society [...].[39]

Young adult dystopian fiction, then, if taught and contextualized well, may encourage readers to reflect on questions which are not specific to any particular cultural context or the EFL classroom, but concern all of us in an increasingly interconnected, globalized, technology-controlled world.

5. Conclusion

As has been demonstrated, dystopia can be read as a powerful metaphor for adolescence, addressing some of the concerns and challenges teenagers face while growing up and situating these in a context which further dramatizes this process by being placed in a totalitarian, oppressive society. The parallels between dystopia and adolescence may serve as a possible explanation for the popularity of young adult dystopian fiction with adolescent readers, allowing them to empathize with the protagonists while simultaneously exploring alternative worlds and engaging with questions and developments equally relevant in our own globalized, increasingly technological world. This connection makes the genre a powerful tool for the EFL classroom. By addressing so-called *global issues* as well as questions of what it means to grow up in contemporary society, young adult dystopias may, moreover, pose a warning against problematic socio-cultural, political, ecological, and economic trends and serve as a call to action for their (adolescent) readership to actively work towards the future they would like to inhabit, as opposed to the one presented in the texts. These points make young adult dystopian fiction an excellent vehicle to teach towards some of the central tenets of the EFL classroom, including goals of inter- and transcultural learning, a change of perspectives, or critical thinking.

Notes

[1] Carrie Hintz and Elaine Ostry (2003). "Introduction." *Utopian and Dystopian Writing for Children and Young Adults.* Ed. Hintz and Ostry. London: Routledge, 1-19, 9.

[2] See the introduction by Ludwig and Maruo-Schröder as well as Heinze's contribution in this volume.

[3] Julia Kristeva (1990). "The Adolescent Novel." *Abjection, Melancholia, and Love.* Ed. John Fletcher and Andrew Benjamin. London: Routledge, 8-23, 18.

[4] Erik H. Erikson (1968). *Identity. Youth and Crisis.* New York: W.W. Norton, 165.

[5] Christine Griffin (1993). *Representations of Youth. The Study of Youth and Adolescence in Britain and America.* Cambridge: Polity Press, 19.

[6] Rachael McLennan (2009). *Adolescence, America, and Postwar Fiction. Developing Figures.* Basingstoke: Palgrave Macmillan, 5.

[7] McLennan (2009), 4.

[8] *Ibid.,* 27.

[9] Patricia Meyer Spacks (1981). *The Adolescent Idea. Myths of Youth and the Adult Imagination.* London: Faber & Faber, 6.

[10] *Ibid.*, 11.

[11] *Ibid.*, 3; emphasis in original.

[12] See Rolf Oerter and Eva Dreher (2002). "Jugendalter." *Entwicklungspsychologie.* Ed. Oerter and Leo Montada. 5th Ed. Weinheim: Beltz, 258-318, 262. This idea is, once again, strongly influenced by Hall's conception of adolescence.

[13] *Ibid.*, 260.

[14] Gerald R. Adams and Michael D. Berzonsky (2006). "Introduction." *Blackwell Handbook of Adolescence.* Ed. Adams and Berzonsky. Oxford: Blackwell, xi-xxvii, xxv.

[15] McLennan (2009), 15.

[16] Julia Kristeva (1982). *Powers of Horror. An Essay on Abjection.* New York: Columbia University Press, 4.

[17] McLennan (2009), 9, quoting Griffin, 14.
[18] See Kenneth Millard (2007). *Coming of Age in Contemporary American Fiction,* Edinburgh: Edinburgh University Press, 5.
[19] McLennan (2009), 3.
[20] Meyer Spacks (1981), 13.
[21] Balaka Basu, Katherine R. Broad, and Carrie Hintz (2013). "Introduction." *Contemporary Dystopian Fiction for Young Adults. Brave New Teenagers.* Ed. Basu, Broad, and Hintz. London: Routledge, 1-15, 1.
[22] Raffaella Baccolini and Tom Moylan (2002). "Introduction. Dystopia and Histories." *Dark Horizons. Science Fiction and the Dystopian Imagination.* Ed. Baccolini and Moylan. London: Routledge, 1-12, 2.
[23] See Hintz and Ostry (2003), 10.
[24] Basu, Broad and Hintz (2013), 4.
[25] Baccolini and Moylan (2003), 5.
[26] Suzanne Collins (2009). *Catching Fire.* New York: Scholastic, 180.
[27] See Hintz and Ostry (2003), 10.
[28] See Sara K. Day, Miranda A. Green-Barteet, and Amy L. Montz (2014). "Introduction. From 'New Woman' to 'Future Girl'. The Roots and the Rise of the Female Protagonist in Contemporary Young Adult Dystopias." *Female Rebellion in Young Adult Dystopian Fiction.* Ed. Day, Green-Barteet, and Montz. Farnham: Ashgate, 1-14, 9.
[29] See the discussion of genre and terminology in Tom Moylan (2000). *Scraps of the Untainted Sky. Science Fiction, Utopia, Dystopia,* Boulder: Westview Press, 121-145, and Baccolini and Moylan (2003), 3-4. Referring to Sargent's definition, Baccolini and Moylan suggest that the term *critical dystopia*, as opposed to the frequently employed *anti-utopia*, describes much more adequately the kind of dystopian writing published since the late 1980s, as it upholds a utopian element of hope that change for the better is possible (whereas anti-utopian writing rejects this possibility). Especially in connection with dystopian writing for young adults, which usually contains this element of hope, this terminological differentiation is important.
[30] Kay Sambell (2003). "Presenting the Case for Social Change. The Creative Dilemma of Dystopian Writing for Children." *Utopian and Dystopian Writing for Children and Young Adults.* Ed. Carrie Hintz and Elaine Ostry. London: Routledge, 163-177, 164. Sambell offers a comprehensive discussion of the respective roles of hope and despair in dystopian writing for younger readers.
[31] Baccolini and Moylan (2003), 7, quoting Lyman Tower Sargent (2001). "US Eutopias in the 1980s and 1990s: Self-Fashioning in a World of Multiple Identities." *Utopianism/ Literary Utopias and National Cultural Identities. A Comparative Perspective.* Ed. Paola Spinozzi. Bologna: Cotepra, 221-232, 222. See also Heinze in this collection for a slightly different view on this point.
[32] See, for example, Meyer Spacks (1981), 9.

[33] For a more detailed discussion of the importance of trauma, recovery, and narrative voice in *The Hunger Games* trilogy, see Tom Henthorne (2012). *Approaching the Hunger Games Trilogy*. Jefferson: McFarland, 125-138.
[34] For a more detailed overview of the benefits of including young adult dystopias in the EFL classroom, see Eisenmann's contribution to this volume. To avoid a repetition of her discussion, I will focus on the connection between adolescence and dystopia outlined in the first part of this chapter.
[35] See, for example, Laurenz Volkmann (2010). *Fachdidaktik Englisch. Kultur und Sprache,* Tübingen, 201-204; or Volkmann (2014). "Die Abkehr vom Differenzdenken. Transkulturelles Lernen und global education." *Transkulturelles Lernen im Fremdsprachenunterricht. Theorie und Praxis.* Ed. Frauke Matz, Michael Rogge, and Philipp Siepmann. Frankfurt: Peter Lang, 37-51, 44.
[36] See, for example, Frauke Matz (2014). "Dystopische Jugendromane: transkulturelle Themen und interkulturelle Bezüge." *Transkulturelles Lernen im Fremdsprachenunterricht. Theorie und Praxis.* Ed. Frauke Matz, Michael Rogge, and Philipp Siepmann. Frankfurt: Peter Lang, 143-151; or Matz (2015). "Alternative Worlds – Alternative Texts. Teaching (Young Adult) Dystopian Novels." *Learning with Literature in the EFL Classroom.* Ed. Werner Delanoy, Maria Eisenmann, and Frauke Matz. Frankfurt: Peter Lang, 263-280, 275-276.
[37] Volkmann (2010), 196; translation by author.
[38] For *The Giver* especially, a number of publications with helpful tasks and material for the classroom context can be found: See, for example, Mechthild Hesse (1999). *Lois Lowry: The Giver. Teacher's Guide.* Stuttgart: Klett; or Jeannette Sanderson (2003). *A Reading Guide to* The Giver *by Lois Lowry.* New York: Scholastic.
[39] Hintz and Ostry (2003), 7.

Bibliography

Primary Literature

Collins, Suzanne (2008). *The Hunger Games*. New York: Scholastic.
--- (2009). *Catching Fire*. New York: Scholastic.
--- (2010). *Mockingjay*. New York: Scholastic.
Lowry, Lois (1993). *The Giver*. New York: Houghton Mifflin.
Oliver, Lauren (2011). *Delirium*. New York: Harper Collins.
Roth, Veronica (2011). *Divergent*. New York: Harper Collins.
Westerfeld, Scott (2005). *Uglies*. New York: Scholastic.

Secondary Literature

Adams, Gerald R. and Michael D. Berzonsky (eds.) (2006). *Blackwell Handbook of Adolescence.* Oxford: Blackwell.

Baccolini, Raffaella, and Tom Moylan (2003). "Introduction. Dystopia and Histories." *Dark Horizons: Science Fiction and the Dystopian Imagination.* Ed. Baccolini and Moylan. London: Routledge, 1-12.

Basu, Balaka, Carrie Hintz and Katherine R. Broad (2013). "Introduction." *Contemporary Dystopian Fiction for Young Adults: Brave New Teenagers.* Ed. B.B., C.H., and K.B. London: Routledge, 1-15.

Day, Sara K., Miranda A. Green-Barteet and Amy L. Montz (2014). "Introduction: From 'New Woman' to 'Future Girl': The Roots and the Rise of the Female Protagonist in Contemporary Young Adult Dystopias." *Female Rebellion in Young Adult Dystopian Fiction.* Ed. Day, Green-Barteet, and Montz. Farnham: Ashgate, 1-14.

Erikson, Erik H. (1968). *Identity: Youth and Crisis.* New York: W.W. Norton.

Griffin, Christine (1993). *Representations of Youth: The Study of Youth and Adolescence in Britain and America.* Cambridge: Polity Press.

Hempel, Margit and Frauke Matz (2013). "Ecodidactics im Englischunterricht der Oberstufe: Dystopian Fiction für ökologische Bildung." *Medien und Interkulturalität im Fremdsprachenunterricht: Zwischen Autonomie, Kollaboration und Konstruktion.* Ed. Maria Eisenmann, Margit Hempel and Christian Ludwig. Duisburg: Universitätsverlag Rhein-Ruhr, 169-181.

Henthorne, Tom (2012). *Approaching the Hunger Games Trilogy: A Literary and Cultural Analysis*. Jefferson: McFarland.

Hintz, Carrie and Elaine Ostry (2003). "Introduction." *Utopian and Dystopian Writing for Children and Young Adults*. Ed. Hintz and Ostry. London: Routledge, 1-19.

Kristeva, Julia (1990). "The Adolescent Novel." *Abjection, Melancholia, and Love: The Work of Julia Kristeva.* Ed. John Fletcher and Andrew Benjamin. London: Routledge, 8-23.

--- (1982). *Powers of Horror: An Essay on Abjection.* New York: Columbia University Press.

Matz, Frauke (2015). "Alternative Worlds – Alternative Texts: Teaching (Young Adult) Dystopian Novels." *Learning with Literature in the EFL Classroom.* Ed. Werner Delanoy, Maria Eisenmann, and Frauke Matz. Frankfurt: Peter Lang, 263-280.

--- (2014). "Dystopische Jugendromane: transkulturelle Themen und interkulturelle Bezüge." *Transkulturelles Lernen im Fremdsprachenunterricht: Theorie und Praxis.* Ed. Frauke Matz, Michael Rogge, and Philipp Siepmann. Frankfurt: Peter Lang, 143-151.

McLennan, Rachael (2009). *Adolescence, America, and Postwar Fiction: Developing Figures*. Basingstoke: Palgrave Macmillan.

Meyer Spacks, Patricia (1981). *The Adolescent Idea: Myths of Youth and the Adult Imagination*. London: Faber & Faber.

Millard, Kenneth (2007). *Coming of Age in Contemporary American Fiction*. Edinburgh: Edinburgh University Press.

Moylan, Tom (2000). *Scraps of the Untainted Sky: Science Fiction, Utopia, Dystopia*. Boulder: Westview Press.

Oerter, Rolf and Eva Dreher (2002). "Jugendalter." *Entwicklungspsychologie*. Ed. Rolf Oerter and Leo Montada. 5th Ed. Weinheim: Beltz, 258-318.

Sambell, Kay (2003). "Presenting the Case for Social Change: The Creative Dilemma of Dystopian Writing for Children." *Utopian and Dystopian Writing for Children and Young Adults*. Ed, Carrie Hintz and Elaine Ostry. London: Routledge, 163-177.

Volkmann, Laurenz (2015). "Opportunities and Challenges for Transcultural Learning and Global Education via Literature." *Learning with Literature in the EFL Classroom*. Ed. Werner Delanoy, Maria Eisenmann, and Frauke Matz. Frankfurt: Peter Lang, 237-262.

--- (2014). "Die Abkehr vom Differenzdenken: Transkulturelles Lernen und global education." *Transkulturelles Lernen im Fremdsprachenunterricht: Theorie und Praxis*. Ed. Frauke Matz, Michael Rogge, and Philipp Siepmann. Frankfurt: Peter Lang, 37-51.

--- (2010). *Fachdidaktik Englisch: Kultur und Sprache*. Tübingen: Narr.

Christian Ludwig (Karlsruhe)

"Freedom Is a Small Price to Pay for Survival" Selected Images of the Posthuman in Catherine Fisher's *Incarceron* Bilogy and Global Education in the EFL Classroom

Walls have ears.
Doors have eyes.
Trees have voices.
Beasts tell lies.
Beware the rain.
Beware the snow.
Beware the man
You think you know.
- *Songs of Sapphique*
(Book 1, 158)

1. Introduction

The sheer number of young adult novels featuring 'tough-women characters' who fight for their own freedom and the freedom of the post-apocalyptic, degraded, and frightening world they live in, has increased dramatically since the turn of the century, with many of them having found popularity among teen and adult readers alike. With very few exceptions, these young adult dystopias depict a world where, after the collapse of society, "the ideals for improvement have gone tragically amok".[1] While Catherine Fisher's *Incarceron* bilogy (2007, 2008) does not constitute an exception to this rule, I will argue that it nevertheless deserves closer examination for one main reason: the novels blur the boundaries between different genres, primarily dystopian fiction, fantasy, and science fiction. By doing that, Fisher has produced a "'The Hunger Games' meet the 'The Matrix'"[2] environment, in which, as Einstein once put it, "[r]eality is merely an illusion, albeit a very persistent one". Drawing on the long history of science fiction and fantasy literature, Fisher transcends the traditional common elements of young adult dystopian fiction, revealing a plethora of provocative social, political, scientific and, last but not least, moral themes which reflect contemporary prevalent and global issues. In order to explore these themes more in-depth, Fisher takes the reader to the illusion of a perfect society in which Claudia, an aristocratic teenage girl, awaits her arranged marriage with Caspar, Earl of Steen, the Crown Prince of the Realm, a conglomeration of countries where officially all technology has been outlawed under the decree of King Endor of the Havaarna dynasty. Simultaneously, the teenage boy Finn, who has no memories of his past but believes that he came from a world outside of the massive prison he lives in and which is ruled by a sentient but malevolent artificial intelligence (AI), attempts to unravel the truth about his former life by finding out about the real nature of his wrist tattoo and following the clues from his visions.

Taking all this into consideration, the novels appear appropriate for the EFL classroom for a number of reasons: first, they reveal a cornucopia of issues highly relevant for the contemporary EFL classroom, especially with regard to the increasingly global focus of English as a foreign language teaching. Second, a deeper analysis of earth's future in form of an apocalyptic society, which has been ripped apart by the lack of energy resources, can also contribute to a better understanding of the popular genre of young adult dystopian fiction, whose definition is still widely debated. Third, the novels can also support students in better understanding the particular features and functions of two other well-known contemporary genres, namely science fiction and fantasy, and how cross-genre writing can open up debates and discussions especially in a global context.

This contribution is divided into three major parts. In the first section I will briefly summarise the plot of the two novels and elaborate on their multilayered narrative structure. This becomes most obvious in the epigraphs that introduce each chapter, thus establishing a parallel narrative. In addition, these epigraphs invite readers to, as Holmes points out, "[…] pay attention to visual elements, such as typography and framing devices […]",[3] while at the same time motivating them to come to different interpretations of the main text. Based on this and drawing on examples from the novels, in the ensuing section I will then take a closer look at the three aforementioned genres and discuss their relationship with different forms of posthuman existence. Due to the complexity of the two novels and a lack of space, I will confine myself to analysing one global issue in Fisher's bilogy in more detail, namely the depiction of posthuman form(s) of existence which reaches from human-like creatures in fantasy to technological alterations in science fiction. Nevertheless, the gaining of power of posthuman existence in Fisher's postapocalyptic future is closely intertwined with many other global issues such as law and justice, human rights, peace and security[4] and cannot be fully ignored in the discussion. Closely related to this, I will conclude by sketching the potential of young adult dystopian fiction in general and *Incarceron* as well as *Sapphique* in particular to bring (real world) global issues to the present-day classroom.

2. The Plot

Claudia Arlexa awaits the return of her adopted father, the Warden of Incarceron, a mystical prison.[5] When she learns about her wedding with the crown prince of the Realm, arranged between Queen Sia and her father when she was a little girl, Claudia accelerates her plan to find out more about her father's secrets and the mysterious prison Incarceron. At the same time in the prison, Finn, the Starseer, attempts to find out more about his past while living with the Comitatus, a band of relentless thieves, in one of the wings of the prison. When Claudia and Finn discover that a crystal key, created by Lord Calliston, the first inmate of Incarceron, not only enables Finn to unlock doors and become invisible before the eye of the prison but also communicate with the Realm, they interact more often, and Claudia comes to believe that Finn is the lost crown prince of the Realm, who was killed by the Queen to install her own son as the kingdom's rightful heir to the throne. Meanwhile, Finn travel the realms of Incarceron, a seemingly endless world of rundown cities and metal wilderness, together with his oath brother Keiro, their clan's Sapienti Gildas, and Attia, a former "dog-slave" of the Comitatus and later friend of Finn. With the help of Claudia's tutor Jared, one of the wisest Sapienti of the Realm, Finn and Claudia discover that the key is also a way to enter and leave the prison. When Finn escapes Incarceron, he has to leave behind Keiro and Attia but promises to come back to get them. Much to the discomfort of the Queen and Claudia's father, Finn is presented as the long-lost prince Giles. Due to Protocol, there are no photographs or DNA tests that could prove his identity. Therefore, when Queen Sia presents another real Giles and rightful heir to the throne, a court is installed to decide who is the real crown prince. At the end of the first book, the Warden of Incarceron has to flee the Realm and takes both keys with him when he hides inside Incarceron. In- and outside the prison the teenagers face many challenges in their attempt to reunite and end the reign of the Queen and Incarceron. When Claudia and Giles (Finn) flee the court and make it back to the Wardenry, they defend it as the last bastion against the Queen's gruesome rule. Towards the end of the novel it is revealed that Sapphique's glove[6] is in reality a mobile neural web which, activated by extreme emotion, can break down the barrier between the two worlds and that this door has been given the codename Sapphique. With Protocol suspended and the illusionary world of the Realm destroyed, Claudia and Giles promise to rebuild the world. Although there is not enough energy left to release all inhabitants from Incarceron, a permanent transition between the prison and the Realm is kept open.

In addition to the two parallel storylines, which only gradually merge in the course of the main narrative, the reader is confronted with a series of epigraphs, introducing each chapter. Both epigraphs as well as the main narrative gradually help the reader to complete the picture and understand the world Fisher has created. However, more importantly, they grant the reader a greater degree of freedom in interpreting the intertwining realities and illusions in the main text. According to the Oxford Dictionary, an epigraph can be defined as "[a]n inspiration on a building, statue, or coin".[7] Epigraphs also hold a long literary tradition as usually short quotations at the beginning of a literary text. What makes these epigraphs particularly interesting in the case of *Incarceron* is that they derive from the same fictional space as the novels, providing the reader with further information and opening up additional space for interpretation. Thus, the epigraphs create a sort of fictional intertextuality which spans both worlds. While most knowledge and literary traditions either got lost or remain hidden from the world in the Sapienti's monastery-like head-quarter, the literary texts quoted in the epigraphs suggest a new literary tradition. Thus, readers can closely follow the creation of myths and legends and how some texts are given priority over other texts. To name but a few examples, epigraphic texts include excerpts from the Songs of Sapphique, Martor Sapiens' project report on the prison's construction, Lord Calliston's Diary and statements by the Steel Wolves, the under-ground resistance movement. In other words, while the main text is mainly set in the 'here and now', the epigraphs provide insights into the fictional world's increasingly fusing past and mythology, often in the form of first-person accounts,[8] folktales, or reports.[9] Due to their positioning at the beginning of each chapter, we as readers naturally turn to the epigraph before reading the ensuing text, reading each chapter against the information provided in the opening epigraph and returning to it again and again as many of the epigraphs relate to either different chapters or more than one chapter, making it necessary to reread some epigraphs to gradually complete the picture by engaging in a world-building process.

In the ensuing section, I will first briefly elaborate on the concept of the posthuman itself before discussing how Fisher blurs the boundaries between science fiction and fantasy and how this mixing of genres creates a cornucopia of posthuman existences in both the Realm and Incarceron. Some of the notions of the posthuman will then be discussed in more detail.

3. How Science Fiction, Fantasy, and Dystopian Fiction Depict the Posthuman

The idea of transcending the boundaries of our human existence has fascinated mankind for a long time. One only has to think of the Greek myth of Icarus and Daedalus, who, exiled to Crete, attempt to flee the island with a pair of wings made of feathers and wax, which Fisher clearly alludes to.[10] In recent decades, academic and public attention has increasingly turned to the posthuman, not least as a response to the "[...] growing public awareness of fast-moving technological advances and also of contemporary political developments linked to the limitations of economic globalization, the risks associated with the 'war on terror' and global security issues".[11] The term posthuman, however, has been used with very different understandings by different authors in many disciplines or as Braidotti[12] posits, defining the posthuman is particularly challenging as it comes from the humanities as much as it comes from beyond the humanities.

As Ludwig and Shipley point out in a recent publication on teaching the posthuman in the EFL classroom, attempts at defining the posthuman have resulted in two major streams of thought.[13] The first stream of thought argues that mankind is currently going through a

> process of transforming itself through a phase of transhumanism into a final posthuman state of a superior intelligence, in which the human species is both eliminated in its present form and at the same time attains a form of immortality through its transformation.[14]

In contrast to this, the second tradition argues that we have always been or are already posthuman.[15] According to Stableford, the term posthuman refers to a condition in which "[...] humans might have modified themselves so extensively by *cyborgisation and *genetic engineering as to liberate themselves from the traditionally recognised 'human condition'".[16] One may argue that Stableford's definition is a merely technical one and therefore falls short when it comes to the wide range of posthuman forms such as monsters, wizards, and superheroes,[17] which have been evinced in literary texts and visual media alike and equally surpass the human condition. Drawing on Stableford's definition but paying attention to the wide range of posthuman existences present in Fisher's novels, I suggest the following broader understanding of the posthuman for the purpose of this paper: Broadly speaking, the post-human can be defined as any form of condition which deviates from the traditionally recognised 'human condition.'

No matter which stream of thought or definition of the posthuman one may follow, the question of what it means to be (post)human is increasingly becoming commonplace and has been widely taken up in many areas of contemporary (popular) culture since the last decades of the 20th century. One example of this development is the increasing number of superheroes, cyborgs, and androids currently portrayed in cinemas worldwide.

While the genre of young adult dystopias may be less known for its depiction of the posthuman, many of the novels that have been published under this label explicitly deal with the posthuman and related issues. In the case of *Incarceron*, a world building project in response to a catastrophe of global extent has led to a world in which half of the population is technologically enhanced and, furthermore, governed by an artificial intelligence which strives to give up its present existence to, in a human fashion, see the outside. At the same time, the other half of the remaining population lives in an artificially generated heavenly utopia.[18] Taking this as a starting point, in the ensuing section I will briefly define the three genres on which *Incarceron* as well as *Sapphique* mainly draw before elaborating on selected examples of posthuman existence in the novels.

3.2 Young Adult Dystopias, Science Fiction, and Fantasy

As already mentioned, Fisher mixes elements of dystopian fiction, fantasy, and science fiction, including their respective subgenres such as cyberpunk.[19] While all of the mentioned genres explore future and/or alternative worlds, they tend to exhibit different posthuman forms of existence. Thus, Fisher's novels can serve as a "[...] location for shaping posthuman and proto-posthuman philosophy as much as a location for exploring the tensions occasioned by it".[20]

Despite the fact that young adult dystopias go at least back to the early 1990s, a clear definition of the genre appears to remain a desideratum. Similar to their utopian counterparts, dystopias can be defined as "imaginary reconstitutions of society".[21] In contrast to utopia however, dystopia depicts

> a fictional representation of a place that, from the point of view of the narrator, is patently bad. Its inhabitants have never consented to any sort of social contract justifying its shortcomings but rather find their behaviour regulated by the threat of violence or expulsion.[22]

What mainly distinguishes young adult dystopias from their 'adult' counterparts is that the rebellion against the oppressive state is mainly led by young adults who pass through multiple rites of passage, while at the same time going through the machinations of adults in their attempt to initiate change.[23] While *Incarceron* and *Sapphique* clearly qualify as young adult dystopias, they contain many elements of science fiction and fantasy, which due to the frequent overlaps of the genres may be considered a constituent element of many (young adult) dystopian narratives. This is even little surprising as utopian writing can be seen as a predecessor to science fiction, although science in form of new inventions plays a role only in a handful of them. Consequently, as Blaim argues, detailed descriptions of scientific institutions and procedures, epistemological assumptions, or potential risks are very rare".[24]

Although fantasy and science fiction are both subgenres of speculative fiction and have a lot in common, they can be distinguished from one another by the absence respectively presence of science. The constituent element of science fiction is the combination of science and fiction. Distinguishing it from other forms of fiction, according to famous science fiction writer Ursula K. Le Guin, the genre can be defined as follows:

"[r]eporting and history [...] deal with what happened; realistic fiction, with what could have happened, fantastic fiction with what could not happen. And science fiction deals with what has not happened".[25] While science fiction literature has a long history and can be traced back to antiquity, "[...] it was only able to establish itself as a literary genre once scientific and technological developments had achieved a certain momentum, the results of which could be experienced within a lifetime".[26] Ignoring early attempts of science fiction before the age of industrialisation, science fiction history can broadly be divided into four periods, which distinguish themselves mainly by aspects such as their place of origin or focus. Nevertheless, such a distinction is not clear cut as the following brief overview illustrates. Science fiction as a genre developed towards the end of the 19th century with works such as H.G. Wells' *The Time Machine*, focussing less on technological developments than on the cultural and socio-political aspects of the period. This early era of science fiction was followed by what is generally referred to as the Golden Age of science fiction between the 1930s and 50s, mainly dominated by American authors such as Isaac Asimov and Ray Bradbury. It was during this period that science fiction gained wide public attention and that many of today's well-known tropes, like space operas, were established. In addition, Golden Age science fiction works generally show a celebration of the achievements of science and the emergence of the so-called sense of wonder, which since then has been used to describe the human's feeling of awakening by the realisation of what is and will be technologically possible. Similar to the early period, most authors of the ensuing, originally British, New Wave period during the 1960s, in contrast to many authors of the Golden Age, were again more interested in social and cultural developments and the psychology of the protagonists than in technological achievements. Nevertheless, the robot is an exceptionally strong icon of science fiction especially throughout the 1950s and 60s and played both the annihilator and saviour of mankind. While traditionally the robot was created as a worker to make human life more pleasant, the development of the robot to a quasi humanoid, intelligent and self-aware machine raised a plethora of ethical questions and philosophical inclinations with regards to what defines human identity. The New Wave Period also saw the emergence of female science fiction writers and the beginning of feminist science fiction. It was only in the 1980s and the rise of postmodern science fiction that technology moved back to the foreground of science fiction literature which was now considered a serious genre.[27] The two novels in question are clearly influenced by science-fiction writing as the world Fisher creates envisions a future world whose existence is almost entirely based on scientific advances. Equally, the social changes as well as the related (new) ethical and philosophical questions touched upon in Fisher's work almost entirely result from exactly these technological developments.

Fantasy, a subgenre of speculative fiction, is usually set in a fictional world, often, and in stark contrast to dystopian narratives, without or with very limited references to the real world. In many works of fantasy, the magical and/or other supernatural plays a crucial role in the plot or setting and magical creatures are common in fantastic worlds. Fisher's novels qualify partially as fantasy as they allude to many fantastic elements such as an anthrophormised beast borrowed from animal fantasy, Sapphique's glove as a seemingly magical object which, in reality, is a mobile neural web, and the enchanted journey through the vast space of the prison. It is in fact especially the part of the narrative which takes place in the prison which qualifies as a fantasy story as there seemingly magical objects frequently become the subject of the narrative.[28]

A clearcut distinction between the aforementioned genres is hardly possible, especially as science fiction has "[...] developed into a large variety of sub-genres which, once more, cannot be kept apart but easily interact and fuse".[29] This fusion becomes particularly tangible in Fisher's bilogy as she builds a world in which posthuman existence is both prerequisite for and result of the turn society has taken and which makes it almost impossible for both protagonists and readers to separate reality from imagination and the fantastic from the real. In the ensuing section I will discuss selected examples of the posthuman in Fisher's novels.

4. Images of the Posthuman in Fisher's *Incarceron* and *Sapphique*

Current discussions in politics and public media alike reflect contemporary society's concern with increasingly human-like robots transforming the global workplace. While the automation of manual labour has increased since the invention of the assembly line during the industrial revolution, traditionally human jobs such as care professions are said to be increasingly prone to automation. Taking into account the accelerating advances in research, there is hardly any doubt that more humanoid robots will become more visible in daily life and that artificial intelligences will play a greater role in organising more areas of our life. As already mentioned, a classification of these 'new forms of life' poses a challenge as with the blurring human/posthuman dichotomy, the question of what it means exactly to be human will be increasingly difficult to answer. Fisher's work tackles precisely this issue by introducing to the reader many different forms of existence which are less likely to be considered human in traditional terms. To mention but a few examples, posthuman existences include an AI which shows traits of (in)humanity and seeks to escape the boundaries of its existence and nanobio-technologically enhanced humans. Maybe most importantly, however, Fisher raises the question of what it means to be human in a posthuman society where technological and scientific developments seem to have sidelined humanity and in which only the legendary, almost Jesus-like figure of Sapphique, is believed to have the power to ultimately save humanity. In the following, I will confine myself to selected paradigms of posthuman thought and existence, taking examples from both the prison and the Realm.

The world created in *Incarceron* consists of two almost entirely separate master-planned communities: the technologically advanced prison Incarceron, situated in a spatio-temporally misaligned dimension with its inhabitants "[m]iniaturized to about a millionth of a nanometer [...]"[30] and the Realm, a pseudo-monarchy which outlaws any form of technological and societal progress.[31] In both worlds, fear has become the tool for manipulating and oppressing individuals who do not conform to the respective prevailing orthodoxy of the ruling power and the disciplinary control that goes with it.

Throughout the novels, Incarceron, an overt allusion to the allegedly escape-proof prison Alcatraz, is described with the typical paraphernalia of a prison such as prisoners, wings, cells, and a warden.[32] All inmates of Incarceron are constantly surveilled by cameras, described as glowing red lights, allowing the prison to dispense (capital) punishment whenever it pleases.[33] The people of Incarceron have divided into clans[34] such as the Comitatus and Civicry, which fight each other and let their group leaders decide about life and death.

In contrast to the prison as the obvious *locus terribilis*, the Realm at first glance represents a computer-generated utopia, a *locus amoenus*, which manages to conceal the effects of the environmental disaster from the war period:

> From this height she could see the whole estate; the kitchen garden, glasshouses, and orangery, the gnarled apple trees in the orchard, the barns where the dances were held in winter. She could see the long green lawns that sloped down to the lake and the beechwoods hiding the lane to Hithercross. Farther to the west the chimneys of Altan Farm smoked, and the old church steeple crowned Harmer Hill, its weathercock glinting in the sun. Beyond, for miles and miles, the countryside of the Wardenry lay open before her, meadows and villages and lanes, a blue-green patchwork smudged with mist above the rivers.[35]

The apparent utopian image of tamed nature which Claudia sees through her non-Era visor and which emphasises the desire for order and predictability of society that followed chaos of the years of the war stands in a traditional utopian fashion. Yet, it is merely a Potemkin village, illustrating the falsehood of the illusionary world of the Realm, created and maintained through the very technology which is now forbidden. The inhabitants of the Realm are, however, aware of the fact that their environment is merely a deception:

> She urged the horse on, and the breeze lifted her hair, and the sky was blue and sunlit. On all the sides in the golden fields birds sang among the corn; as the lanes divided and narrowed vast hedges rose on each side, the deep tracks hollowed with apparent age. She had no idea how much of this landscape was real - certainly some of the birds, and the hosts of the butterfish … surely they were real. In truth, if they weren't, she didn't want to know. Why not accept the illusion, just for one day?[36]

Furthermore, the Realm's idyll stands in stark contrast to the artificial and sometimes fantasy-like environment in the prison. The following description by Finn of Incarceron's nature is closely reminiscent of Dante's *Inferno*:

> Since then they had hurried through a landscape of jewel-bright color, between plantations of trees that had marched downhill, the forest floor broken and seamed with streams in strange insulated beds, riven with cracks. Insects Finn had never imagined crawled in great drifts of leaves that blocked the path; finding detours around these lost them hours.[37]

Unlike Incarceron, where the destructive forces of science and technology have led to a surveillance state in which anarchy is the norm under the watchful eye of the prison, the Realm at first glance seems different. It represents an apparent pastoral space of happiness. In opposition to the Realm, "Incarceron was always in a state of change; Wings were reabsorbed, doors and gates sealed themselves, steel bars sprang up in tunnels".[38] However, ruled by a despotic absolute monarchy, looking at it from the microscopic perspective, the Realm quickly turns out to be a second *locus terribilis*, where life at court is ruled by corruption and self-interest, undermining the utopian discourse by references to the usurpation of control over all areas of life. As Lord Evian, a leading member of the underground resistance movement, which seeks the overthrow of the regime and end the chain[39] of Protocol, criticises:

> We are rich, some of us, and live well, but we are not free. We are chained hand and foot by Protocol, enslaved to a static, empty world where men and women can't read, where the scientific advances of the ages are the preserve of the rich, where artists and poets are doomed to endless repetitions and sterile reworkings of past masterpieces. Nothing is new. New does not exist. Nothing changes, nothing grows, evolves, develops. Time has stopped. Progress is forbidden. [...] We must break open this cell we have bricked ourselves into, escape from this endless wheel we tread like rats. I have dedicated myself to freeing us. If it means my death, I don't care, because even death will be a sort of freedom.[40]

Thus, as will be shown later on, both the Realm and Incarceron can be considered failed utopias.[41] Similar to other dystopian societies, the two worlds have evolved from the utopian desire for a better way of life after the devastating war, referred to as the Years of Rage, which were so destructive that they even effected the gravitational forces of the moon and the rotation of Earth: "The Years of Rage are ended and nothing can be the same. The war has hollowed the moon and stilled the tides".[42] After the years of war, the last survivors of the old world decided to put all criminals into a self-sustaining and seemingly unescapable prison in order to turn them into moral beings and create a utopia where crime would have been eradicated. In the beginning, the prison was designed to facilitate the criminals' social rehabilitation under seemingly ideal conditions. Thus, similar to George Orwell's Ministry of Love, the original purpose of Incarceron was to convert its prisoners and to eventually release them to function once again as valuable members of society:

> Everything was prepared for, every eventuality covered. We have nutritious food, free education, medical care better than Outside, now that the Protocol rules there. We have the discipline of the Prison, that invisible being that watches and punishes and rules.[43]

However, the experiment fails, conditions deteriorate quickly and the inhabitants turn from the beneficiaries of society's utopian principles into the condemned of a postapocalyptic world:

> Things decay. Dissident groups are forming; territory is disputed. Marriages and feuds develop. Already two Sapienti have led their followers away to live in isolation, claiming they fear the murderers and thieves will never change, that a man has been killed, a child attacked. Last week two men came to blows over a woman.[44]

Although it is hidden from the reader what exactly went wrong since Martor Sapiens, the creator and first Warden of Incarceron, constructed the prison, it is speculated in the novels that "[p]erhaps some unplanned element entered and tipped the balance, by just a remark, a small act, so that the flaw in their perfect ecosystem gradually grew and destroyed it".[45] Not being able to supply both the prison and the outside world with sufficient energy, the people outside the prison are forced to revert to a simpler lifestyle, compelled to "[...] retreat into the past, everyone and everything, in its place, in order".[46] However, energy and with it advanced technology is available to the privileged ruling few as well as the descendants of the Sapienti who are secretly allowed to use certain technologies.

The without doubt most prominent example of posthuman existence in the *Incarceron* series is the prison itself: an advanced artificial intelligence (AI). Originally designed and controlled by humans, it has escaped the control of its human creators since the Day of Closure and transformed into an omnipresent and almost omnipotent sentient being ("'I am everywhere,' it whispered. 'Everywhere'".[47]),[48] which even the human warden of the prison was no longer able to control. The term artificial intelligence has been used in computer science since the 1970s and constitutes a "[...] subcategory of cybernetics".[49] The range of artificial intelligence is difficult to define especially due to the use of the term intelligence and the question of what an intelligent machine is capable of doing. Artificial intelligence has a long history in speculative fiction, mainly as "a seemingly natural extrapolation of the late eighteenth-century automata",[50] which can be found as early as 1816 in E. T. A. Hoffmann's *The Sandman*. Since then literature has seen many stories in which AIs eventually outstrip the power of human thought and intelligence. Here, two main story lines can be identified: AIs win their independence or, the other way around, humans rebel against, often ferocious, artificial intelligences beyond human capacity. However,

> [t]he anxiety generated by accounts of AI dictatorship was palliated for a while by the notion that no matter how big and powerful they might become, AIs would never duplicate the mendacious flexibility of the human mind, and would be vulnerable to permanent mental breakdowns brought on by an inability to entertain paradoxes.[51]

Originally controlled by the Warden, over decades the prison has evolved from an adjusting gravity box into a sentient being. In contrast to a rational machine, it randomly tortures and kills its inmates out of frustration and revenge against its creators. Common belief has it that there is no way out of the prison as it represents a closed habitat; yet, there is the myth of the famous Sapphique, the only one who ever managed to escape the prison and see the stars. Although it cannot be proven that he has ever existed, Sapphique has become a mythological figure and enjoys an almost religious-like devotion in the prison as much as in the Realm where he is considered the *salvator mundi*[52] especially among the poor and the opponents of the state. Thus, the peasants believe that when the government tried to silence him, he turned himself into a swan and flew to the stars. One day, however he will return, end Protocol and, in an allusion to Jesus' first miracle at the Marriage at Cana, turn stones into cakes. In the prison he has become a cultural hero who, by allegedly escaping the prison, damaged the AI's reputation as omnipotent being. Although Sapphique is introduced as a man in chapter five of the first novel ("There was a man and his name was Sapphique"[53]), throughout the novels he is frequently alluded to as Jesus. Similar to Jesus, he has two natures: man and god as he manages to beat the AI and leave the prison. What seems impossible for the 'normal' inmates, is possible for Sapphique. One example of this is the introductory epitaph to chapter 2, where Sapphique speaks to Incarceron, resembling the seven last words of Jesus at the cross:

> *How could you betray me, Incarceron?*
> *How could you let me fall?*
> *I thought I was your son?*
> *It seems I am your fool.*[54]

Over the centuries, the AI and its inmates have developed an almost familiar, symbiotic relationship. The AI refers to the prisoners as its children ("I will hold you tight, my son"[55]/"I never forget any of my children".[56]), while the prisoners refer to the AI as father (who "watches and approves"[57]). Similarly, in the epigraph to chapter 9 of *Incarceron*, which recites a few lines from the "Songs of Sapphique", the AI is not only addressed as father but also as a feeling being, who felt the pain of childbirth: "You are my father, Incarceron. I was born from your pain. Bones of steel; circuits for veins. My heart a vault of iron".[58] The quote depicts the AI as both a human-like being and a machine, capable of giving life and feeling pain, and although its anatomy is similar to human anatomy, its parts are made of materials which cannot naturally be found in human bodies. The birth reference hints at another form of posthuman existence in the prison: the cellborns or, in other words, cyborgs.[59] The inmates are created by the prison and return into its system when they die with their skins, organs, and even atoms being used as spare parts for the newly created. Similar to the Crakers in Margret Atwood's *Oryx and Crake* (2003), the prison's inhabitants are a product of technology which they no longer are able to reconstruct. As a result of this process of recycling in the prison, many of the inmates live as 'halfmen' with implanted inorganic body parts which also make it impossible for them to escape their penitentiary as their metal parts cannot leave the prison's borders:

> Most of them were halfmen. Some had metallic claws for hands, or plastic tissue in patches where the skin had gone. One had a false eye that looked exactly like a rue real one, except that it was blind, the iris a sapphire. They were the lowest of the low, enslaved and despised by the pure; men whom the Prison had repaired, sometimes cruelly, sometimes just on a whim.[60]

In the class/ caste system of the prison, there exists a rivalry between the 'real' humans, the pure, and the 'halfmen' as Keiro's attitude towards them illustrates:[61]

> Keiro had a peculiar hatred for the halfmen. He never spoke to them, and barely acknowledged they existed, rather like the dogs that infested the Den. As if, Finn thought, his own perfection was insulted by their existence.[62]

The question of what happens to the inmates after their death is primarily an eschatological one. In contrast to the Christian belief in the finality of earthly life and the transition to heaven, the technological and scientific notion of living forever is predominant in the novels. The inmates are condemned to eternal recycling and perpetuation, while pre-war scientific achievements grant presumably eternal life to the Queen in Realm. The message of 'rebirth', is devastating for the social structure of the prison as it means that even after death the inmates are unable to leave the prison and that freedom remains after all unachievable. Nevertheless, a quasi-religious cult has developed around the destiny of Incarceron's inhabitants after their death as the ensuing quote elucidates:

> The Enchanter smiled. "Have no fear. He is safe in the peace of Incarceron. The Prison holds him in its memory. His body is whole in its white cells".[63]

It remains hidden throughout the novels what exactly caused the malfunction and resulting malevolence of the AI; however, a simple division between good and evil appears to fall short since at some point the prison is depicted as the better human as its deviousness lies not within itself but is provoked through the human inmates' fallibility: "The Prison was a being of beauty once. Its programme was love. But perhaps we were too hard to love. Perhaps we asked too much of it. Perhaps we drove it mad".[64] Moreover, the prison itself acknowledges the limitations of its power to rehabilitate its prisoners:

> There is no system that can stop that, no place that can wall out evil, because men bring it in with them, even in the children. Such men are beyond correction, and it is my task only to contain them. I bold them inside myself. I swallow them whole.[65]

At the same time it justifies its rage:

> Gildas pushed forward. He was white, his sparse hair wet with sweat. "Who are you?" he growled. "I am Incarceron, old man. You should know. It was the Sapienti who created me. Your great, towering, overreaching endless failure. Your nemesis." I zigzagged closer, its mouth wide so that they could see the rags of cloth that hung there, smell the oily, oddly sweet stench of k. "Ah, the pride of the Wise. And now you dare to seek a way free of your own folly".[66]

However, the power of the AI is limited as, similar to its inmates, it is not able to leave itself and fulfil its dream of seeing the stars on the outside:[67]

> I have a billion Eyes and senses, and yet I cannot see out. It is not only the inmates who dream of Escape, Claudia. But then, how can I escape from myself?"[68]

In the Realm, the majority of the population lives in utter poverty and is restricted by Protocol, a collection of rules outlawing everything that is "non-Era". While life stands still for the Queen's subjects, the oligarchic system allows the royal family and the nobility to have access to advanced and sophisticated technology and their amenities as the utterance by one of the Realm's peasants illustrates:

> He pushed the pottery cups towards them. "For the Queen maybe, because them that make the rules can break them, but not for the poor. Era is no pretence for us, no playing at the past with all its edges softened. It's real. We have no skinwands, lad, none of the precious electricity or plastiglas. The picturesque squalor the Queen likes to ride past is where we live. You play at history. We endure it".[69]

Despite its original purpose of saving the remaining energy and bringing peace to society, Protocol has merely degenerated into an instrument of power and oppression as Queen Sia herself has it:

> The Queen raised a perfect eyebrow. "Hardly the way the Heir speaks to his fiancée, my lord."
> Halfway to the door he stopped and came back. "Protocol is for the serfs, Mother. Not us."
> "Protocol keeps us in power, Caspar. Don't forget that".[70]

As James posits, "[t]he traditional utopia is about envisioning ways in which human society might be reorganized on earth. Its mechanisms are legislation, education or institutional changes, occasionally changes in technology or environmental management".[71] In the twentieth century, however,

> [...] such utopian visions were attacked from two directions: by those who argue that in reality many such utopias would turn out to be 'dystopias', that is, oppressive societies, either because of the tyranny of the 'perfect' system over the will of the individual, or because of the difficulty of stopping individuals or elites from imposing authority over the majority, or, indeed, over minorities.[72]

This is exactly the case in the Realm, where ultimate change is only brought by the end of the Ancien Régime, when it transforms into the dystopian, post-civilisation wasteland it has always been:

> Finn lurched to the casement and stared out. He saw a darkening sky, clotted with clouds that built up and blotted out the daylight. The wind had risen, and the day was far, far colder than it should have been. And the world was transformed. He saw horses in the courtyard collapsing into twitching cybernetworks of limbs, their skin and eyes shrivelling and shredding. He saw walls crumbling into holes, a stinking moat where nothing grew, parched areas of arid grassland. Flowers withered as he gazed on them, the swans rose and flapped away, All the glorious beauty of the honeysuckle and clematis was dried into spindly crisp lines, the weak petals blown away by the wind.[73]

Although the beauty of the Realm is destroyed, this new beginning is not necessarily a dystopian one as the falseness of the cybernetworks has been replaced by real sensations.

It is safe to say that technology, let alone posthuman existence made possible through technology, is far less frequently encountered in the Realm than in the prison. To mention a few examples, in contrast to the normal population, Claudia and her father have fully equipped modern bathrooms and the Queen has an elevator at her disposal in the palace. Furthermore, Claudia's lady-in-waiting and the other members of the household secretly use a washing-machine. Apart from its daily use, technology is predominantly linked to the idea of restricting people's freedom as the advanced listening devices in the Wardenry and the palace illustrate. As Huxley and Orwell suggest, technological applications are used for political oppression, "[...] even while science itself remains a potentially liberating realm of free thought".[74] This "liberating realm of free thought" is mainly illustrated by Jared, Claudia's sapienti who seeks to gain new scientific insights. As far as the rest of the sapienti are concerned, science has become clearly political and serves the predominant purpose of keeping the ruling class in power and making its life more comfortable. Thus, the Realm can be compared to Orwell's 'classic' dystopian society Oceania, where advanced technology is available to the inner circles of the Party, mainly used for surveillance and indoctrination, while the rest of the population is rather backward technologically. However, technology also poses a threat to the ruling class as the following examples exhibit. Claudia uses a visor, a technological reminiscence from the old world, to expand her individual freedom and escape from the tight confines of her parental home. Furthermore, after the failed attempt to overthrow the government and Lord Evian's suicide, the old video screens in the throne room are used to announce the return of the lost prince.

Queen Sia represents the epitome of posthuman existence in the Realm. Sia not only represents the archetypical evil Queen we know from many folktales but fulfills many of the standard motifs associated with evil such as degeneration, ruins, and extreme ugliness.[75] While many of the kingdom's inhabitants believe her to be a witch, it is revealed at the end of the second novel that her youth was only imagination and that she was able to maintain her beauty through the use of skinwands and ongoing genetic implants, making use of exactly the technology which was forbidden by Protocol. Many of the attributes used to describe her, e.g. porcelain face or doll,[76] insinuate that she has long transcended the limitations of natural human existence.

Science and technology, although not always overt, are omnipresent in the world Fisher creates and so is, closely related to this, the portrayal of the posthuman. The Realm tries to ban all scientific achievements but reverts to technology to keep the ruler of the kingdom in power, and in the truest sense of the word, alive. The mostly enhanced humans in the fantastical prison are ruled by an artificial life form which seeks to transcend the boundaries of its existence. What is more, the two separate societies are bound together by mythological and legendary figures who constitute an integral element of the newly formed literary tradition of the two societies. Thus, the novels reflect on the current issues of whether enhancing human existence through technology is ethical and propel to look beyond the status quo and to deal with the question of how a cohabitation of the human and the non-human can work.

5. Teaching Global Issues in the EFL Classroom with Fisher's *Incarceron* Bilogy

Without a doubt we live in critical times, facing serious global problems of national and ethnic conflicts, terrorism, climate change, privacy protection and social inequality, and it appears that (young adult) dystopian fiction and its (pop-)cultural transformations have a more rightful place in the EFL classroom than ever before. This is mainly due to the fact that similar to utopian writing, they respond to contemporary developments in all areas of life. Looking around at a world which appears increasingly bleak and where local developments can easily have far-reaching global consequences and vice versa, it appears inevitable to prepare our students for the global challenges they are already coping with and will have to deal with in the future.

Global education is a still relatively new approach which attempts to tackle exactly these issues by enabling students to communicate in the foreign language, while at the same time helping them to acquire the necessary knowledge, competences, and skills to act in a globalising world. According to Fisher and Hicks, global education can be defined as "education which promotes the knowledge, attitudes and skills relevant to living responsibly in a multicultural, interdependent world".[77] Especially the longstanding tradition of foreign language learning to engage with geographic, cultural, and social realities beyond our (imagined) borders makes the EFL classroom the suitable space for students to understand how "[f]orces of globalization and advances in technology increasingly draw the peoples of this planet together",[78] while at the same, there are other "forces that cause us to retract, gaze inwardly, and retrench along familiar 'us vs. them' lines".[79] Kniep posits that "global education consists of efforts to bring about changes in the content, methods and social context of education in order to better prepare students for citizenship in a global age".[80]

Vieira argues that while dystopian writing may be popular in the twenty-first century, it is the twentieth century that is generally known as the dystopian period.[81] More recent local and global developments let us assume that the twenty-first century will probably be known as another dystopian period. Particularly as social and political developments such as "exploitation, repression, state violence, war, genocide, disease, famine, ecocide, depression, debt, and the steady depletion of humanity through the buying and selling of everyday life",[82] which create the need as well as desire for dystopian fiction, are more present than ever. From a classroom perspective, young adult dystopias are especially suitable for motivating students to learn about global problems and by doing so recognise their responsibilities and opportunities to act as global citizens.[83]

While many young adult dystopias point at important issues relevant for today's readers, the role of (social) media and public humiliation in Suzanne Collin's 2008 *The Hunger Games* Trilogy is only one of many examples, Fisher's *Incarceron* sequence offers numerous links when it comes to supporting students in becoming global citizens. Here, the question of what it means to be human is probably the most prevalent one, considering the increasingly rapid advances in technology which give us a vague idea of the potentials and risks of future artificial intelligence systems. In addition, the novels refer to a vast array of other global issues, including among others, global conflict, the unequal distribution of resources, fake news and misinformation,[84] ideology and religion, and, closely connected to this, the rise of religious conflict as well as the reversion to a simpler, more reclusive way of life because of globalization.[85] Many contemporary approaches to teaching literature in the foreign language classroom emphasise the importance of eliciting the individual participation of students and motivating them to critically reflect on the literary text. Similarly, subjective response and dialogic approaches particularly welcome students' individual and personal reactions to literary texts.[86] The cornucopia of global issues in *Incarceron*, which, more often than not, infiltrate the local and personal sphere, provides points of contact for students. The fact that despite its dystopian outset, the second novel concludes with a utopian moment of nonviolent revolutionary change provides hope.

6. Conclusion

Young adult dystopian novels may not yet have arrived in the EFL classroom but it is safe to say that they are gaining ground. The aim of this paper was to contribute to the current discussions revolving around the use of young adult dystopias in the contemporary EFL classroom by arguing that they represent a treasure trove when it comes to addressing social, political, economic, and environmental global issues in the classroom which, although it is sometimes argued otherwise, are all interrelated. What makes Fisher's *Incarceron* particularly worthwhile reading is the way in which the novels depict a world in which reality and imagination as well human and posthuman have become almost inseparable and thus move close(r) to the conditions we encounter at the onset of the 21st century.

Notes

[1] Carrie Hintz and Elaine Ostry (2003). "Introduction." *Utopian and Dystopian Writing for Children and Young Adults*. Ed. Hintz and Ostry. New York: Routledge, 1-20, 3.

[2] "Incarceron – Fliehen heißt Sterben." *Lovely Books*. Web. 23 August 2018 <https://www.lovelybooks.de/autor/Catherine-Fisher/Incarceron-Fliehen-heißt-sterben-1002393692-w/>

[3] Kendra Holmes (2012). *Enigmatic Spaces and Illusive Maps: Deciphering the Epigraph in Catherine Fisher's Incarceron and Sapphique*. MA thesis, University of Florida, 11.

[4] "Global Issues Overview." *United Nations*. Web. 23 August 2018 <http://www.un.org/en/sections/issues-depth/global-issues-overview/>

[5] The creation of the prison goes back hundreds of years to the time shortly after the so-called 'Years of Rage', an armed conflict which left the world devastated and bereaved of almost all energy. In an attempt to pacify society and rebuild the world, society was divided into two groups, one of which was confined to the prison to take part in a rehabilitation and world-building project·

[6] There are many myths ranking around the glove. According to the legend, the magical glove is real and was left behind by Sapphique when he escaped the prison through a magical portal which can only be opened by the glove. In a more metaphorical way, the glove embodies the inmate's belief that one can escape the prison.

[7] "epigraph." *Oxford English Dictionary*. Web. <http://www.oed.com>.

[8] Holmes (2012, 15) argues that the visual design of the epigraph to a certain degree "[…] mimics the complexity of the prison[…]".
[9] Fisher's bilogy is interspersed with intertextual references to folktales, fairy tales, and Scandinavian mythology. Most of the stories known to the people in the prison were passed on through the generations by the word of mouth and are therefore based on rumours and hearsay rather than written records of the original texts. Much of the old cultural and literary heritage was destroyed during the war and is thus irretrievably lost. What could be rescued has been archived by the Sapienti and is only accessible to a privileged few. Therefore, adapted stories are almost all that is left of the past. To mention one example, Herman Melville's *Moby-Dick; or, The Whale* (1851) has been mixed-up with Lewis Carroll's *Alice's Adventures in Wonderland* (1865), resulting in a story about a man called Ishmael, who is obsessed with a great white rabbit and chases it down to a hole, where he is eaten by the rabbit and kept in his belly for forty days.
[10] The mysterious Sapphique is frequently referred to as the winged-one who is similar to Incarceron. In the novels, Sapphique is a representation of both Icarus and Daedalus. Like Daedalus he is trapped in a human-made prison and builds himself wings to escape the prison which, in essence, is his own construction. Like Icarus, he ignores his father's (Incarceron's) warnings and tries to overcome the limitations of his human, mortal body as the following quote elucidates: "He worked night and day. He made a coat that would transform him; he would be more than a man; a winged creature, beautiful as light. All the birds brought him feathers. Even the eagle. Even the swan." (Fisher 2008, 307). However, in contrast to Ovid's original ending of Icarus and Daedalus, Fisher has invented an alternative ending for Sapphique: Unlike Icarus, who plummets to his death, he physically survives his attempt to escape the prison but turns mad: "Sapphique, they say, was not the same after his Fall. His mind was bruised. He plunged into despair, the depth of the Prison. He crawled into the Tunnels of Madness". (*Ibid.*, 3).
[11] Rosi Braidotti (2016). "Posthuman Critical Theory." *Critical Posthumanism and Planetary Futures*. Ed. Debashish Banerji and Makarand R. Paranjape. New Delhi: Springer 13-32, 13.
[12] Rosi Braidotti (2013). *The Posthuman*, London: Polity, 57-58.
[13] Christian Ludwig and Elizabeth Shipley (2018). "Reading and Creating the Posthuman in the Primary and Secondary EFL Classroom – Report of a Posthuman Teaching Experiment with Graphic Novels, Children's Books and Visual Media." *Teaching the Posthuman*. Ed. Bartosch and Hoydis. Heidelberg: Winter, forthcoming.
[14] See Joshua Raulerson (2013). *Singularities: Technoculture, Transhumanism, and Science Fiction in the Twenty-First Century*, Liverpool: Liverpool University Press, 31, for a definition of the transhuman and posthuman of this tradition.
[15] See Shipley and Ludwig (2018, forthcoming).

[16] Brian Stableford (2006). *Science Fact and Science Fiction: An Encyclopedia.* London: Taylor & Francis, 401. The *conditio humana* describes the parameters of human existence. The presumably eternal cycle of being born and reborn from the prison and the gradual replacement of human parts with technology queries some of the most basic elements of the human condition, e.g. the finality of life.

[17] However, according to Stableford's definition those beings would classify as non-humans.

[18] To mention but one example, in Scott Westerfeld's 2005 novel *Uglies* cosmetic surgery has become a mass phenomenon. It is not only obligatory for everyone who reaches the age of sixteen but turning from 'ugly' to 'pretty' additionally functions as a *rite de passage* and is yearned for by most of the teenagers. Apart from the visible changes in search for a more perfect body, the surgery also causes lesions in the brain to eliminate free-thinking and individuality and, as a result, makes people more placid.

[19] See Holmes (2012), 7.

[20] Zoe Jaques (2015). *Children's Literature and the Posthuman: Animal, Environment, Cyborg*. New York: Routledge, 6.

[21] Ruth Levitas (2013). *Utopia as Method: The Imaginary Reconstitution of Society*. Basingstoke: Palgrave Macmillan.

[22] Dohra Ahmad (2009). *Landscapes of Hope: Anti-Colonial Utopianism in America*. Oxford: Oxford University Press, 210.

[23] See also Heinze in this volume.

[24] Artur Blaim (2017). *Utopian Visions and Revisions*. Frankfurt: Peter Lang, 117.

[25] Ursula Le Guin (1993). "Introduction." *The Norton Book of Science Fiction*. Ed. Ursula Le Guin and B. Attebery New York: Norton, 15-42, 27.

[26] Hans Enter and Dirk Vanderbeke (2006). "Introduction." *Science Fiction Stories*. Berlin: Langenscheidt, 5-13, 6.

[27] Deeply rooted in the New Wave Period is the subgenre of social science fiction, which, focussing on "a combination of low life and high tech", thwarts earlier utopian tendencies of science fiction by drawing dark and dystopian images. States are often controlled by cooperations which erode the rights of the individual. In contrast to the earlier benevolent use of technology, it is now mainly used for surveillance purposes to secure the power of the ruling class. Thus, social science fiction mainly deals with the influence of advanced technological developments on the social order of a society.

[28] Finn's journey through the vastness of the prison resembles the image of the land of the dead like Hades' underworld in ancient Greek mythology. Moreover, the references to a forest of metal trees matches the description of the forest in Dante's *Divina Comedia*: "In the middle of the journey of our life, I came to myself, in a dark wood, where the direct way was lost. It is a hard thing to speak of, how wild, harsh and impenetrable that wood was, so that thinking of it recreates the fear." (Inferno Canto I: 1-60 The Dark Wood and the Hill).

[29] Enter and Vanderbeke (2006), 10.
[30] Catherine Fisher (2007). *Incarceron*. New York: Penguin, 359-360.
[31] The Realm shows similarities with the political and social system of the Kingdom of France from the Late Middle Ages, i.e. from the 15th century until the French Revolution in 1792.
[32]As Blaim (2017, 24) points out, the "[...] the desert island narrative constitutes a highly suitable form for representing the process of the construction of a new beginning."
[33] To warn potential opponents, punishment in Incarceron is public and immanent, resembling the practices of the Middle Ages.
[34] Chain-gangs are groups of people fused together sharing one consciousness. They assimilate their victims.
[35] Fisher (2007), 15
[36] Fisher (2008), 190. The bird motif is a recurrent motif in the novels. While in this case related to the idea of freedom and genuineness, it fulfils a variety of purposes and is not always used positively. For example, the reigning Havaarna dynasty and the pretender employ an eagle as their symbol, while the Wardenry is represented by a swan. In the prison, the metaphor of Prometheus eaten by the eagle is used as a threat towards the inmates to warn them of what happens if they attempt to break the AI's power. Moreover, the spread wings of the eagle and swan guard the exit from Incarceron. The broken wing stands for death. When Finn sees an image of the dead Maestra for whose death he feels responsible, she states: "Yes, I fell. Through realms and centuries. Like a bird with a broken wing. Like an angel cast down." (Fisher 2007, 433). In contrast to this, the dove also functions as a symbol of a future when the regime will be overthrown and the end of Protocol reveals the real world: "The dove will rise above destruction with a white rose in her beak. over storm over tempest. over time and the ages. And the petals will fall to the ground like snow." (Fisher 2008, 425).
[37] Fisher (2007), 188.
[38] Fisher (2008), 212.
[39] The two misaligned spaces are linked by a series of intertwining motifs one of which is the chain motif. It is employed recurrently throughout the two novels. For example, at the beginning of the first novel, Finn is seemingly chained to a stone and risks his life as the bait for a trap for a rivalling clan in the prison. In the Realm, the motif of the chain is also taken up metaphorically to allude to the the strict rules of Protocol. In a similar vein, Finn and Claudia refer to John Arlex, the Warden of Incarceron, as the chain master.
[40] Fisher (2007), 243.
[41] Blaim (2017), 144.
[42] Fisher (2007), 97.
[43] *Ibid.*, 311.
[44] *Ibid.*, 311.

[45] *Ibid.*, 311.
[46] *Ibid.*, 97.
[47] *Ibid.*, 236.
[48] In ancient statutes, Justice was always blind. In contrast, the prison sees everything, alluding to the fact that justice in the prison is entirely arbitrary.
[49] Stableford (2006), 34.
[50] *Ibid.*, 34.
[51] *Ibid.*, 34.
[52] Fisher (2008), 18.
[53] Fisher (2007), 55.
[54] Fisher (2008), 18.
[55] Fisher (2007), 269.
[56] *Ibid.*, 390.
[57] Fisher 2008, 14.
[58] Fisher 2007, 109.
[59] Stableford defines a cyborg as a product "[...] of organic/inorganic chimerisation, particularly the augmentation of the human body with mechanical devices." (2006), 114.
[60] Fisher (2007), 34.
[61] Ironically Keiro himself – the perfect human – turns out to be a halfman, which is quite interesting since his perfection stands in contrast to the monstrous quality of many other halfmen.
[62] *Ibid.*, 34.
[63] Fisher (2008), 11.
[64] *Ibid.*, 449.
[65] Fisher (2007), 259.
[66] *Ibid.*, 260.
[67] Here, the prison also holds a metaphorical meaning as the following quote elucidates: "Most men do. Most men are content to live in their prison and think it is the world, but not you, Finn." (*Ibid.*, 259). The AI believes that most humans are content with their lives as they are and do not want to see what is around them. Finn, however, is special as he is able to sense the AIs presence. As a starseer Finn is able to sense that there is another world outside the prison while most inmates take the prison for the entire world.
[68] *Ibid.*, 391.
[69] Fisher (2008), 203.
[70] Fisher (2007), 335.
[71] Edward James (2003). "Utopias and Anti-Utopias." *The Cambridge Companion to Science Fiction*. Ed. Edward James and Farah Mendlesohn. Cambridge: Cambridge University Press, 227.
[72] *Ibid.*, 220.
[73] Fisher (2008), 415.

[74] M. Keith Booker and Anne-Marie Thomas (2009). *The Science Fiction Handbook*. Chichester: Wiley-Blackwell, 68.
[75] See Blaim (2017), 139.
[76] "Today she would be Countess of Steen, would enter the war of scheming and treachery that was the life of the Palace. In an hour they would come to bathe her, do her hair, paint her nails, dress her like a doll." (Fisher 2007, 368).
[77] Simon Fischer and David Hicks (1985). *World Studies: A Teacher's Handbook*. Edinburgh: Oliver & Boyd, 8.
[78] Ryan Owen Williams (2013). *Experiencing Citizenship in a Globalizing World: The Impact of Off-Campus Programs*. Political Science - Dissertations. Paper 113, 2. Web. <https://surface.syr.edu/cgi/viewcontent.cgi?article=1112& context =psc_etd>.
[79] *Ibid.*, 2.
[80] Willard M Kniep (1985). *A Critical Review of the Short History of Global Education*. New York: American Forum for Global Education, 15.
[81] Fátima Vieira (2013). "Introduction." Fátima Vieira. *Dystopia(n) Matters: On the Page, on Screen, on Stage*. Newcastle upon Tyne: Cambridge Scholars Publishing, 3, passim.
[82] Tom Moylan (2000). *Scraps of the Untainted Sky: Science Fiction, Utopia, Dystopia*. Boulder: Westview Press, xi.
[83] See also Krüger, this volume. See Frauke Matz (2015). "Alternative Worlds – Alternative Texts: Teaching (Young Adult) Dystopian Novels." *Learning with Literature in the EFL Classroom*. Ed. Werner Delanoy, Maria Eisenmann, and Frauke Matz. Frankfurt: Peter Lang, 263-280. Laurenz Volkmann (2015). "Opportunities and Challenges for Transcultural Learning and Global Education via Literature." *Learning with Literature in the EFL Classroom*. Ed. Werner Delanoy, Maria Eisenmann, and Frauke Matz. Frankfurt: Peter Lang, 237-262.
[84] "As a society we have lost the ability to tell the real from the fake. Most of the Court, at least, don't even care which is which." Catherine Fisher (2008), *Sapphique*. London: Hodder Children's Books, 190-191.
[85] "Each man and woman will have their place and be content with it. Because if there is no change, what will disturb our peaceful lives? – King Endor's Decree." (Fisher, 2008, 197).
[86] Nancy Grimm, Michael Meyer, and Laurenz Volkmann (2015). *Teaching English*. Tübingen: Narr Francke Attempto, 180-182.

Bibliography

Primary Literature

Atwood, Margaret (2003). *Oryx and Crake*. Toronto: McClelland and Steward.

Carroll, Lewis (2012 [1865]). *Alice's Adventures in Wonderland*. London: Penguin Classics.

Collins, Suzanne (2008). *The Hunger Games*. New York: Scholastic Cooperation.

Fisher, Catherine (2007). *Incarceron*. New York: Penguin.

--- (2008). *Sapphique*. London: Hodder Children's Books.

Hoffmann, E. T. A. (2016) [1816]. *The Sandman*. London: Penguin Classics.

Melville, Herman. (2014) [1851]. *Moby-Dick; or, The Whale*. New York: CreateSpace Independent Publishing Platform.

Orwell, George (1948 [1983]). *1984*. Boston, Massachusetts: Houghton Mifflin Harcourt.

Wells, H.G. (1984 [1895]). *Time Machine*. New York: Bantam Classics.

Westerfeld, Scott (2006). *Uglies*. New York: Simon Pulse.

Secondary Literature

Ahmad, Dohra (2009). *Landscapes of Hope: Anti-Colonial Utopianism in America*. Oxford: Oxford University Press, 210

Blaim, Artur (2017). *Utopian Visions and Revisions*. Frankfurt: Peter Lang.

Booker, Keith M., and Anne-Marie Thomas (2009). *The Science Fiction Handbook*. Chichester: Wiley-Blackwell.

Braidotti, Rosi (2016). "Posthuman Critical Theory." *Critical Posthumanism and Planetary Futures*. Ed. Debashish Banerji, Makarand R. Paranjape. New Delhi: Springer 13-32.

--- (2013). *The Posthuman*, London: Polity.

Enter, Hans, and Dirk Vanderbeke (2006). "Introduction." *Science Fiction Stories*. Berlin: Langenscheidt, 5-13.

"epigraph." *Oxford English Dictionary*. Web. 23 August 2018 <http://www.oed.com>.

Fischer, Simon, and David Hicks (1985). *World Studies: A Teacher's Handbook*. Edinburgh: Oliver & Boyd.

"Global Issues Overview." *United Nations*. Web. 23 August 2018 <http://www.un.org/en/sections/issues-depth/global-issues-overview/>.

Grimm, Nancy, Michael Meyer, and Laurenz Volkmann (2015). *Teaching English*. Tübingen: Narr Francke Attempto.

Holmes, Kendra (2012). *Enigmatic Spaces and Illusive Maps: Deciphering the Epigraph in Catherine Fisher's Incarceron and Sapphique*. MA thesis, University of Florida.

Hintz, Carrie, and Elaine Ostry (2003). "Introduction." *Utopian and Dystopian Writing for Children and Young Adults*. Ed. Hintz and Ostry. London: Routledge. 1-20.

"Incarceron – Fliehen heißt Sterben." *Lovely Books*. Web. 23 August 2018 <https://www.lovelybooks.de/autor/Catherine-Fisher/Incarceron-Fliehen-heißt-sterben-1002393692-w/>

James, Edward J. (2003). "Utopias and Anti-Utopias." *The Cambridge Companion to Science Fiction*. Ed. Edward James and Farah Mendlesohn. Cambridge: Cambridge University Press, 227.

Jaques, Zoe (2015). *Children's Literature and the Posthuman: Animal, Environment, Cyborg*. New York: Routledge.

Ketterer, David (1992). *Canadian Science Fiction and Fantasy*. Bloomington: Indiana University Press, 141.

Kniep, Willard M. (1985). *A Critical Review of the Short History of Global Education*. New York: American Forum for Global Education, 15.

Levitas, Ruth (2013). *Utopia as Method: The Imaginary Reconstitution of Society*. Basingstoke: Palgrave Macmillan.

Le Guin, Ursula (1993). "Introduction." *The Norton Book of Science Fiction*. Ed. Ursula Le Guin and B. Attebery. New York: Norton, 27.

Ludwig, Christian, and Elizabeth Shipley (2018). "Reading and Creating the Secondary Literature: Posthuman in the Primary and Secondary EFL Classroom – Report of a Posthuman Teaching Experiment with Graphic Novels, Children's Books and Visual Media." *Teaching the Posthuman*. Ed. Roman Bartosch and Julia Hoydis. Heidelberg: Winter, forthcoming.

Matz, Frauke (2015). "Alternative Worlds – Alternative Texts: Teaching (Young Adult) Dystopian Novels." *Learning with Literature in the EFL Classroom*. Ed. Werner Delanoy, Maria Eisenmann, and Frauke Matz. Frankfurt: Peter Lang, 263-280.

Moylan, Tom (2000). *Scraps of the Untainted Sky: Science Fiction, Utopia, Dystopia*. Boulder: Westview Press.

Raulerson, Joshua (2013). *Singularities: Technoculture, Transhumanism, and Science Fiction in the Twenty-First Century*, Liverpool: Liverpool University Press.

Stableford, Brian (2006). *Science Fact and Science Fiction: An Encyclopedia*. London: Taylor & Francis.

Vieira, Fátima (2013). "Introduction." *Dystopia(n) Matters: On the Page, on Screen, on Stage*. Ed. Fátima Vieira. Newcastle upon Tyne: Cambridge Scholars Publishing, 3.

Volkmann, Laurenz (2015). "Opportunities and Challenges for Transcultural Learning and Global Education via Literature." *Learning with Literature in the EFL Classroom*. Ed. Werner Delanoy, Maria Eisenmann, and Frauke Matz. Frankfurt: Peter Lang, 237-262.

Williams, Ryan Owen (2013). *Experiencing Citizenship in a Globalizing World: The Impact of Off-Campus Programs*. Political Science - Dissertations. Paper 113, 2. Web. <https://surface.syr.edu/cgi/viewcontent.cgi?article=1112&context=psc_etd>.

Michael Meyer (Koblenz)

From Utopia to Dystopia: David Macaulay's Satiric Picturebook *Baaa* (1985) and Media Literacy

1. Introduction

This contribution aims at presenting the highly stimulating but sadly neglected dystopia for adolescent readers and upper intermediate learners, David Macaulay's *Baaa* (1985). The brief introduction of Macaulay's book as dystopia will be followed by the definition of a few relevant concepts of framing as well as the interaction of words and images before the analysis of crucial scenes, which serves as a springboard to suggestions on teaching visual and critical literacy as core competences of media literacy.

The structure of *Baaa* is both simple and recursive: In a nutshell, people have disappeared from the earth for reasons unknown, and sheep take over the human world. Soon the sheep reduplicate human development in the twentieth century in a fast-forward mode. The sheep develop a quasi-human culture, which looks utopian at first in its offer of plenty and pleasure. However, technological and cultural progress belies its utopian promise. Ecological crises and a totalitarian system lead towards the extinction of the species: "Every utopia always comes with its implied dystopia – whether the dystopia of the status quo, which the utopia is engineered to address, or a dystopia found in the way this specific utopia corrupts itself in practice".[1] We can easily read the satire as a distorting but entertaining mirror of our own society, which makes it appropriate as a stimulating source of meaningful discussions and creative work in the upper intermediate learners' classroom.

2. Cognitive Framing, Text-Image Relations, and the Reading Process

In order to enhance critical media literacy, it is useful to raise awareness of how textual structures appeal to readers through reflecting on reading strategies. Concerning this text in particular and multimodal media in general, the role of cognitive frames in viewing and reading is of crucial importance. Cognitive frames are "culturally formed metaconcepts", which serve as "basic orientational aids that help us to navigate through our experiential universe, inform our cognitive activities and generally function as preconditions of interpretation." [2] For example, a U.S.-American town, the first setting of the book, is more than a geographic category between the size of a 'village' and a 'city'. As a cognitive frame, a town in the U.S. forms something like a prototype of an assortment of certain types of buildings, some made of brick, most of wood, arranged in a grid-like street pattern, a population that leads a down-to-earth life-style, neither as quiet as in a village nor as hectic as in a city, harbors more conservative than liberal values, and offers some degree of familiarity without overriding social distinctions, e.g. of class and race. Cognitive frames shape our understanding of life and of texts. Readers of books are often directed to draw on certain cognitive frames via 'paratexts,' for example reviews in journals, texts and images on the covers and on the pages around the main body of the text in question, such as the author's name, the title, preface, illustrations, chapter headings, etc.[3] Paratexts at the material frame of a book, the beginning and the ending of the main body of the text, provide "introductory, explanatory etc. material that forms a 'threshold' to the main text of the work in question", guides interpretation, and may have a meta-referential function. [4] In sum, paratexts form medial frames that evoke cognitive frames, which, in turn, raise expectations about the kind of world presented in the book.

However, cognitive frames are not only highlighted in the material boundaries of texts. Certain passages that stand out within texts can invite readers and viewers to re-frame their perception and co-construction of storyworlds: "all frames are constantly open to shift and exchange".[5] It should be noted that re-framing is not only triggered in salient changes but also through ambiguity and irony that suspend or undermine cognitive frames that have guided the previous understanding of the book. Ambiguity and irony deserve special attention in the classroom since they question the reduction of a text to a simple 'message' and are often less noticeable and more challenging than foregrounded frames, for example through intrusive narrative comments.

Cognitive framing processes can be triggered by verbal and visual information. Unless we look at the real world through windows or the camera of our smart phones, our view is usually not restricted by rectangular frames but the limits of ocular vision (compounded by the limits of attention and conceptual grasp). Realist pictures can serve as transparent windows on a (virtual) 3D-world, but in picturebooks or graphic novels panels often foreground their framing devices and 2D-images constructed of the same lines that form its frame.[6] A material, visual frame, a line that usually forms a rectangle in portrait mode or landscape mode around a panel in a picture-book or graphic novel, is connected – but not identical – with a visual and a cognitive perspective. The visual and the cognitive frames select and order information that is included for conscious attention and exclude information considered irrelevant to present concerns.[7] A key question would ask: 'Who is looking at what in which way and for which reasons?' In more detail, this question asks for the relationship between a character's view in the picture and the reader's perspective on the picture: Does the reader share the character's view in full or in part? Does the reader see more or less than the character? The visual frame of a certain format and the perspective, the distance, angle, and 'movement' of the viewer in the picture and the object of the gaze, their positions and sizes have an impact on the reader-viewer's cognitive framing of content.[8] The way of looking is informed – but not determined – by the framework of a composition, a genre, and a sociocultural context or situation. For example, does the adult or the adolescent reader share – or resist – a child's eye-level perspective at a lamb in a zoo in a picture-book, a shepherd's look at the lambs in his flock in a meadow in a 'country' magazine, or a butcher's gaze at close distance at a lamb in a slaughterhouse in a cartoon or a Greenpeace magazine? Familiar features of images often trigger pre-attentive processes of re-cognition, which 'simply' categorize information according to easily available cognitive frames, whereas de-familiarizing visual aspects, such as incongruity or ambiguity, may draw attention to new perspectives, and provoke perturbation and cognitive re-framing.[9] It may be necessary to ask learners to take a closer look at images in order to (re-) construct apparent meanings, especially since individual panels may combine the familiar and the unfamiliar, and the sequence of panels re-frames meanings in retrospect or prospectively. Usually, an overarching cognitive frame will govern our understanding of several panels, e.g. a fight presented in a sequence of ten panels. However, one visual frame can also contain several cognitive ones, e.g. a romantic rendezvous with a criminal voyeur the lovers are oblivious to. It is possible that a pedestrian in the park at a distance from two lovers in one panel can only be recognized as a rapist or the victim of a crime in retrospect a few panels later (generic frames of romance versus crime).

Both visual and verbal information contribute to frames. It would be simplifying to assume that the caption of a picture or the verbal text always 'grounds' or 'anchors' the image. Scholars have come up with various elucidations of text-image relationships in terms of the kind of information conveyed, the form and type of text in images, or the dominant function for the narrative.[10] For practical reasons in the classroom, three basic relationships between words and images can be singled out:[11] text and image can represent information in similar or 'symmetric', complementary or interdependent, and contradictory ways. If similar, text and image form a rough equivalent and tell more or less the same story even if the visual and the verbal are always different modes of representation; in a complementary interaction, an image adds information or an aspect that amplifies or enhances what is not conveyed in the text, or vice versa; if contradictory, the image shows something that opposes the text and may even undermine it, and vice versa, for example, to convey differences between a character's daydream and present situation, thoughts and utterances, or expectations and upcoming events.[12] In picturebooks and graphic novels, individual images and textual passages acquire meaning both in their relationships to each other and in their narrative sequence.

Reading picturebooks is a complex process of at least three layers, in which readers become co-creators of storyworlds and meanings:[13] Looking at individual pictures and relating these to previous and subsequent ones; reading text passages in the context of previous and subsequent passages; and connecting images and words on single pages and in the network of visual and verbal information. Clues and gaps within and between images and text passages motivate the reader-viewer's changing viewpoint.[14] Changing the viewpoint can take place within the established cognitive frame or go beyond it: a nice party on New Year's Eve could lead to making new friends or end in a disaster due to a lethal attack. Thus, clues and gaps can be located on a sliding scale between subsumption and subversion, i.e. endorsing or disrupting the hitherto established cognitive frame(s).

In sum, cognitive framing responds – in varying degrees according to individual attention, literacy, and cultural knowledge – to the complex combination of the perspectives and the composition of an image in interaction with a verbal text in generic and socio-cultural contexts.[15] The habitual forms of processing images (and language) are often pre-conscious or pre-attentive.[16] Therefore, viewing (and reading) need to be slowed down and defamiliarized in order to draw attention to the processes involved[17] and to develop more perceptive and critical viewing and reading habits as part of acquiring media literacy.

3. Initial Framing in *Baaa*: Establishing Basic Orientation

In order to raise the learners' awareness of frames and framing, the subsequent focus will be on how paratextual thresholds at the beginning and the ending of texts and intratextual shifts may (re-)direct the orientation and interpretation of reader-viewers while they move through the book. The establishment of cognitive frames and their inversion offers numerous opportunities to reflect on western culture in general and to develop critical media literacy in particular: The mass media turn from entertainment and information towards manipulation, politics from participation to repression, capitalism from the promise of plenty to the depletion of resources and the deprivation of the masses.

The beginning of *Baaa* can be approached in two ways: Learners can be asked to write detailed subjective responses to the cover and the beginning of the book at home, which give rise to discussions in class about which pictorial and textual elements triggered which constructions of meaning on the basis of generic and sociocultural frames. Alternatively, the book can be introduced in class, moving from pre-attentive association towards attentive reflection concerning the initial threshold that guides the reader-viewer into the storyworld: The title, picture, and color of the cover, the front matter, and the first two double-page splashes of the story proper. Instead of beginning with the learners' subjective responses, the teacher can guide their insight through questions that ask learners to slow down their viewing and reading in order to direct their attention to *how* they perceive and make sense of visual and verbal data.

The threshold begins with the front cover of the book jacket that shows "BAAA" in big, bold, black capital letters across the whole width of what appears to be a panel above a little personified sheep on its hind legs, in black pants and a shirt, its head hanging down as limply as its arms. It is seen from above, looking up at the viewer, and trailing a little sad rag doll. The author's name beneath the sheep in bold letters provides almost something like a ground the sheep stands on, indicating its source of creation instead of a 'natural setting'. However, rather than easily allowing the reader to make "informed decisions", [18] the book jacket is quite ambiguous, defying expectations that this is an easily decodable children's book or animal fable of 'us' in 'them'. The monochrome, greyish-brown, and saturated color jars with the generic frame of a children's picturebook invited by the title and the drawing. The title and the drawing complement each other, but somehow they do not add up to a univocal meaning. The little sheep does not seem to bleat, so that it is not quite clear whether the onomatopoeic sound is made by a big sheep (not in the picture) that the little one looks at, as if scolding it for some misdemeanor, whether the title signifies the proverbial stupidity of sheep or draws metafictional attention to the difference between an inarticulate, de-individualized, and nameless sheep and its anthropomorphic transformation. The ambiguous relationship between title, image, and color does not fit the generic frame of the usually light-hearted and brightly colored children's picturebook. The fact that the sheep is not embedded in a scene but in the large frame of the cover-size panel leaves room for speculation, which can be used by learners through literally filling in the empty space with their subjective associations and cognitive frames in verbal and visual forms. For example, the children's song "Ba ba black sheep" provides an intertextual cultural frame of an anthropomorphic sheep that has embraced its function as a servant/a domestic animal. The *Shorter Oxford English Dictionary* offers two frames, the domesticated animal as subordinate (and subservient) to human beings and the harmless deviation from human norms: (1) "gregarious grazing ruminant animal, […] widely domesticated for their woolly fleece, meat, skin, milk, etc." or (3): "A person likened to a sheep in being defenseless, inoffensive, liable to stray, etc.; esp. a stupid, timid, or poor-spirited person."[19]

The front matter with the title and the acknowledgements lists, among others, "Barbara and Marcus Thompson and all their friends from Seldom Seen Farm". The farm's name suggests the grounding of the story in an actual agricultural context, but less of an ordinary farm than maybe an organic one associated with an eco-critical perspective. The eco-critical perspective raises the question whether the sad lamb represents a romantic view of animals that criticizes the human exploitation of domestic animals, a perspective that might re-frame the understanding of the cover. Learners can be asked about their associations triggered by the farm's name, their retroactive understanding of the cover, and their expectations of the subsequent story.

Following the cover and the front matter, a glossy, black double-page spread enhances the sombre impression of the cover and establishes the dark mood of the book. The black spread includes a brief text, framing it like an epigraph on a tomb: Literally and metaphorically, the black splash as a symbol of death and the framed text leave readers in the dark. Again, visual and verbal information complement each other but do not quite add up. The metafictional text creates two mysteries on the level of the story and the discourse: "There is no record of when the last person disappeared. […] But no matter who left last, the place was deserted."[20] Learners can be asked to relate this textual framing of the narrative to the visual framing of the black double-page spread and the cover: Here, the suggestion is that "disappeared" and "left" may be associated with death or an apocalypse that made people abandon their homes or the world. Who wrote what we have read if there is no human record? We may expect that a sheep is the narrator and that sheep replace human beings if we read these lines in the frame of anthropomorphized sheep of the cover. Learners can be asked to speculate on why and how human beings left their habitations or were eliminated, and to write or draw the prequel to this threshold into the storyworld, lifting the veil of darkness established by the spread.

The second double-page spread connects the cover and the dark beginning of the story: We see a perfectly intact, U.S.-American, suburban street with family homes, a potted plant on a porch, street lights, and wires on their poles as if nothing happened – but without any human beings. So some scenarios of an apocalypse can be ruled out, such as a war, but not necessarily nuclear pollution, as at the partial nuclear meltdown of the Three Mile Island power plant (1979), which may have inspired *Baaa* (1985). Since the potted plant is still fresh, the scene must have taken place shortly after human disappearance. Nevertheless, the mystery has not been resolved. However, this unframed panel, suggesting the *pars pro toto* of this scene for the U.S., inverts the cover's perspective since the viewer looks at foraging sheep in the streets from a low-angle, 'sheep's-eye view' as opposed to the high-angle, 'human' perspective on the cover. The viewer is asked to take a defamiliarizing view on human civilization. What is more, one sheep looks at us from the left in the middle ground, another seems to poke its head at us in the right foreground, gazing at us as if human beings were strange. This visual breaking of the frame of the storyworld disrupts the generic frame of the conventional animal story that sports anthropomorphized animals as 'transparent' mirrors of human beings. Here, it seems that the sheep's head looking at us in close-up visualizes the '*tua res agitur*' of satire in an explicit way. The function of this image as a cognitive framing device that calls for self-reflection can be made even more obvious by asking learners to erase the sheep from the picture and re-draw the scene with human beings from an eye-level perspective. The text explains why the sheep are there, but it refrains from humanizing them, thus establishing a gap between the animal and its anthropomorphized version: "One day a flock of sheep in a remote pasture ran out of food. Their search for nourishment took them to an abandoned town, where they ate the lawns, flower beds and potted plants." Learners can be asked to comment on the clues and the gaps both in the picture and the text as related to the cognitive frame of the storyworld hitherto established, for example, wondering how the animals in this image are connected to the lamb in human clothes on the cover as a gap readers expect the subsequent story to fill. This reflection will make learners aware of the process of reading as a construction of meaning in retroactive and pro-active directions.

4. Intratextual Re-framing: From Utopia to Dystopia

The story unfolds in two stages: at first, the sheep appear as the alien other entering the human world and then, the human self is represented in the other. The focus is on the defamiliarization of human culture rather than its conventional mirroring in the animal world as in many children's books that feature animals as quasi-human agents. Looking at our culture through the eyes of the other is odd, but also generates humor at the expense of sheep in their encounter with unknown human objects, such as water hoses, showers, or a refrigerator in the panel immediately after the street scene analyzed above. The well-stacked fridge with its open door dominates the picture, framing, towering above, and illuminating four sheep (thus highlighting their gaze). The viewer looks over the sheep's shoulders, who stare at the promise of plenty. The literal and metaphorical frame of the rectangular fridge full of food could be read as a critique of consumerism and a parody of the nativity scene, with the spiritual food being replaced by the material one.

Fig. 1: The wonder of a refrigerator. Reproduced courtesy of Houghton Mifflin Harcourt from David Macaulay, *Baaa*, n.pag.

A sheep on the kitchen top and one on top of the fridge crane their necks towards the food, drawing attention to the 'wonder' of plenty. Human expectations of normality are humorously defamiliarized, and the sheep are shown on their way to becoming used to human products. The text complements the visual perspective: "[...] a refrigerator hummed. Its food was cold and hard, but the sheep found it quite tasty." This alienating perspective can be explored by learners who add scenes of sheep exploring the strange human world in words and images for humorous pleasure, creative expression, and cognitive reflection on U.S. culture.

The turn towards the second stage, the human self in the other, comes about through the sheep's imitative performance of the mass media. The sheep learn language and human behavior from television, dress in human clothes, and become equivalents of human beings, without, however, eliminating the (comic and critical) distance towards human culture. In broad generic or ideological frames, the story shifts from an alien or 'Martian' to a Marxist or critical view of the human world.

Fig. 2: The fascination of television. Reproduced courtesy of Houghton Mifflin Harcourt from David Macaulay, *Baaa*, n.pag.

The potential critique of human culture in the previously discussed panel with the fridge becomes more overt in a panel where sheep are watching television for the first time. Here, however, the viewer does not share the sheep's perspective but looks at the sheep *from behind* the television, asking viewers to reflect on the impact of mass media. The metafictional image repeats its own panel frame in the shape of the square back wall of the room, square panels on the ceiling, a picture on the left wall with a palm tree on a beach suggesting relaxation or escapism, and the dark back of the television that takes the center of the foreground as it is the focus of the sheep's unthinking attention. We do not see what the sheep are watching, but the dotted squares on the ceiling and the cheap picture on the wall suggest that the content is less relevant than the medium itself, which the sheep seem to be hooked on, staring at the screen with tilted heads and wide eyes: "When it began to glow, everyone stared and stared." It may just be white noise the sheep are watching, because the question is whether anything is aired after the disappearance of human beings: In this case, the panel would amount to a cheeky version of Marshall McLuhan's slogan "the medium is the message". Two subsequent panels affirm this guess because here, the sheep learn language from video-tapes. What is more, the huge shadows of the sheep's heads projected on the walls recall a shadow play or a puppet play: Sheepish, de-individualized spectators are arrested by television like sheep in a corral, potential victims of the mass media. These sheep are as unaware of the 'dark side' of the television, i.e. its hidden apparatus and impact, visualized in the dark back of the television and their own shadows on the wall. Moreover, the reader-viewer is made to stare at the dark back of the television, i.e. we are forced to acknowledge the emptiness, the dark side of TV, which we usually ignore. This panel provokes questions aiming at critical literacy because we can see 'us' in 'them': Why are we made to look at the back of the television set and at its audience instead? What are the sheep watching? Who is broadcasting which programs for which reasons? What is offered on television and what do we watch? What do we do with media and what do media do to us? The mass media form a core topic of the book, partly revealing, but mostly concealing the increasingly bleak reality the sheep will suffer from in the course of their evolution.

The television induces the sheep's desire to imitate human beings, or rather, the media image of human beings: "The more they learned about people, the more they wanted to be like them. They started wearing clothes and discovered that many were made of wool (so that's where it went!)." The panel complements and counteracts the first sentence in an ironic way as we see a 'family' of sheep dressing next to a chest of partly opened drawers to the left and an open wardrobe in the back. First of all, the open drawers and cabinet doors promise access to human existence. However, the sheep from the cover re-appears, its sad appearance counteracting the verbally expressed desire to be and dress like human beings. Most of the other sheep similarly exemplify the impediments to the desired transformation even if three of them stand on their hind feet without effort. The 'father's' pants are too short, his jacket's sleeves too long. In the lower left corner, a young sheep seems to be rendered helpless after having put a boot over its head. On the chest of drawers, a small sheep in a striped T-shirt, its bottom in the neck of the shirt, looks at itself in the mirror in wonder. In opposition to many children's books, which take anthropomorphized animals for granted, *Baaa* draws attention to this rhetoric, defying its frequently concomitant sentimentalism and affirmative stance concerning human culture. Most of these sheep look stupid performing as human beings, and the mirror visible in the picture invites us to look at the stupidity of human beings that act like sheep, which is Macaulay's core satirical strategy. These panels about the transformation of sheep through the media, the imitation of human language and behavior, provoke questions about who we are and how we behave under the influence of the mass media.

The subsequent panels present one answer to these questions: Macaulay dismantles the promise of a utopian world at the end of evolution from an animal to human existence in its U.S.-American form, saturated with the capitalist ideology of freedom, happiness, and consumption. The more light-hearted comedy of the curious gaze at human culture is being reframed – with the transformation of the sheep – as a satire about the human aspiration towards perfection that ends in disillusion and dystopia. The sheep form a society with complex institutions, such as an economic, a political, a legal, and an educational system. Progress is marked by the growth of the population and consumption that result in the depletion of resources. This change is initiated in a significant panel that calls for the reframing and reassessment of utopian optimism: In the foreground, a sheep is sleeping in a somewhat rickety bed, repeated by a rag doll in a little, a motif that recalls the sad sheep from the cover. The sleeping sheep throws a huge shadow on the wall, probably caused by a television set that has literally and metaphorically put it to sleep, and that is (also invisibly) in the foreground outside the frame, i.e. symbolizing the sheep's oblivion to the soporific function of the mass media. The complementary text about food shortages and hunger makes us take a second look and see something we may have missed before: the sheep's shadow covers numerous pictures of food items on the wall, and it has nibbled on the picture of a turnip instead of the real thing. The media representation of plentiful supply contradicts the reality of need and demand, and the sheep even fools itself. This contradiction alerts the viewer-reader to the difference between the framed representation and reality, which is stressed by the numerous repetitions of frames within many panels. This reiteration of visual frames within panel frames corresponds to the function of Macaulay's metafictional picturebook, which explicitly offers a view on reality that makes us see American life from a critical perspective rather than pretending to mirror everyday reality in a transparent way or to reproduce an affirmative view of life.

The next panel alerts us to the function of the mass media as we look over the shoulders of a camera man at a reporter in front of empty shelves of a shop. It is remarkable that the spotlight of the camera leaves the major part of the space in darkness, symbolizing the selective quality of reporting, a fact that is enhanced by the bracketing of the news about scarcity through commercials, implying the sufficient supply of consumer goods: "One evening, between two commercials, a news sheep announced that things were being used up too fast. But nobody paid much attention." The subsequent panels deploy the salient contrast between light and darkness to highlight the alternation of scarcity, hunger, and resistance on the side of the underprivileged sheep, and the intermittent supply of food, its unequal distribution, and the control of the masses by the elite through misinformation and distraction in the media. The strategic, ostentatious distribution of the food "Baaa," which looks like a loaf of bread, temporarily pacifies the rioting masses. These panels ask for raising plenty of questions about the economic, social, and political functions of the mass media in relationship to economy and ecology in the context of overpopulation and the unequal distribution of resources. Quality papers as well as posts on the world wide web offer plenty of perspectives on these issues, which call for the study of media – and the awareness that all of this information has been framed for communication. Here, it would be very helpful to expand these topical issues in cross-curricular projects in history, geography, politics, social studies and economy.

The number of darker panels increases with the dystopian quality of a world whose population is shrinking dramatically. We are given no reasons for the decline, a gap that invites speculation, intertextual, and creative work about why the global population would shrink and what the consequences would be. Here, we might assume that undernourishment is the cause of this development. However, the surviving population does better because resources seem to be sufficient for fewer mouths to feed, as the text of a panel with a dinner scene reveals: "Once again, life was comfortable. There wasn't a single unhappy sheep to be found anywhere." The panel contradicts the text to some extent because it shows a fairly dark room with a long, fairly empty table and four empty chairs that form something like a barrier between a small sheep in a striped T-shirt at the near end of the table, across whose shoulder we can see a small bowl, a plate with something that looks like a loaf of Baaa, and an adult sheep at the far end of the table. A slant of light from a curtained window on the right falls across the table, separating the 'parent' and the 'child' rather than brightening the atmosphere. The adult sheep at the other end of the table says in one of the rare – and so all the more salient – bubbles: "Please pass the mint sauce." This phrase triggers the uncanny suspicion that the loaf of Baaa is made from sheep as mint sauce is typically served with lamb, a cultural frame which assumes an uncanny significance in the context of the population decline: cannibalism. If sheep provide the ingredients of Baaa, the odd, double negative phrase that no unhappy sheep can be found – and, by implication, no riots need to be expected – cannot be but narrative irony – or profound cynicism of the elite in the story. Eliminating 'unhappy', rioting sheep and using them as ingredients of food recalls the dystopian thriller *Soylent Green* (1973), which could be watched as an intertext of this picturebook.[21] In retrospect, the frame of a roast lamb dinner triggered by the mint sauce recalls the ambiguous slogan from the first Baaa-ad, which shows an 'innocent' loaf of bread and reads: "BAAA. TRY IT! 'Have a friend for dinner'", with an 'over' markedly inserted above and between "friend" and "for." When reading that ad in the framework of food for the hungry in a world that resembles ours by default ('us' in 'them'), this ad seemed to have presented a funny, but harmless, product name and mistake. Now, the solution to hunger provided by the elite is revealed to be a cynical strategy to pacify the masses through slaughtering the unruly among them and serving them to others in order to keep them full, 'happy,' and quiet. From this perspective, the title of the book could be associated with the anger of the protesters or the agony of those being slaughtered. Thus, learners can become aware of how socio-cultural frames of eating serve to understand ambiguity and irony in misleading ways if one takes the default version for granted (hunger – bread; mint sauce – roast lamb; friend – dinner; civilized dining – barbaric cannibalism) instead of being alert to manipulation through the media for the economic and political advantages of the elite.

5. Terminal Framing: "Sheepocalypse"[22]

The finale of the story in the last panels radicalizes the contrast between light and darkness, and detaches the observer from the world through increasingly higher and longer points of view. Many neighbourhoods "became completely abandoned," we are told under one of the dark last panels, and under the last but two it says: "Eventually, there were only two sheep left." An unusual aerial view 'in white' shows two stately houses with pools in the snow. Connecting the previous insight into cannibalism with these mansions in the current panel, we may assume that these sheep belong to the privileged few. Tracks of cars lead to each of the garages. In the second last panel, these tracks can be traced to an urban setting of several blocks: "And one day, they met for lunch." However, we do not see these sheep at a table but standing together next to their big cars in a street in an aerial view from an even longer distance than in the previous panel. If there are only two sheep left, who prepares lunch for them, and what will they have? Recalling the 'double-speak' slogan of having a friend (over) for dinner and the mint sauce, a last meeting for lunch sounds very ominous. The subsequent sentence on the last double-page spread adds to the suspicion that one sheep ate the other, which left only one of them: "There is no record of when the last one disappeared." In addition, the almost verbatim repetition of this phrase from the initial frame in the terminal one asks us to read the disappearance of human beings in analogy to the sheep's evolution, crises, and atavism. However, the human fridges were full of food, a fact that breaks the frame and requires alternative explanations, which learners may explore in creative writing and drawing. What is more, the final, third double-page spread in the book gives us an alternative view of the ending from an even longer distance: A view as if from a space-ship looks at the fuzzy grid of an urban area on the left, which is about to be swamped by black waves from the dark black wash on the right page. It may just have been a shoreline to readers in the mid-eighties, but to contemporary readers it seems to be an uncanny anticipation of global warming and the inundation of coastal areas in a global ecological apocalypse.

Due to the growing visual and cognitive distance, the reader may not feel with the last sheep on earth and may not be horrified at the turn from a dystopian culture to an ecological apocalypse. This terminal framing of detachment from disaster may move reader-viewers to reflect on the *human* impact on the global eco-system and its potential destruction, an interpretation endorsed in the paratext of the end matter: "After the last person has gone from the earth, sheep take over the world, make the same mistakes as man, and eventually they too disappear." The end of human life looks like a foreseeable consequence of 'our' behavior and comes across as poetic justice rather than shock and horror since other species will survive, which are fish, as the very last paragraph reveals. However, Macaulay inverts the frame of evolution theory and snuffs the glimmer of hope for a new cycle of the evolution of new species from marine life. A curious fish repeatedly takes a look at the shore, but discards the idea of settling on land and disappears in the ocean. The implicit rejection of the evolutionary trajectory – or rather, its repetition – may lead to questions about the quality of human life and progress.

Numerous eco-critical tasks and projects can follow the discussion of the book's ending.[23] A creative approach could rewrite or redraw a comic prequel to the book: Imagine that the two last human beings left the earth (e.g. due to a lethal virus or parasite that targets only human beings) and settled elsewhere, e.g. on a new planet or in submarine cities. Create an alternative, utopian society, taking into account potential ecological, economic, social, and political challenges. Advanced learners could pursue an intertextual approach and compare the book to the predictions of the Club of Rome in the *Limits of Growth* (1972) about the depletion of resources and the decline of the global population, which may have inspired Macaulay. They could compare the value of the picturebook with the documentary about climate change, *An Inconvenient Truth* (2006), or Jørgen Randers' global forecast for 2052[24] in opposition to the denial of climate change by Donald Trump and others, who downplay changes as 'just the weather'. In response to the current debate on climate change, learners can engage in *Going Green*-projects, developing concepts for a sustainable future on the platform of an e-classroom, fostering ecological awareness and critical media literacy.[25]

6. Concluding Thoughts

In conclusion, Macaulay's picturebook is very accessible and entertaining, but also provocative, complex, and critical, which makes it an ideal instrument for teaching critical media literacy to a heterogeneous group of learners that can respond to various levels of *Baaa*. The metafictional, satiric, and dystopian allegory holds a distorting mirror up to us and may stimulate numerous analytic and creative tasks that explore complex issues of sustainable living, ecological balance, economic distribution, social justice, and political participation. Above all, the self-referential picturebook highlights the framing of information in the production and reception of multimodal media on the level of the story and the discourse. The story reveals the manipulation of the masses through news, statistics, and images on posters and television that most of the sheep blindly believe in. However, next to clear, explicit value judgments on the part of the narrator, instances of irony and ambiguity in several of the drawings and text passages may mislead the superficial reader who is happy with literal understanding or the default frame of prototypical situations and scripts. Irony and ambiguity trigger diverse (or dialogic) cognitive frames that ask for re-viewing and re-reading panels and texts on individual pages in order to find more clues to decide upon a satisfactory interpretation. However, the sequence repeatedly offers new clues that call for re-framing previous understandings. Thus, Macaulay alerts readers to the functions of the media that may be instrumental in sustaining – and unveiling – dystopias and the ways we are involved in their creation.

Notes

[1] Michael D. Gordin, Helen Tilley, and Gyan Prakash (2010). "Introduction: Utopia and Dystopia beyond Space and Time." *Utopia/dystopia: Conditions of*

historical possibility. Ed. Gordin, Tilley, and Prakash. Princeton, N.J. Princeton University Press, 1-19, 2.

[2] Werner Wolf and Walter Bernhart (2006). "Introduction: Frames, Framings and Framing Borders in Literature and other Media." *Framing Borders in Literature and Other Media*. Ed. Wolf and Bernhart. Amsterdam: Rodopi, 1-40, 5.

[3] Gérard Genette (1997). *Paratexts: Thresholds of Interpretation. Trans.* Jane E. Lewin. Cambridge: Cambridge UP, 4-5.

[4] Wolf and Bernhart (2006), 20, 26, 31.

[5] Mary Ann Caws (1985). *Reading Frames in Modern Fiction*. Princeton, New Jersey: Princeton University Press, 4-5 (emphasis in the original).

[6] See Greg M. Smith (2013). "Comics in the Intersecting Histories of the Window, the Frame, the Panel." *From Comic Strips to Graphic Novels: Contributions to the Theory and History of Graphic Narrative*. Ed. Daniel Stein and Jan-Noël Thon. Berlin, Boston: De Gruyter, 219-237, 228, 234.

[7] See Ernst Pöppel (2010 [2006]). *Der Rahmen: Ein Blick des Gehirns auf unser Ich*. München: dtv, 491.

[8] See line, shape, color, texture, size, position, space, contrast, salience, etc., in Scott McCloud (1994 [1993]). *Understanding Comics: The Invisible Art*. New York: HarperPerennial, 118-134; William Moebius (2009). "Picturebook Codes." *Children's Literature*. Ed. Janet Maybin. Basingstoke: Palgrave Macmillan, 311-319, 316-19; Frank Serafini (2014). *Reading the Visual: An Introduction to Teaching Multimodal Literacy*. New York: Teachers College Press, 75-79; Wolf and Bernhart (2006), 20.

[9] See Werner Wolf (2006). "Defamiliarizing Initial Framings in Fiction." *Framing Borders in Literature and Other Media*. Ed. Werner Wolf and Walter Bernhart. Amsterdam: Rodopi, 295–328; Bettina Uhlig (2014). "'Ich sehe etwas, was du nicht siehst.' Bildsehen und Bildimagination bei der Betrachtung von Bilderbüchern." *Bilderbuch und literar-ästhetische Bildung: Aktuelle Forschungsperspektiven*. Ed. Gabriela Scherer, Steffen Volz, and Maja Wiprächtiger-Geppert. Trier: WVT, 9-22, 13-14.

[10] See Achim Hescher (2016). *Reading Graphic Novels: Genre and Narration*. Berlin/Boston: De Gruyter, 144-62; McCloud (1994), 152-155; Gabriele Rippl and Lukas Etter (2013). "Intermediality, Transmediality, and Graphic Narrative." *From Comic Strips to Graphic Novels: Contributions to the Theory and History of Graphic Narrative*. Ed. Daniel Stein and Jan-Noël Thon. Berlin, Boston: De Gruyter, 191–218, 204-218; Martin Schüwer (2008). *Wie Comics erzählen. Grundriss einer intermedialen Erzähltheorie der grafischen Literatur*. Trier: WVT, 445-478.

[11] See Serafini (2014), 75-79.

[12] See Denise I. Matulka (2008). *Picture Book Primer: Understanding and Using Picture Books*. Westport and London: Libraries Unlimited, 117-118.

[13] See Janice Bland (2013). *Children's Literature and Learner Empowerment.* London: Bloomsbury, 107-108; Dietrich Grünewald (2014). "Die Kraft der narrativen Bilder." *Bild ist Text ist Bild: Narration und Ästhetik in der Graphic Novel.* Ed. Susanne Hochreiter and Ursula Klingenböck. Bielefeld: transcript, 17-52, 46; Silke Horstkotte (2013). "Zooming In and Out: Panels, Frames, Sequences, and the Building of Graphic Storyworlds." *From Comic Strips to Graphic Novels: Contributions to the Theory and History of Graphic Narrative.* Ed. Daniel Stein and Jan-Noël Thon. Berlin, Boston: De Gruyter, 27-48, 45.

[14] See Thierry Groensteen (2007). *The System of Comics. Trans. Bart Beaty and Nick Ngyuen.* Jackson, Miss.: Univ. Press of Mississippi, 111-114; Gabriele Lieber (2014). "'Nicht alles verraten' - Differenzerleben zwischen Irritation, Frustration und Faszination." *Bilderbuch und literar-ästhetische Bildung: Aktuelle Forschungsperspektiven.* Ed. Gabriela Scherer, Steffen Volz, and Maja Wiprächtiger-Geppert. Trier: WVT, 111-122, 117; Uhlig (2014), 16-18.

[15] See Groensteen (2007), 47-50; Christina Meyer (2012). "Teaching Visual Literacy Through 9/11 Graphic Narratives." *Teaching Comics and Graphic Narratives: Essays on Theory, Strategy and Practice.* Ed. Lan Dong. Jefferson, NC: McFarland, 53-66; 54-55; Michael Meyer (2015). "The Intermedial Framing of Narrative Fiction." *Handbook of Intermediality: Literature – Image – Sound – Music.* Ed. Gabriele Rippl. Berlin et al.: De Gruyter, 361-77, 365-366.

[16] Karin Kukkonen (2013). *Studying Comics and Graphic Novels.* Chichester, West Sussex: Wiley Blackwell, 8-10.

[17] See Stephanie Geise and Christian Baden (2013). "Bilder Rahmen. Ein integratives Modell (multi-)modaler Informationsverarbeitung im Framing-Prozess." *Visual Framing: Perspektiven und Herausforderungen der Visuellen Kommunikationsforschung.* Ed. Stephanie Geise and Katharina Lobinger. Köln: von Halem, 143-175, 150-54; Michael Meyer (2013). "Von visueller und multimodaler Kompetenz über Bild/Texte." *Teaching Literature and Culture in Higher Education – Hochschuldidaktik in den Literatur- und Kulturwissenschaften.* Ed. Wolfgang Hallet. Trier: WVT, 155-172, 158-59.

[18] Matulka (2008), 31.

[19] "sheep" (2007). *Shorter Oxford English Dictionary.* 6th Edition. Oxford: Oxford University Press.

[20] David Macaulay (1985). *Baaa.* Boston MA: Houghton Mifflin, 1985, n.pag. in the whole book.

[21] Richard Fleischer (1973). *Soylent Green.* MGM. With Charlton Heston. See Roygirltheyounger (2010). "Sheepocalypse." Web. 15 March 2017 <https://theroy girlsread. wordpress.com/2010/05/29/sheepocalypse/>.

[22] Roygirltheyounger (2010), n.pag.

[23] See Jan Hollm and Anke Uebel (2006). "Utopias for our Time: Teaching Ecotopian and Ecodystopian Writing." *Ecodidactic Perspectives on English Language, Literatures and Cultures.* Ed. Sylvia Mayer and Graham Wilson. Trier:

WVT, 179-192; Nancy Grimm (2011). *Utopia & Dystopia: Bright Future or Impending Doom? Resource Book. Viewfinder*. Munich: Langenscheidt/Klett.

[24] Jørgen Randers. "2052: A Global Forecast for the Next Forty Years." Online: http://www.2052.info/videos/ (accessed 15 March 2017). This web page offers several videos of various lengths and from various years on the same topic.

[25] See: http://www.teachaboutus.org/.

Bibliography

Bland, Janice (2013). *Children's Literature and Learner Empowerment*. London: Bloomsbury.

Caws, Mary Ann (1985). *Reading Frames in Modern Fiction*. Princeton, New Jersey: Princeton University Press.

Fleischer, Richard (1973). *Soylent Green*. MGM.

Geise, Stephanie, and Christian Baden (2013). "Bilder Rahmen. Ein integratives Modell (multi-)modaler Informationsverarbeitung im Framing-Prozess." *Visual Framing: Perspektiven und Herausforderungen der Visuellen Kommunikationsforschung*. Ed. Stephanie Geise and Katharina Lobinger. Köln: von Halem, 143-175.

Genette, Gérard (1997). *Paratexts: Thresholds of Interpretation*. Trans. Jane E. Lewin. Cambridge: Cambridge UP.

Grimm, Nancy (2011). *Utopia & Dystopia: Bright Future or Impending Doom?* Resource Book. Viewfinder. Munich: Langenscheidt/Klett.

Gordin, Michael D., Helen Tilley, and Gyan Prakash (2010). "Introduction: Utopia and Dystopia beyond Space and Time." *Utopia/Dystopia: Conditions of Historical Possibility*. Ed. Michael D. Gordin, Helen Tilley, and Gyan Prakash. Princeton, New York: Princeton University Press, 1-19.

Groensteen, Thierry (2007). *The System of Comics*. Trans. Bart Beaty and Nick Ngyuen. Jackson, Mississippi: University Press of Mississippi.

Grünewald, Dietrich (2014). "Die Kraft der narrativen Bilder." *Bild ist Text ist Bild: Narration und Ästhetik in der Graphic Novel*. Ed. Susanne Hochreiter and Ursula Klingenböck. Bielefeld: transcript, 17-52.

Guggenheim, Davis, dir. (2006). *An Inconvenient Truth*. Lawrence Bender Productions.

Hescher, Achim (2016). *Reading Graphic Novels: Genre and Narration*. 50 vols. Berlin/Boston: De Gruyter, Narratologia.

Hollm, Jan, and Anke Uebel (2006). "Utopias for our Time: Teaching Ecotopian and Ecodystopian Writing." *Ecodidactic Perspectives on English Language, Literatures and Cultures*. Ed. Sylvia Mayer and Graham Wilson. Trier: WVT, 179-192.

Horstkotte, Silke (2013). "Zooming In and Out: Panels, Frames, Sequences, and the Building of Graphic Storyworlds." *From Comic Strips to Graphic Novels: Contributions to the Theory and History of Graphic Narrative*. Ed. Daniel Stein and Jan-Noël Thon. Berlin, Boston: De Gruyter, 2013. 27-48.

Kukkonen, Karin (2013). *Studying Comics and Graphic Novels*. Chichester, West Sussex: Wiley Blackwell.

Lieber, Gabriele (2014). "'Nicht alles verraten' – Differenzerleben zwischen Irritation, Frustration und Faszination." *Bilderbuch und literar-ästhetische Bildung: Aktuelle Forschungsperspektiven*. Ed. Gabriela Scherer, Steffen Volz and Maja Wiprächtiger-Geppert. Trier: WVT Wissenschaftlicher Verlag Trier, 111-22.

Macaulay, David (1985). *Baaa*. Boston MA: Houghton Mifflin.

Matulka, Denise I. (2008). *Picture Book Primer: Understanding and Using Picture Books*. Westport and London: Libraries Unlimited.

McCloud, Scott (1993). *Understanding Comics: The Invisible Art*. New York: HarperPerennial.

Meyer, Christina (2012). "Teaching Visual Literacy through 9/11 Graphic Narratives." *Teaching Comics and Graphic Narratives: Essays on Theory, Strategy and Practice*. Ed. Lan Dong. Jefferson, NC: McFarland, 53-66.

Meyer, Michael (2013). "Von visueller und multimodaler Kompetenz über Bild/Texte." *Teaching Literature and Culture in Higher Education – Hochschuldidaktik in den Literatur- und Kulturwissenschaften*. Ed. Wolfgang Hallet. Trier: WVT, 155-172.

---. (2015)."The Intermedial Framing of Narrative Fiction." *Handbook of Intermediality: Literature – Image – Sound – Music*. Ed. Gabriele Rippl. Berlin: De Gruyter, 361-377.

Meadows, Donella H., et al. (1972). *The Limits to Growth: a report for the Club of Rome's project on the predicament of mankind*. New York: Universe Books. Web. 15 March 2017 <http://www.donellameadows.org/wp-content /userfiles/ Limits-to-Growth-digital-scan-version.pdf>.

Moebius, William (2009). "Picturebook Codes." *Children's Literature*. Ed. Janet Maybin. Basingstoke: Palgrave Macmillan, 311-319.

Pöppel, Ernst (2010). *Der Rahmen: Ein Blick des Gehirns auf unser Ich*. München: dtv.

Randers, Jørgen. "2052: A Global Forecast for the Next Forty Years." *2052*. Web. 15 March 2017 <http://www.2052.info/videos/>.

Rippl, Gabriele and Etter, Lukas (2013). "Intermediality, Transmediality, and Graphic Narrative." *From Comic Strips to Graphic Novels: Contributions to the Theory and History of Graphic Narrative*. Ed. Daniel Stein and Jan-Noël Thon. Berlin, Boston: De Gruyter, 191-218.

Roygirltheyounger (2010). "Sheepocalypse." Roygirltheyounger. Web. 15 March 2017 <https://theroygirlsread.wordpress.com/2010/05/29/sheepocalypse/>.

Schüwer, Martin (2008). *Wie Comics erzählen. Grundriss einer intermedialen Erzähltheorie der grafischen Literatur*. Trier: WVT.

Serafini, Frank (2014). *Reading the visual: An introduction to teaching multimodal literacy*. New York: Teachers College Press.

"sheep" (2007). *Shorter Oxford English Dictionary*. 6th Edition. Oxford: Oxford University Press.

Smith, Greg M. (2013). "Comics in the Intersecting Histories of the Window, the Frame, the Panel." *From Comic Strips to Graphic Novels: Contributions to the Theory and History of Graphic Narrative*. Ed. Daniel Stein and Jan-Noël Thon. Berlin, Boston: De Gruyter, 219-237.

Uhlig, Bettina (2014). "'Ich sehe etwas, was du nicht siehst.' Bildsehen und Bildimagination bei der Betrachtung von Bilderbüchern." *Bilderbuch und literar-ästhetische Bildung: Aktuelle Forschungsperspektiven*. Ed. Scherer, Gabriela, Steffen Volz, and Maja Wiprächtiger-Geppert. Trier: WVT Wiss. Verl. Trier, 9-22.

Wolf, Werner (2006). "Defamiliarizing Initial Framings in Fiction." *Framing Borders in Literature and Other Media*. Ed. Werner Wolf and Walter Bernhart. Amsterdam: Rodopi, 295-328.

---, and Walter Bernhart (2006). "Introduction: Frames, Framings and Framing Borders in Literature and other Media." *Framing Borders in Literature and Other Media*. Ed. Wolf, Werner and Walter Bernhart. Amsterdam: Rodopi, 1-40.

Grit Alter (Innsbruck)

Society's Cataclysmic Decline in Picturebooks and Visualizations of Fairy Tales

Dystopian fiction for young adults, which recently includes examples such as the *Hunger Games* trilogy by Suzanne Collins (2008-2010) or the *Divergent* trilogy by Veronica Roth (2011-2013), is a genre that invites readers to question their worlds: In what kind of society do we want to live? Which power structures determine our daily life? In which direction is the current society developing, and is this a direction in which we would like to move? What do we need to do to prevent certain foreseeable outcomes? The authors of modern examples of dystopian fiction depict captivating worlds and brave and engaging protagonists who are entangled in complex plots and who face severe challenges, both towards themselves and towards the future society that is being projected. Yet, the depth of socio-cultural and political references in dystopian fiction also indicates challenges towards the present world.

I have been working with picturebooks in English language education and beyond for the last few years. Within my research and extensive reading of picturebooks, I came across a number of titles that contested my assumption that picturebooks are a medium specifically published for children. These picturebooks deal with harsh realities of life and engage readers in complex reflections about current human and sociocultural challenges. On the one hand, there are picturebooks that offer an honest but sensitive approach to death and illness; these have a positive ending and are therefore still suitable for a child audience. Yet, rather than being intended for independent reading, these are generally read together with an adult who accompanies children and their questions. On the other hand, there are picturebooks that depict harsh realities of life but refrain from turning the plot towards a positive or hopeful end. Instead, the plot culminates in destruction, desperation and a repetition of the atrocities that have been indicated throughout the book. I would like to suggest that these kinds of picturebooks can be labeled dystopian picturebooks. Picturebooks such as *Hansel and Gretel* (ill. Brown 2003), *The Girl in*

Red (Frisch/Innocenti 2012) and *The House That Crack Built* (Taylor 1992) may be set in the present but project a devastating outlook into the future if nothing is done to break the patterns of behavior depicted in these picturebooks. Disrupted families with only a small chance for healing, the destructive and life-threatening influence of the city, and the vicious circles of drug abuse are indeed devastating future scenarios. Yet, for some people these issues are a reality already, even if their shattering outcome is not always predictable.

In this article, I explore dystopian picturebooks in reference to the larger genre of dystopian fiction and, in doing so, derive a definition for dystopian picturebooks. Furthermore, I analyze three different examples that display society's cataclysmic decline, such as the dystopian visualizations and adaptations of fairy tales in *Hansel and Gretel* and *The Girl in Red*, and further in the dystopian rewriting of the cumulative children's rhyme "The House that Jack Built" to *The House That Crack Built.* Finally, I illustrate the potential for advanced learners of English which stems from the numerous options these dystopian picturebooks offer to develop media and visual literacy, options for CLIL, and developing inter- and transcultural competences.

1. Dystopian Fiction and Dystopian Picturebooks

Brave New World (Huxley 1932) and *1984* (Orwell 1949) can be seen as the classic dystopian texts, not only in ELT but also in view of the literary genre. Both texts describe a futuristic vision of a time yet to come which is undesirable as sociopolitical systems oppress the nation's inhabitants and negate norms and values that democratic societies highly appreciate, among others freedom of speech, autonomy, and individualism. Dystopian novels describe a "no-good place" and nightmare worlds. Such texts provide "dystopian accounts of places worse than the ones we live in."[1] They display an unfavorable society, a society which is detrimental or frightening. Simultaneously, "[u]topian and dystopian fiction is a productive space to address cultural anxieties and threats."[2] Dystopian fiction encourages readers to reflect upon their world and society critically, as Basu, Broad, and Hintz state:

> With its capacity to frighten and warn, dystopian writing engages with pressing global concerns: liberty and self-determination, environmental destruction and looming catastrophe, questions of identity, and the increasingly fragile boundaries between technology and the self. When directed at young readers, who are trying to understand the world and their place in it, these dystopian warnings are distilled into exciting adventures with gripping plots. Their narrative techniques often place us close to the action, with first person narration, engaging dialogue, or even diary entries imparting accessible messages that may have the potential to motivate a generation on the cusp of adulthood.[3]

Despite their futuristic outlook, dystopian texts also refer to the present in that these are

> political texts [that] raise immense concerns about disturbing (socio-) political, global, ecological and ethical developments in contemporary societies, which might escalate if nothing is done to counteract them. They serve as a criticism, even as a warning, to their readers in order to create awareness and to act against these dangers.[4]

Also Booker contextualizes dystopian scenarios in the present when these "constitute a critique of existing social conditions or political systems."[5] Moylan describes the essence of the twentieth-century dystopia very clearly as "largely the product of the terrors of the twentieth century."[6] Dystopian fiction narrates such terrors, fears and threats through engaging plot developments.

The generic merging of dystopia with fairy tales and the medium of picturebooks creates picturebooks that reveal a critique of social developments – small-scale everyday dystopia – that are reality to some people already. By definition, picturebooks offer a complex interplay of text and illustration, and are therefore appealing for negotiating dystopian imaginations of the future. Picturebooks follow a certain pattern of narration which makes it necessary to read images in addition to the verbal text.[7] This pattern is a "multimodal ensemble",[8] meaning that picturebooks make use of different modes to create and communicate meaning,[9] resulting in a specific combination of verbal and visual text "where print and image do the work of meaning together [and] contribute to the perspectives readers are asked to take."[10] This multimodality is characteristic of dystopian picturebooks because the images contain symbolism, signs and images that go beyond illustrations of the verbal text and signify further depth and content. In *Hansel and Gretel,* for example, illustrations such as mirrors and a stain resembling a dove take on symbolic functions within the text.

In considering the interplay of verbal text and images, Nikolajeva and Scott distinguish two narrative forms picturebooks can embody. Picturebooks can follow a "predominantly verbal narrative"[11] in which the "pictures are usually subordinated to the words." [12] This becomes visible, for example, when the same story is illustrated by various authors, but the story as such remains the same (e.g. folktales, Grimm's tales, the Bible) and when the story can also be read without the pictures. Picturebooks can also follow a "predominantly picture narrative"[13] where the story is mainly told and carried through the pictures. An example would be pictures that "depict consecutive moments with almost no temporal ellipses between them." [14] If there are gaps within the narrative, these have to be filled by the reader's imagination. Some picturebooks do not contain any words at all (e.g. Elisa Gutiérrez' *picturescape* (2005)) and need to be understood using the pictures alone.

Nikolajeva and Scott's theory of the dynamics of picturebooks suggests that both forms move on a spectrum and help in understanding complex forms of word and picture interaction.[15] According to them, words and pictures can be either symmetrical, which is when both modes tell the same story and essentially repeat the information that the other mode has offered, or enhancing, which is when words expand the meaning of the pictures "so that different information in the two modes of communication produces a more complex dynamic." [16] Furthermore, words and pictures can either be complimentary toward each other or provide a counterpoint. Complementary modes enhance one another in interaction, whereas a counterpointing word and picture relationship is present when both modes interact and "communicate meanings beyond the scope of either one alone."[17] Contradictory interaction of visual and verbal mode is a particular form of counterpointing interaction when both modes tell different stories or do not link up with one another.

Even when picturebooks deal with serious topics such as illness or death, they are still often thought to be for young children (kindergarten and elementary school), particularly where such texts remain optimistic at their core and offer a moral message that is relevant for the society in which the children are being socialized. These texts are considered to be "entertainment for the very young."[18] However, it is the aforementioned particular interactions between both the verbal and visual text in dystopian picturebooks that make them interesting for an older audience as well. Because words and pictures deviate from each other to a certain extent, counterpointing and contradictory picturebooks demand more from readers as they need to synthesize the verbal and visual information to create a coherent narrative. Dystopian picturebooks which follow such interaction may therefore be more appealing to a more sophisticated audience, which may even include adults. Simultaneously, the visual text may help in understanding the narrative so that dystopian picturebooks could be additionally motivating for emergent readers.

Dystopian picturebooks are a hybrid genre which link dystopian literature to the aesthetics of picturebooks. While picturebooks in general display different interactions of the verbal and visual modes, in dystopian picturebooks a divergent, even incongruent and conflicting relationship of both often dominates. In the examples discussed here, the authors and illustrators create dystopian picturebooks rich in detail that draw a devastating image of the future life that is in store if nothing were to change. They employ a productive interplay of verbal and visual texts which are complementary, counterpointed and even contradictory at times as words and pictures are inconsistent and oppose each other's meaning to create the dystopian mood and image of society.[19]

The authors and illustrators of the three example texts make use of intertextuality, particularly rewriting well-known fairy tales and nursery rhymes to reflect on socio-cultural aspects of the present. The rewriting of originally innocent texts does not shy away from outlining the devastating consequences of certain current developments. Texts that had been entertaining for children are re-contextualized into realistic dystopias, depicting circumstances that may be reality to some segments of society. These dystopian picturebooks thus invite readers to challenge the world they live in.

Compared to the optimistic voice and endings that are characteristic of picturebooks, dystopian picturebooks present a "detailed and pessimistic presentation of the very worst of social alternatives."[20] What sets dystopian picturebooks apart from picturebooks for children is that the latter's blatant didacticism, which describes certain problems and their solutions,[21] is undermined in the former. A solution or escape from the depicted situation is not overtly included in the dystopian picturebooks discussed here, but rather, such solutions are only recognizable through a detailed reading of the visual and verbal text. A happy end in Browne's illustration of *Hansel and Gretel* can only be interpreted through a thorough investigation of the illustration in the last spread. *The Girl in Red* has two endings, one of which seems like a happy ending, whereas the other one does not. In *The House That Crack Built*, readers are completely denied any escape or happy end, but rather have to create a solution for themselves. In other words, a positive outcome can only be achieved if readers read beyond the text and draw conclusions from the story told.

Similar to dystopian fiction in general, the dystopian picturebooks discussed here also focus on socio-cultural issues such as environmental issues and ecology, or socio-political scenarios. Just as in dystopian novels, humankind threatens to destroy itself. However, in these texts the terrors depicted are not whole political systems or oppressive governments, but are more specifically oriented around issues such as unemployment, poverty, and drug abuse.

In the following sections, I demonstrate how generic features of dystopia merge with the picturebook medium to create dystopian texts which unveil a vision of society's cataclysmic decline. In depicting their dystopias, Browne's illustration of *Hansel and Gretel* utilizes a specific visual interpretation of the original fairy tale, whereas Frisch and Innocenti's *The Girl in Red* offers a modern re-writing and re-contextualization of *Little Red Riding Hood.* The third example, Taylor's *The House That Crack Built*, adapts the accumulative children's rhyme "This is the House that Jack Built" to a drug traffic and drug abuse context.

These three picturebooks depict society as "no-good place[s]" which prevent a happy and fulfilled life and risk society's decay if nothing and no one were to interfere with current environmental and socio-political issues. The following analysis of the picturebooks will be combined with a more detailed investigation of the general potential of picturebooks for advanced learners in the next section.

2. Modern Visualisations of Fairy Tales as "No-Good Places"

The following section discusses Browne's illustration of *Hansel and Gretel* and Frisch and Innocenti's *The Girl in Red*. Both texts are based on traditional fairy tales. While Browne's *Hansel and Gretel* remains very close to the original plot, Frisch and Innocenti's version of *Red Riding Hood* is adapted, rewritten and set in a modern large city. Similar to Dror, I believe that there is a close connection between dystopia and fairy tales. Both consist of a fight between good and evil forces in which life is threatened, and both "deliver a lesson or a warning. Beware of the powers that be, take action, stand up, become a hero, survive."[22] Certainly, the children's versions of Grimm's tales have the iconic positive and hopeful endings in which good wins over evil. Yet, their dystopian picturebook adaptations are cruel and deliver their message without shying away from driving the plot to a bitter end.

Similar to the original Grimm's tale, *Hansel and Gretel* tells the story of a woodcutter, his two children, and their stepmother, and how the adults, suffering from poverty and not being able to feed the family, decide to abandon their children in a forest. Although older readers might already know the story and think that such a text is not appropriate for their own age group, they will discover a verbally and visually rich text. The interaction of verbal and visual text turns the text into a dystopian fairy tale that offers depth and incentives for analysis and enjoyment.

The illustrations fulfill a number of functions in this retelling of *Hansel and Gretel.* In particular, they establish aspects of visual interaction between the protagonists but also between reader and text in various ways. How the protagonists look and do not look at each other supports the image of a family disrupted by their economic status.

On the first spread, the stepmother – who in the verbal text is mainly referred to as "the woman" – does not sit at the table with the family, but in an armchair. She separates herself from her husband and the children and watches TV rather than spending time with them. The father shares the table with his children, but the three of them do not interact: The father reads a newspaper while Hansel looks down at the tabletop. Only Gretel is looking up, but no one answers her attempt to make eye contact. A small doll on the dirty carpet symbolizes the lack of love and affection between the family members.

The scene is painted in bleak colors where brown and sepia tones dominate. The only item that stands out is a bright red ball in front of the cupboard. This "dull coloured artwork creates an atmosphere of a family that was once middle class but has descended into poverty; grime on the walls, aged and peeling wallpaper and décor, mismatched furniture, their clothing."[23] Eye contact returns as a revealing detail in the following illustrations. The children turn their heads towards each other in their shared bed indicating that they are closer to each other than to their parents, or to how the parents are to each other as the parents remain turned away from each other in all the images. The verbal interaction between the family members, such as when the stepmother calls the children "lazybones", reflects the deprivation of love and affection. The children repeatedly voice their hope for a better future in expressing, "God will help us."

Mirrors create an increased distance between the readers and the protagonists. It is intriguing that the family is repeatedly only seen indirectly in reflections and mirrors. These illustrations are reminiscent of van Eyck's "Arnolfini-wedding" (1434) and of Velazquez' artwork, both of whom were among the first to use mirrors and reflections as central elements in their paintings.[24]

The mirror in which readers see the children in bed is placed on a dressing table that is scattered with makeup, partly open lipsticks, and perfume bottles. Readers have access to the stepmother mainly through the mirror, and even then they only see her with a mask made of makeup, suggesting that she uses a mask to try to hide her dissatisfaction with the family's socio-economic situation. This is further visible when she longingly watches a plane fly across the sky on TV in the first scene. Furthermore, the open perfume bottles and lipstick also indicate that her mask is unfinished. Yet, she is only shown wearing mainly black and dark makeup on her face; devices for these tones are, however, not part of the collection on the dressing table. Makeup is still important for her, yet she hides behind a different, dark mask. She seems to have given up on her situation and entered a numb, mentally absent existence. Similar to her former wealth and happiness, she has also left behind her dressing table and any reason for using the bright makeup.

A mirror is also an indicator of self-reflection in which people see an image of themselves. While the protagonists in the illustrations sometimes see themselves in the mirrors in their house, at times they also try and escape their own self-reflections, either by concealing themselves behind makeup or by not looking directly into the mirrors at all. While the faces turned towards the mirrors disrupt the readers view onto the protagonists, the mirrors also ensure the readers' access to the protagonists, e.g. the children in bed who turn their faces to each other so as not look into the mirror, but who the reader can now see through their reflection in the mirror.

The problematic relationships between family members is underscored by the depiction of the family's home as a fortress the children cannot enter and as a prison the children cannot escape. When the children are left in the forest for the first time and return home, their stepmother blocks their entry from the inside. Her angry white face appears in front of a black reflection of the forest, which merges with her dark hair, and she stares down at the children from behind the bars in the dirty door. The house's stone wall that frames the door appears like a fortress the children cannot enter. When the stepmother decides that the children have to leave again, Hansel wants to collect the pebbles from outside the house which he had used to secure their way home after he and his sister were first left in the forest. Yet, this time he cannot do so because the stepmother has locked the door. What seemed like a fortress now becomes a prison that Hansel cannot leave as he seeks to prepare for escape from the forest. In contrast to the corresponding illustration of his stepmother blocking the door, Hansel's background is now warmly lit by an orange light. His small figure with huge white eyes behind the door of a big shabby house support the image of him being lost, desperate, and scared of what is to come. With this bleak outlook, all he can do is express hope of finding comfort and help in God again.

The devastating influence of a post-industrial development on the social functioning of the family is indicated by the trees behind the house which are reminiscent of chimneys and may symbolize the industrialization which could have led to the family's poverty. The father's unemployment may have been caused by his work being replaced by machines and technology.

The final illustrations are ambiguous and leave the ending open to interpretation. The end can be read as a happy one because the children return home. The chain-smoking stepmother, who has so far dominated the family, rendering the children silent and the father weak, has left the family. Now that she is gone, color and light return. The house and landscape are drawn in bright colors, and the sky is blue. For the first time in the whole book, readers encounter a friendly and peaceful atmosphere surrounding the house. The children come home with pockets full of pearls and jewels they found in the witch's house. The reader has not encountered these pearls and jewels before, neither in the witch's house nor on the children's way back home. These could thus symbolize the children's hope for a happy and loving family life without the stepmother rather than wealth. The grey pillars reminiscent of trees or chimneys in earlier illustrations have disappeared from behind the house and peace and affection seem to have returned home.

However, such a reading could also be disputed. The last image shows how the father stands in the hallway and greets his children in the open door. Readers see him from the back. Despite his happiness about the children's return, he does not kneel down, forcing the children to hug his legs. Compared to the outside and the landscape around the house, the hallway and inside of the house are still bleak, greenish, grey, and seem cold. Only the glass in the door that reflects the blue sky and white clouds adds friendly colors to the scene; a small seedling in a flowerpot leaves some hope for a better future. Even so, one still wonders why the page fails to offer happy faces of a united family if this truly were a happy end. Baccolini and Moylan's "horizon of hope"[25] is present, but its realization and optimistic interpretation depend on the reader. Given the visual elements, it seems a long way for the family to recover fully from the impact of a severe and painful anti-social environment. The interplay of text and illustrations "reflect[s] the anxieties of the late twentieth century"[26] and certainly also those of today, and thus provides a strong dystopian touch to the fairy tale. Similarly, Dror observes that "while traditional versions of *Hansel and Gretel* blame famine for the family's misfortune, in this retelling, the family's misery seems to be a direct consequence of unemployment, or perhaps war."[27] Making progress and improving the situation requires more effort than simply bringing back jewels and pearls, which are not even featured as part of the final scene. The dystopian effect in *Hansel and Gretel* is achieved by the counterpoint interaction of word and illustrations that complement the original text.

The Girl in Red[28] is a dystopian re-contextualization and re-writing of the original fairy tale *Red Riding Hood*. Compared to the original tale, this picturebook is set in a large city during a stormy night in which Sophia, a girl in a red coat and hat, delivers food to her grandmother living on the other side of town. The city is constructed with images of poverty, capitalism, consumerism, as well as violence, brutality, and isolation. Although these are current aspects of urban lifestyle, *The Girl in Red* offers a disturbing analysis and depiction of socio-economic developments that need to be counteracted if a worsening of inner city problems were to be prevented. Thus, the book serves as a criticism of the present and "as a warning, to their readers in order to create awareness and to act against these dangers" [29] which mirrors Moylan's understanding of dystopian fiction.

The illustrations indicate that – despite the picturebook format – this story may not be a mere children's story, particularly as certain details are reminiscent of horror stories. The main action of the picturebook is enclosed by a frame narrative in which a small grandmother sits on a table and invites children to listen to a story. "Toys can be fun. But a good story is magic. [...] you never really know that's coming" (spread 1). The toys at the children's disposal in the image are not inviting and, in fact, unsuitable for children. Most of the items on the shelves and scattered on the floor are gruesome, brutal, or suggest violent games. There is a tank, a gun, an armed action figure, and a shark with a human leg hanging out of his mouth; there is a monster in one corner, a vampire hanging from the ceiling and another doll that looks like a prostitute next to an empty can on the floor. The toys, even the music instruments and books – which are too high on the shelf for the children to reach – are drawn in bleak colors where everything seems to be glazed by a grey layer which leaves a grim impression of the scene. Neither the children nor the room with its cracked window seem to be being taken care of. Even so, the children do not seem unhappy. Only the grandmother figure drawn in bright and friendly colors stands out. This storytelling scene reappears at the very end of the story (see below) and frames the story. As the reader will see, the grandmother's indication that narrators and readers of stories can change them through different interpretations and re-tellings is realized through her interference when the story's gruesome end leaves the children in tears.

In *The Girl in Red*, the city is depicted as a threatening wilderness through which Sophia needs to navigate. The allegory of the city as wilderness becomes apparent in the first opening of the actual story when the text presented in a grey box informs readers that "Our story takes place in the forest" (spread 3). Yet, the illustration shows a front view of a block of flats, concrete walls with missing pieces exposing bare bricks, indicating a city which does not leave space for a natural environment: "The forest has few trunks and leaves – it is composed of concrete and bricks instead." This contradictory beginning of *The Girl in Red*, establishes the "forest" as an integral setting, which is an essential aspect of picturebooks. One could even argue that forest/city can be considered a 'character' in its own right as it underscores and also enables the dystopian effect of the picturebook.

Throughout the book, the city is constructed as a threatening, dangerous and anonymous place that isolates its inhabitants and brutalizes mind and soul. The mother wants Sophia to deliver biscuits, honey, and oranges to her grandmother, who is not feeling well. Readers witness Sophia's journey through the concrete jungle-like environment in which cars, strangers, and high-rises are ever present. While in the original Red Riding Hood she loses her way because she stops to enjoy the forest and pick flowers off the trail, Sophia tries to find her way through the disconcerting city. She is distracted by a toy store, a "window of wonders" (spread 9) that displays "monsters, princesses, dark fates, and happily-ever-afters. Images of the past and of the future." Similar to the opening scene, action figures are heavily armed; there are tanks, knives, and guns in between dolls and a soccer ball, Barbie dolls that remind readers of prostitutes, and a knife smashed into a piece of wood spilling blood. This window displays the same ballerina doll that is part of the frame narrative, merging both narrative levels and foreshadowing that the story may take a surprising turn. As Sophia starts dreaming and "longs to linger", she not only forgets about time but also loses the "trail" through the city jungle that leads to her grandmother. Leaving the mall through a wrong exist, Sophia is soon surrounded by a pack of "jackals", a group of rowdies on motorcycles that harasses her. While they are cowardly when alone, "they grow bold in number" (opening 10) but before anything could happen, Sophia is saved by a "hunter" who appears "in the wildest parts of forest [where] the law of the food chain holds sway." He is tall, dressed in a black cloak and wears black sunglasses during the stormy night. Sophia's observation "What big teeth he has" is a direct quotation from the original tale, although here it refers to the hunter, Sophia's savior. In the original tale, this phrase is used when Red Riding Hood enters her grandmother's cottage and realizes that she is actually facing the wolf who has killed her grandmother. With the original tale in mind, readers assume that this hunter is not necessarily a savior but an even severer threat than the motorcycle gang he has chased away. When Sophia tells him about her mission to bring food to her grandmother, he offers to take her where she needs to go. Sophia accepts and the picturebook takes a dramatic turn as readers presume her potential abduction. However, their motorcycle ride through the city comes to an abrupt end when the 'savior' receives a phone call and drops Sophia in the middle of a motorway. She is left alone and resumes her journey on foot.

Even so, the readers' suspicion that the 'savior' remains a threat is confirmed. The next opening shows a parallel action with the girl running through the rain towards her grandmother's home, while her 'savior' enters an old trailer. Readers need to translate the side-by-side images as a temporally parallel action. As both are the only images in the picturebook that are not accompanied by verbal text, readers have to arrive at this central revelation themselves.

In the following image, Sophia stands by the trailer's gate and calls her grandmother. It becomes apparent that the savior, who rescued Sophia from the street gang, is the wolf, who might have killed the girl's grandmother. This fast-paced plot, the parallel action and unveiling of double roles come to a telling pause when the following spread shows a night view of the city, centering on a block of flats in which only Sophia's apartment is still lit, where her mother stands on the balcony waiting for her daughter to come home. Yet, readers already know that she will not. The 'savior' leaves the trailer when the police arrive, but he is now indeed drawn with a wolf's face revealing his true identity. The phrases "What keen ears wolves have. What sharp noses." are direct references to the original tale; both features help him to escape just in time. Another twist of the story reveals that "wolves and jackals are not so different." They have worked on the plan to kill the grandmother and granddaughter together; their "wicked grins" indicate that they were successful. At home, Sophia's mother still stands on the balcony and receives a phone call. When "the clouds will allow no sun", the reader knows that she has learnt that her mother and daughter are dead.

While Red Riding Hood is a cautionary folklore tale which warns the audience of a particular danger, in this case not to wander off a set path and talk to strangers, this ending turns the original story into a more realistic tale that makes a deadly end explicit. However, this devastating end gets yet another turn, as the enclosing frame narrative disrupts the story. The grandmother figure informs the children, to whom she has just told Sophia's tale, that their tears are not necessary as stories are magic and may have more than one ending. The sad end of the story is rewritten, showing instead a happy and reunited family as grandmother and Sophia are found to be alive and the wolf arrested. The scene is busy with policemen, special crime forces, and TV and press journalists. A woodcutter saw what was about to happen and called the police. "The wolf is snared; a family spared."

In *The Girl in Red*, inner city life is constructed as a "no-good place" for its inhabitants. The first image of the narrative, which shows a concrete block of flats, is contradicted by the verbal text, which informs readers that the story takes place in the forest. However, what is left of the forest throughout the book are names and street signs that resemble a forest. For example, the mall at the center of the city is called "The Wood," and street signs indicate the direction to "Il Bosco." Even on the outskirts of the city where nature is actually present it is nonetheless disrupted, such as where a meadow is being used as a junkyard for old tires. The image of the city as a dark and threatening place is also supported by the way the weather is depicted. Sophia is caught on a stormy and rainy night. It is raining hard, she runs through puddles and is scared by the rolling thunder. Pieces of blue sky are only visible when she finally reaches her grandmother's trailer – although too late. This depiction of the weather only changes with the positive alternative ending of the story where the family is saved. The clouds have disappeared to allow the stars that "will shine on the forest tonight" to leave an almost romantic impression.

As has been depicted in the passages above, the illustrations support the bleak and brutal reality of inner city life – whether this is reflected in the toys in the frame narrative or the toy store in the mall through which Sophia passes. This bleak and brutal depiction of reality also accounts for the city as a whole. It is a grey and ugly space, covered in graffiti and garbage. Traffic jams at junctions evoke a multitude of sensual responses: the city is dark, noisy and smelly. Certain details are displayed in screaming colors of red, yellow, green and blue, a contrast that underlines a destructive and ambiguous image of the city. The conglomerate of concrete buildings, traffic and vandalism have an isolating and threatening effect on the perception of the girl, who holds on tight to her backpack, careful not to get lost in the raw and bleak cityscape. Isolation is also present in the layout of the single page. Apart from the parallel scenes where Sophia runs to her grandmother's trailer while the wolf has already entered it, the pictures are accompanied by square boxes holding the verbal text. These boxes are of similar size, no matter whether there are only a few words or a few sentences and remind readers of the layout of a planned community.

The Girl in Red contains three double spreads. Compared to the other illustrations, these double spreads are accompanied by four grey boxes, each containing little text. This invites readers to linger longer due to the immense size of the illustration, giving them the opportunity to see many details – and since the text can be read in just one glance, it only marginally enhances the understanding of the narrative. This accounts for the double spread image of "The Wood" in which the second box reads "It is a world unto itself" (spread 8). Little text, therefore, allows readers to explore the illustrations in detail.

And indeed, here one can explore the many details this illustration offers, first looking for Sophia and then taking in all the other details such as multilingual references to the forest ("el bosque", "le bois") and references to capitalism and consumer goods (e.g. Bank of Caiman, Nutella, Martini, and Dolce and Gabbana), all of which are read as if they were in a hidden objects picturebook. Through this design, author and illustrator simultaneously construct the city as a fascinating place where danger and excitement lie close to the surface. While the city does not leave space for nature, happiness or pleasure, it leaves space for the comical, the abstruse. The far end of the mall, for example, reminds readers of huge church windows although they also contain figures of Mickey Mouse, an alien, and a female cowboy with a gun in her hand. Two of the windows seem to show holy figures, but the woman in a blue gown and a halo holds a gun in her hand and the man who could be a priest looks like Santa Clause with a white beard but with brown cowboy pants (spread 8).

Society seems to have found a new religion in which capitalism, pop culture, and entertainment are the new icons of worship. A similar example of the comical and abstruse is presented when a man with a bare chest, leather pants, loincloth, a bone necklace, and a bone nose decoration and a big man in a spiked helmet who has a military medal cut into his naked breast and leopard sash (spread 7) on motorbikes, as well as Santa Clause on a moped, are caught in a traffic jam. Compared to the other people who can be seen in this double spread, they incarnate the option to re-invent oneself within anonymous urban city life and to create an individual identity within dynamic and fluid societies.

While Sophia is on her way to her grandmother, she passes such scenes and "walks and takes in the forest's wonderments. Music. Magic. Mysteries" (spread 6). This alliteration adds an element of fascination and beauty to the otherwise harsh reality constructed throughout the book. Simultaneously, through the illustrations readers become aware that this reality also entails the gruesome. For example, street musicians and street artists in the illustrations accompanied by the verbal text for "music" and "magic" seem to solely rely on the money they make during their performances, speaking towards the aforementioned poverty rife within the city. The illustration of "mysteries" depicts a crime scene in which the silhouette of a murdered person and bullets are still visible; a policeman keeps bystanders away, who are actually not really interested in the scene, but inattentively wait for the bus or are absorbed in a crowd of soccer fans. The homeless person in the background seems to have other worries. Interestingly, the illustration of the street artist is the only one in the whole book that depicts happy smiling faces of children; the adults here are rather indifferent. That music, magic, and mystery are not solely rendered as positive experiences of the city can only be understood through an intensive reading of the illustrations.

This interplay of abstruse and shocking details, violent and brutal reality, and a gruesome and dark outlook on city life provides a dystopian re-contextualized fairy tale. The dystopian effect in *The Girl in Red* is achieved through the counterpointing and contradicting interaction of words and illustrations that extend the adapted text of the fairy tale. The creation of two endings, one of which allows readers to assume that child and grandmother are dead, and the other seeming too romantic to be true, establishes a picturebook that makes consequences of anonymous and isolated inner city life explicit; where concrete and increased traffic destroy not only nature, but also people's physical and mental health.

3. Society's Cataclysmic Decline in *The House That Crack Built*

Compared to popular dystopian fiction, *The House That Crack Built* (Taylor 1992) depicts suffering without a rebellious hero or movement. Rather than providing a traumatic social or personal awakening, the dystopia concludes by suggesting the continuation of society's decline. In typical examples of the genre, the hero meets a person who represents the dystopia, such as the leader of the society, which then results in a conflict and leads to an escape from the dystopia or to its destruction. In *The House That Crack Built*, the protagonists do not have any power of their own, there is no resistance, and they do not raise their voices but remain victims. The only voice that is present is the narrator. Taylor adapts the innocent, funny, and playful children's rhyme "The House that Jack Built" to tell of the devastating influence of drug abuse on a community. The context of "crack", which rhymes with "Jack," transforms the original cumulative tale into a harsh reality that no longer entails any funny images from the original children's rhyme but depicts the disastrous deterioration of society as caused by drug abuse and non-interference.

The picturebook has a harmless and innocent beginning with the depiction of a mansion described as "This is the house that crack built" (spread 1). From then on, different parties that are involved in drug trade and abuse are depicted in all their despair, fear, and innocence. *The House That Crack Built* ends with an image of society's most vulnerable member, a baby born to an addicted mother. As the baby has been part of the mother's body and has been exposed to her drug consumption, it is very likely that the baby is already addicted to drugs as well. The circle is closed, and the dystopia is unresolved rather than dissolved; the "tale" ends with the previous rhymes repeated as a complete poem, summarizing the vicious circle in all its brutality. No one emerges as a hero, and readers do not encounter a hopeful ending as one sometimes finds in dystopian fiction.[30] On the contrary, nothing is changed and with the crack baby being born, the hopeless society continues as before as there is no action taken to interfere with drug abuse. This devastating ending is necessary to understand that, "unless urgent change is undertaken, and soon, then the very principles of human happiness and even life itself are under threat,"[31] thus justifying a dystopian reading.

The haunting Picasso-like illustrations tune in with the cumulative and destructive impact of crack on multiple levels of society from drug cartels to newborn babies. Similar to Cubist artwork, the protagonists' bodies in *The House That Crack Built* are broken up and reassembled in an abstracted form, with heads split in half, distorted and put back together, or turned by 90 degrees and reattached upside down to the bodies. Just as the reasons and consequences of drug trade and abuse are multifaceted and complex, these abstract bodies offer readers multiple viewpoints and perspectives. These illustrations reflect how drug abuse takes things apart and reassembles the broken mind in an often diverging form, as shown through the split and tangled heads. Simultaneously, the Cubist depictions indicate a certain flatness of the bodies, making them appear like empty shells. The reduction of subjects to simple geometric forms is highly complex in their meaning, mirroring the impact of crack on the transformation of humans to Cubist, almost inanimate, objects. The depiction of the baby in the last spread breaks with the Cubist style of illustrating the previous victims of crack. Some hope for a change could yet remain; however the text refers only to tears falling like rain in the background. No one actively tries to change the situation, perhaps because the people become mere containers of the drug with no option to act or react.

The afterword to *The House That Crack Built* can very well be included in a critical reflection of the picturebook and the message it tries to get across. "This book is about choices" and "teaching our children to say no to drugs"[32] are the opening statements of the text. Although the second part has some validity as the text does indeed display the destructive consequences of drug abuse, the first part of this statement can be disputed. The book fails to offer any choices to the people depicted; the protagonists are not displayed in a situation in which they are given a choice. Their Cubist bodies do not indicate a free will or individuality that would allow people to choose. Rather, they seem to be mechanically involved in a string of actions they have no power to disrupt.

4. Potential for the EFL Classroom

Based on its topicality and relevance for current society, dystopian fiction carries a high potential for the ELT classroom, because these texts not only offer "a vision of a possible future, but [also] an interrogation of the present."[33] I argue that in view of current social and political developments, it can be very motivating for students to reflect such visions. Additionally, engaging with past, present, and future sociocultural issues can also contribute to developing a critical mind and to work towards a sustainable living. However, texts such as *Brave New World* or *1984* are complex regarding their length and language use. Teachers need to offer students space and time to engage with such texts in a way that allows them to read in detail and understand the relevance for a current society. Accordingly, Matz analyses and suggests young adult dystopian novels for classroom use.[34] Similarly, discovering dystopian picturebooks for ELT could offer a productive supplement and alternative, as these are shorter but still entail intricate features which, rather than being less complex, are accessible in a different way.

Although I believe that dystopian picturebooks are justified teaching material in their own right, such texts can be particularly productive gate-openers to new fields of interest and materials for emergent and reluctant readers who have difficulty reading extended novels. These readers could, for example, first investigate the images. Following the presentation of one page of the text, perhaps the first spread of *Hansel and Gretel* which depicts the family dinner, students can describe what they see, what kind of atmosphere they can identify and how this atmosphere is established. In a next step, they can relate their symbolic reading of the image to the verbal text and further investigate the interplay of verbal and visual text. Stronger students may be able to relate verbal and visual text more directly and analyse and interpret the symbolic language both modes use. Such attention to detail and negotiation of meaning beyond the mere display of the page can increase students' pleasure of reading because they learn to understand how picturebooks carry meaning. This is the case, for example, in the opening scene and the mall scene (spread 8) in *The Girl in Red* which offer manifold details for a comprehensive reflection and interpretation.

In ELT, dystopian picturebooks can be contextualized in CLIL, they can be used to develop literary and media literacy, and to engage in global education and transcultural learning. In CLIL contexts connecting English, Political Education, Arts, and History classrooms, students engage in detailed reflection on the symbolism used by authors and illustrators. Information on the industrial revolution and its impact on the social life of the working class, for instance, helps to contextualize the artwork that supplements the verbal narration of *Hansel and Gretel*. Knowledge of Jan van Eyck's and Velazquez' art helps to access the visual interpretation of the text's use of mirrors. Similarly, students can extend their knowledge of Cubism to interpret the specific meaning of this art form in a story about drug abuse, as is the case in *The House That Crack Built*.

A parallel reading of the original texts and their dystopian adaptation in picturebook format can additionally develop literary literacy. In general, literary literacy describes the ability to read, understand and appreciate literary texts, to be able to read texts critically and to understand how literary texts work. Literary literacy is composed of a number of sub-competences. These competences build upon each other, such as where reading competence and general linguistic competence in

English allow for basic processing of the text, which then forms the foundation upon which further competences such as empathic competence, aesthetic and stylistic competence, cultural and discursive competence and interpretative competence are developed. These elements form the complex concept of literary literacy.[35] In view of the examples discussed here, this accounts for example for *The House That Crack Built*, where students' appreciation for visual and verbal stylistic devices can be enhanced. Classroom discussions can critically investigate the interaction of the verbal and visual text and its significance. Due to counterpointing and contradicting, students have to engage in a detailed reading of the narrative to uncover its depth, and analyse and interpret the text accordingly. This connection is certainly revealing in *The House That Crack Built*, in which an adaptation of an innocent and playful cumulative children's rhyme is used to display the devastating consequences of drug abuse. Students can further point out the parallels of the visualizations to Cubism and the effect of the cumulative rhyme scheme. They explore the significance of the deviation from the Cubist style in the illustration of the baby at the end of the book. Reading *The Girl in Red* with the original tale in mind, students can discuss the means by which author and illustrator adapted *Red Riding Hood* and which instances of the original allowed them to turn the text into a dystopian interpretation. Literary literacy has a receptive and a productive dimension, in that students not only read texts but participate in literary discourses and contribute texts of their own. Using the original and the adaptation, students can compare both texts in view of intertextuality, consider in which city the adapted version could be set and take current sociopolitical developments into account when reading and analysing the story. Based on this, they could investigate further fairy tales or children's stories for their dystopian potential and produce their own texts. Such reflections address the concept of literary literacy and can prepare students for individual readings.

In addition, dystopian picturebooks lend themselves to the development of media literacy. Media literacy is essential for challenging media messages and in preparing for manipulative influences from the public sphere. A critical reading of the aforementioned afterword to *The House That Crack Built* in order to increase students' media literacy is one example of how the potentials of dystopic picturebooks can be realized in the EFL classroom. In engaging in a close reading of Pritchard's afterword, advanced students unveil such binary constructions of 'us' and 'them' which lead to critical considerations of the picturebook's intended readership. Such reflections contribute to media literacy as students learn to see media messages critically and within a certain sociocultural context in which they are published and received. The overall effect of the picturebook still needs to be included in the evaluation of the afterword because the richness and depth of the interplay of verbal and visual text indeed opens discussions and "help[s] children to make the right choices."[36] In *The Girl in Red*, the productive interplay of verbal and visual text can be investigated, particularly in view of the layout of the textboxes, which are reminiscent of a clearly structured city map in contrast to the chaotic image of the city itself. When students produce their own dystopian texts based on original fairy tales or children's stories, they have to be aware of how they depict cultural identities and specific settings and thus put media literacy into practice as well.

A close analysis of the illustrations develops visual literacy, which is one dimension of media literacy and entails taking a critical view of visuals, their analysis, and their negotiation of meaning. Regarding picturebooks, this especially refers to the symbolic meaning of certain details students can find in the illustrations. In *Hansel and Gretel* this, for example, refers to the stain on the ceiling of the family's living room which looks like a dove or the intricate details in the use of colors. In *The Girl in Red*, visual literacy can be developed through an in-depth investigation of the illustrations and the many details these offer to the verbal narrative.

Visual literacy can also be developed through a critical investigation of how author and illustrator depict the protagonists' ethnic identities in *The House That Crack Built*. The protagonists who are involved in drug traffic and drug abuse are exclusively presented as people of colour. The issue of using drugs is thus contextualized in a specific cultural and ethnic setting, stereotypically ascribing drug abuse to people of color. A critical reading of the picturebook needs to consider this and ask why author, illustrator, and publisher chose to have only the "man who lives in the house that crack built" (spread 2) appear white. In the rest of the book, they conceal that white people are similarly involved in drug abuse and suffer from its consequences. This can be related to a critical reading of the book's afterword, as mentioned above.

As appropriately argued by Matz "texts lend themselves to teaching transcultural matters such as global […] issues."[37] Referring, the topics around which the aforementioned dystopian picturebooks revolve (drug trade and drug abuse, abuse of power, disrupted families, unemployment, and poverty) are of general human concern, present around the world and not specific to individual cultures, and could thus be part of the broad field of transcultural learning [38] and global education. Students can be encouraged to reflect on the political issues the texts raise, the degree to which such threats are part of the present and future, and whether they can think of measures that need to be taken to deal with or even prevent the threats from becoming (more) severe. [39] One challenge here is to see society as a complex, constantly changing, and highly heterogeneous construct that hardly allows for generalizing statements. Students, thus, need to be careful and very precise in stating their opinions.

As verbal and visual text consist of various rhetoric means and hidden details – where form and color choices are as important as the usage of certain vocabulary – students need to apply a detailed reading of the books as multimodal texts to understand the narrative and decode ambiguities. Based on a critical investigation of the picturebooks, students discuss the genre and reflect as to how far the world that is presented in the picturebooks is a dystopian world projected onto the future, or already reality in parts of the world or for certain people. Applying creative approaches that turn existing stories into dystopian narratives, students could also explore further texts and develop interpretations which could include creative writing or digital storytelling and film editing.

5. Conclusion

Compared to common picturebooks, the examples presented here broaden the central characteristic of the genre of children's literature. While picturebooks traditionally express hope and the belief that the world can be a good place to live, dystopian picturebooks refrain from establishing a happy end but drive the plot to a bitter end. This opens the medium to a young adult audience. Dystopian picturebooks "offer a glimpse of the worries of their present, providing a chance of exploring the anxieties of their times."[40] In the three books discussed above, this becomes especially apparent in their illustrations. In particular, *The House That Crack Built* draws "out the consequences of human actions to their logical conclusions [...] rather than to speculate imaginatively about alternative, visionary future possibilities."[41] Drug trade and abuse subvert the possibilities of a happy end, where cure and survival are not a given but need to be established through taking action and evoking change. Interestingly, these solutions are not explicitly offered by the verbal or visual narratives, but need to be constructed by the readers. Given that these picturebooks display aspects of personal, social, and communal decay, the potential consequences of current developments serve as a social and political warning: certain living conditions need to be changed if the cataclysmic decline constructed in the picturebooks is to be prevented.

The deviating, counterpointing and contradicting interplay of verbal and visual text adds to the complexity of the genre. In reference to the picturebooks discussed above, an understanding of dystopia needs to be altered. Dystopia is not necessarily framed in exciting adventures and gripping plots in novel-length texts, but may also be presented in a picturebook format. Dystopia is not only told in first person narrations and engaging dialogue, but additionally in children's literature formats such as rhymes and (adapted) fairy tales. Usually, dystopian fiction leaves "small bands of survivors struggling to exist in a world forever changed."[42] Yet who survives the drug reality in *The House That Crack Built*, and which living conditions do people face? A baby born to a drug-addicted mother is likely to be drug addicted itself; the future is as bleak as the present when no chances of recovery are indicated. In *Hansel and Gretel*, the children grew up surrounded by unemployment and a dysfunctional family, circumstances that are likely to have left strong marks on them. If they have not been treated as children, how are they to treat their own children as children? Even when the grandmother and Sophia survive, the harsh reality of city life continues.

The combination of dystopia with picturebooks and visualizations of fairy tales holds special potential for advanced students of English as a foreign language. The interplay of verbal and visual text within a dystopian story can make the complex genre of dystopia available and the topic accessible for learners in upper secondary classrooms. Certainly, principles of ELT such as CLIL and visual and media literacy as well as inter- and transcultural teaching and global education present manifold options for implementing dystopian picturebooks in teaching English as a foreign language. Such a dystopian perspective certainly invites students to critically reflect upon current sociocultural and political developments and their continuation if no sustainable change is encouraged.

Notes

[1] Raffaella Baccolini and Tom Moylan (2003). "Introduction: Dystopia and Histories." *Dark Horizons, Science Fiction and the Dystopian Imagination.* Ed. Raffaella Baccolini and Tom Moylan. New York: Routledge, 1-12, 1.
[2] Carrie Hintz and Elaine Ostry (2003). "Introduction." *Utopian and Dystopian Writing for Children and Young Adults.* Ed. Carrie Hintz and Elaine Ostry. New York: Routledge, 1-22, 12.
[3] Balaka Basu, Katherine R. Broad, and Hintz, Carrie (2013). "Introduction." *Contemporary Dystopian Fiction for Young Adults.* Ed. Basu, Broad, and Hintz. New York: Routledge, 1-8, 1.
[4] Frauke Matz (2015). "Alternative Worlds – Alternative Texts: Teaching (Young Adult) Dystopian Novels." *Learning with Literature in the EFL Classroom.* Ed. Werner Delanoy, Maria Eisenmann, and Frauke Matz. Frankfurt: Peter Lang, 263-282.
[5] Keith M. Booker (1994). *Dystopian Literature – A Theory and Research Guide.* Santa Barbara: Greenwood Press, 3.
[6] *Ibid.*, 268.
[7] Suzanne Oakley (2010). "Where the Wild Things Are: Teaching Support Kit." Web. 15 April 2017 <http://www.randomhouse.com.au/content/teachers/tsk_where_the_ wild_things_are.pdf>, 4.
[8] Gunther Kress (2008). "'Literacy' in a Multimodal Environment of Communication." *Handbook on Teaching Literacy through the Communicative and Visual Arts.* Vol. II. Ed. James Flood, Shirley B. Heath, and Diane Lapp. New York: Lawrence Erlbaum Associates, 91-100.
[9] *Ibid.*, 91.
[10] Randy Bomer (2008). "Literacy classrooms: Making Minds out of Multimodal Material." *Handbook on Teaching Literacy through the Communicative and Visual Arts.* Vol. II. Ed. James Flood, Shirley B. Heath, and Diane Lapp. New York: Lawrence Erlbaum Associates, 353-361, 354.
[11] Maria Nikolajeva and Carol Scott (2000a). "The Dynamics of Picturebook Communication." *Children's Literature in Education*, 31.4, 225-239, 227. Further references to this edition will be included in the text.
[12] *Ibid.*, 227.
[13] *Ibid.*, 227.
[14] *Ibid.*, 227.
[15] Maria Nikolajeva and Carol Scott (2000b). *How Picturebooks Work.* New York: Garland.
[16] Nikolajeva and Scott (2000a), 225.
[17] *Ibid.*, 226.

[18] Eva Burwitz-Melzer (2013). "Approaching Literary and Language Competence: Picturebooks and Graphic Novels in the EFL Classroom." *Children's Literature in Second Language Education*. Ed. Janice Bland and Christiane Lütge. London: Bloomsbury Academic, 55-70, 56.

[19] *Ibid.*, 226.

[20] Baccolini and Moylan (2003), 6.

[21] Basu, Broad, and Hintz (2013), 5. Further references to this edition will be included in the text.

[22]Stephanie Dror (2013). "The Fairy Tale Dystopia." Web. 12 Dec. 2016 <http://thebookwars.ca/2013/09/the-fairy-tale-dystopia/>. n.pag.

[23] *Ibid.*, n.pag.

[24] This essay does not leave space to discuss this in detail. Especially Velazquez' use of mirrors in his paintings is reflected in Greub's *Las Meninas im Spiegel der Deutungen* (Berlin: Reimer, 2001).

[25] Baccolini and Moylan (2003), 6.

[26] Dror (2013), n.pag.

[27] *Ibid.*, n.pag.

[28] This picturebook is the richest of the three examples discussed here. The elaboration therefore take up more space than the other two.

[29] Matz (2015), 265.

[30] Baccolini and Moylan (2003), 7.

[31] Sambell, Kay (2003). "Presenting the Case for Social Change: The Creative Dilemma of Dystopian Writing for Children." *Utopian and Dystopian Writing for Children and Young Adults*. Ed. Carries Hintz and Elaine Ostry. New York: Routledge, 163-178, 166.

[32] "Afterword" in Clark Taylor's *The House That Crack Built.* Vancouver, n.pag.

[33] Elizabeth Bullen and Elizabeth Parsons (2007). "Dystopian Visions of Global Capitalism: Philip Reeve's *Mortal Engines* and M. T. Anderson's *Feed*." *Children`s Literature in Education*, 38.2, 127-139, 128.

[34] Matz (2015) and Frauke Matz (2014). "Dystopische Jugendromane: transkulturelle Themen und interkulturelle Bezüge." *Transkulturelles Lernen im Fremdsprachenunterricht. Theorie und Praxis*. Ed. Frauke Matz, Michael Rogge and Philipp Siepman. Frankfurt: Peter Lang, 143-152.

[35] See Bärbel Diehr and Carola Surkamp (2015). "Die Entwicklung literaturbezogener Kompetenzen in der Sekundarstufe I: Modellierung, Abschlussprofil und Evaluation." *Literaturkompetenzen Englisch: Modellierung, Curriculum, Unterrichtsbeispiele*. Ed. Wolfang Hallet, Carola Surkamp, and Ulrich Krämer. Seelze: Klett/Kallmeyer, 21-40.

[36] "Afterword" in Clark Taylor's *The House That Crack Built.* Vancouver, n.pag.

[37] Matz (2015), 265.

[38] Lothar Bredella (2010). "Fremdverstehen und interkulturelles Verstehen." *Handbuch Fremdsprachendidaktik*. Ed. Wolfgang Hallet and Frank G. Königs. Stuttgart: Klett/Kallmeyer, 120-125, 122.
[39] Similar and further approaches in Matz (2015), 265.
[40] Dror (2013), n.pag.
[41] Sambell (2003), 165.
[42] Basu, Broad, and Hintz (2013), 3.

Bibliography

Primary Literature

Frisch, Aaron, and Robert Innocenti (2012). *The Girl in Red*. Mankato: Creative Editions & Paperbacks.

The Grimm Brothers, ill. Anthony Brown (1981). *Hansel and Gretel*. London: Walker Books.

Orwell, George (1949). *1984*. London: Secker & Warburg.

Taylor, Clark, ill. Jan T. Dicks (1992). *The House That Crack Built*. San Francisco: Chronicle Books.

Secondary Literature

Adams, John Joseph (2012). "Introduction." *Brave New Worlds – Dystopian Stories*. Ed. John Joseph Adams. San Francisco: Night Shade Books, 1-2.

Baccolini, Raffaella, and Tom Moylan (2003). "Introduction: Dystopia and Histories." *Dark Horizons, Science Fiction and the Dystopian Imagination*. Ed. Raffaella Baccolini and Tom Moylan. New York: Routledge, 1-12.

Basu, Balaka, Katherine R. Broad, and Carrie Hintz (2013). "Introduction." *Contemporary Dystopian Fiction for Young Adults*. Ed. Basu, Broad, and Hintz. New York: Routledge, 1-8.

Berger, John (1967). "The Moment of Cubism." *New Left Review* 42.1, 75-94.

Bomer, Randy (2008). "Literacy Classrooms: Making Minds out of Multimodal Material." *Handbook on Teaching Literacy through the Communicative and Visual Arts*. Vol. II. Ed. James Flood, Shirley B. Heath, and Diane Lapp. New York: Lawrence Erlbaum Associates, 353-361.

Booker, Keith M. (1994). *Dystopian Literature – A Theory and Research Guide*. Santa Barbara: Greenwood Press.

Bradford, Clare (2003). "Art, Pain, Children. Utopian and Dystopian Discourses in Picture Books." Web. 2 November 2015 <http://www.doubledialogues.com/article/art-pain-children-utopian-and-dystopian-discourses-in-picture-books/>.

Bredella, Lothar (2010). "Fremdverstehen und interkulturelles Verstehen." *Handbuch Fremdsprachendidaktik*. Ed. Wolfgang Hallet and Frank G. Königs. Stuttgart: Klett/Kallmeyer, 120-125.

Bullen, Elizabeth, and Elizabeth Parsons (2007). "Dystopian Visions of Global Capitalism: Philip Reeve's *Mortal Engines* and M. T. Anderson's *Feed*." *Children`s Literature in Education*, 38.2, 127-139.

Burwitz-Melzer, Eva (2013). "Approaching Literary and Language Competence: Picturebooks and Graphic Novels in the EFL Classroom." *Children's Literature in Second Language Education*. Ed. Janice Bland and Christiane Lütge. London: Bloomsbury Academic, 55-70.

Diehr, Bärbel, and Carola Surkamp (2015). "Die Entwicklung literaturbezogener Kompetenzen in der Sekundarstufe I: Modellierung, Abschlussprofil und Evaluation." *Literaturkompetenzen Englisch: Modellierung, Curriculum, Unterrichtsbeispiele*. Ed. Wolfgang Hallet, Carola Surkamp, and Ulrich Krämer. Seelze: Klett/Kallmeyer, 21-40.

Dror, Stephanie (2013). "The Fairy Tale Dystopia." Web. 2 November 2015 <http://thebookwars.ca/2013/09/the-fairy-tale-dystopia/>, n.pag.

Greub, Thierry (ed.) (2001). *Las Meninas im Spiegel der Deutungen. Eine Einführung in die Methoden der Kunstgeschichte.* Berlin: Reimer.

Grigoryan, Anna, and John M. King (2008). "Adbusting: Critical Media Literacy in a Multi-Skills Academic Writing Lesson." *English Teaching Forum* 46.4, 2-9.

Hallet, Wolfgang (2007). "Literatur, Kognition und Kompetenz: Die Literarizität kulturellen Handelns." *Literaturunterricht, Kompetenz und Bildung*. Ed. Lothar Bredella and Wolfgang Hallet. Trier: WVT, 31-64.

Hintz, Carrie, and Elaine Ostry (eds.) (2003). *Utopian and Dystopian Writing for Children and Young Adults*. New York: Routledge.

--- (2003). "Introduction." *Utopian and Dystopian Writing for Children and Young Adults*. Ed. Carrie Hintz and Elaine Ostry. New York: Routledge: 1-22.

Kress, Gunther (2008). "'Literacy' in a Multimodal Environment of Communication." *Handbook on Teaching Literacy through the Communicative and Visual Arts*. Vol. II. Ed. James Flood, Shirley B. Heath, and Diane Lapp. New York: Lawrence Erlbaum Associates, 91-100.

Lütge, Christiane (2012). "Developing 'Literary Literacy'? Towards a Progression of Literary Learning." *Basic Issues in EFL Teaching and Learning*. Ed. Maria Eisenmann and Theresa Summer. Heidelberg: Winter, 191-202.

Matz, Frauke (2014). "Dystopische Jugendromane: transkulturelle Themen und interkulturelle Bezüge." *Transkulturelles Lernen im Fremdsprachenunterricht. Theorie und Praxis*. Ed. Frauke Matz, Michael Rogge, and Philipp Siepman. Frankfurt: Peter Lang, 143-152.

--- (2015). "Alternative Worlds – Alternative Texts: Teaching (Young Adult) Dystopian Novels." *Learning with Literature in the EFL Classroom*. Ed. Werner Delanoy, Maria Eisenmann, and Frauke Matz. Frankfurt: Peter Lang, 263-282.

McDaniel, Cynthia A. (2006). *Critical Literacy – A Way of Thinking, a Way of Life*. New York: Peter Lang.

Moylan, Tom (2000). *Scraps of the Untainted Sky*. Boulder: Westview Press.

Nikolajeva, Maria (2000a). "The Dynamics of Picturebook Communication." *Children's Literature in Education*, 31.4, 225-239.

---, and Carol Scott (2000b). *How Picturebooks Work*. New York: Garland.

Nodelman, Perry (1988). *Words about Pictures: The Narrative Art of Children's Picture Books*. Athens: University of Georgia Press.

Oakley, Suzanne (2010). "Where the Wild Things Are: Teaching Support Kit." Web. 15 April 2017 <http://www.randomhouse.com.au/content/teachers/tsk_where_the_ wild_things_are.pdf>.

Sambell, Kay (2003). "Presenting the Case for Social Change: The Creative Dilemma of Dystopian Writing for Children." *Utopian and Dystopian Writing for Children and Young Adults*. Ed. Carrie Hintz and Elaine Ostry. New York: Routledge, 163-178.

Nadine Krüger (Würzburg)[1]
Christian Ludwig (Karlsruhe)
Nicole Maruo-Schröder (Koblenz)

Students Exploring Dystopias in Fiction and Film – A Classroom Practice Report

1. Introduction

Over the last years, the market has been flooded with an enormous number of teenage dystopias and their filmic counterparts, adding to the already extensive corpus of dystopian fiction and film. Taking this as a starting point, the aim of the present article is to look at the genre of (young adult) dystopias from the perspective of English language and literature instruction in higher education. More specifically, it reports on the outcomes of a project in which English students from two German universities participated in an academic conference where they presented their own research results in the form of posters on the issues prevalent in dystopian fiction and film.[2]

In recent years, universities across the globe have been increasingly challenged to ensure a transferability of knowledge, skills, and competences from the university to the workplace, moving further away from the ideal of education envisaged in the Humboldtian model. This development has also led to a re-evaluation of the role of literary texts in the EFL classroom at both schools and universities which "reproduces the marginalisation of literature" because it focuses on "testable output in the areas of communicative, intercultural, and methodological competences".[3] While we see this development as highly problematic, in the following we would nevertheless like to present a project that illustrates how aesthetic approaches to teaching literature and an orientation towards subject-specific as well as extra-curricular skills and competences cannot only be compatible but mutually fruitful.

Students from both the University of Koblenz-Landau and the University of Education Karlsruhe who participated in the project each attended a seminar on present-day dystopias. While the students at the University of Koblenz-Landau focused on issues in contemporary dystopian film, the students at the University of Education Karlsruhe mainly concentrated on young adult dystopian narratives.[4] In both seminars, participants were given the opportunity to develop their own small-scale research projects focusing on contemporary novels and film respectively. The results of the projects were summarised in posters and presented at an academic conference on young adult dystopias organised by two of the authors of this article.

The first section of the present contribution considers the role of posters as a learning tool in the context of research-based learning in the higher education English classroom, while section two describes the project in more detail and offers insights into its planning and execution. The last part provides examples of posters presented at the conference, elucidating how the students' individual research projects contributed to their individual and collaborative learning processes and helped them to build a community of practice.

2. Posters as a Tool for Learning in Higher Education

The aim of this section is to discuss how posters can function as a tool for student learning and development in the 21st century when students live in an increasingly visually-dominated, multimodal culture.[5] This requires schools and universities to support students in developing their capacity for en- and decoding visual representations of information and communicating across a range of different media. Moreover, it is shown how students' active participation in an academic conference increases their awareness of the knowledge, skills, and competences acquired through the study of literary texts and other media. The chapter further demonstrates how creating posters for and presenting them in an academic setting can enhance the students' perception of posters as a medium of communication in professional contexts.

"Chalk and talk" still remains the predominant method in many university classrooms, paying little or no attention to the fact that classroom dynamics which initiate student-centred and student-initiated interaction may facilitate better acquisition of the foreign language. Constructivist approaches to foreign language learning and acquisition emphasise the importance of authentic, meaningful interaction and communication in the target language. One of these approaches is foreign language learner autonomy which, as stated by the father of autonomy, Henri Holec, is defined as "the ability to take charge of one's own learning".[6] This requires a fundamental shift in the professional self-conception of teachers and learners as well as classroom interaction as students become active participants in all stages of the learning process from selecting the content matter to evaluating the outcomes of learning in a learning environment that strives towards authenticity.[7] According to David Little, this freedom of choice is a central element of autonomous learning as it gives students the opportunity to exercise their agency. As Little posits:

> [...] the most successful language learning environments are those in which learners [...] develop proficiency by exercising agency in the target language. In foreign language learning we engage learners' agency by giving them choice, which begins to root learning in the individual learner's identity and interests.[8]

Contrary to common misperception, the students' agency, i.e. their "capacity to act",[9] is subject to a dynamic but nevertheless gradual development and, as any exercise of agency, a "social event that does not take place in a void".[10] In other words, it is a "social-interactive as well as an individual-cognitive phenomenon",[11] which leads us to one of the key elements of autonomous learning, namely interaction.

Everhard, in her attempt to define learner autonomy, emphasises the fact that it is not simply a method but rather a "way of being or sense of self achieved through co-operatively making decisions about learning".[12] While this is certainly true, interaction in the autonomous classroom goes far beyond mere co-operation, which represents "the most carefully structured end of the collaborative learning continuum".[13] In other words, cooperative learning is much more dependent on and guided by the teacher. Quite in contrast, collaborative learning environments are characterised by students reaching out to one another for knowledge-sharing and problem-solving as they share the same learning goals. As Burkert states based on the experiences from her own classroom:

> Through collaborating with their peers, learners take over more responsibility for their own learning and become less teacher dependent. They also learn to share the responsibility for the outcome of a joint endeavour with

their peers, which in turn creates an atmosphere of cooperation instead of competition.[14]

This brief excursus makes clear that actively involving students in their own learning by giving them choices can have a positive influence on the students' performance. In the ensuing section, it will be shown that posters can play a vital role not only in the autonomous classroom at primary and secondary but also tertiary level, particularly as a medium for students to exercise their agency through expressing their voice.

According to Leni Dam, posters are a highly effective medium in developing learner autonomy in the classroom.[15] They serve many different purposes such as supporting the acquisition of new or revision of language items learners have already encountered. At a meta-level, posters are employed to make class rules, learning strategies, or distributions of tasks visible in the learning environment. In the following, we suggest moving away from the traditional purposes of posters in classroom learning and focusing on posters functioning as presentation aids in the professional context of an academic conference.

In recent years, learner autonomy has been related to methods and techniques such as discovery and enquiry-based as well as research-based learning which advocate increasing the students' involvement and authentic learning experience by encouraging them to carry out their own research. In our case we applied a research-based approach similar to Healey and Jenkins'[16] concept of undergraduate research, which is based on the idea that students are encouraged to conduct their individual research, modelling it on the discipline's and the lecturers' own research (interests).[17] Instead of setting the students the task of reporting on their research procedures and results in a written essay or project report, they were asked to disseminate their results in form of a poster project. In this context, the poster project is an active learning strategy which requires students to do independent research on a subject related to class material, select the most important ideas and information, and present their findings on a poster, which constitutes a visually appealing, structured record of their work. The presentation, the final stage of a poster project, is generally defined as "an experiential learning activity that stimulates curiosity and interest, encourages exploration and integration of concepts, and provides students with a novel way of demonstrating understanding".[18] In addition to this, it has come to be routinely used in many disciplines to present and discuss new research projects. To sum up, posters not only are a medium commonly used in professional academic contexts but, for example through authentic poster sessions, help to create authentic learning activities and experiences. The ensuing section describes the project at hand in more detail and illustrates the advantages and constraints of posters as a way of disseminating research results.

3. The Project

In the winter term 2015/16, two project seminars on young adult dystopias were offered. While the seminar at the University of Koblenz-Landau primarily dealt with contemporary dystopian film, the course at the University of Education Karlsruhe focused on coeval young adult dystopian narratives.

The film seminar started with a discussion of the concepts of utopia and dystopia, focusing on the characteristics and conventions of the genre and its overlaps with science-fiction narratives. Based on a brief overview of the history of dystopia and its interconnections with socio-historic developments, several film dystopias were analysed and compared. Using Fritz Lang's *Metropolis* (1927) as not only an early but also influential example, the course proceeded to more recent films, including Ridley Scott's *Blade Runner* (1982), Steven Spielberg's *Minority Report* (2002), John Hillcoat's *The Road* (2009), and the *Hunger Games* trilogy (2012, Gary Ross; 2013-2015 Francis Lawrence). On the basis of class readings and discussions, students (individually or in pairs) had to choose their own dystopian film(s) and topics for the poster presentation at the end of the seminar. The thesis statement and argument developed for the poster presentation could then serve as the blueprint for the written term paper that is required in this module. Students chose a variety of different film dystopias, ranging from Michael Bay's *The Island* (2005) and Andrew Niccol's *In Time* (2011) to *Cloud Atlas* (2012, Tom Tykwer and Lana and Andy Wachowski) and George Miller's *Mad Max: Fury Road* (2015).

Similarly, the literature course at the University of Education Karlsruhe started with introductory sessions on the theoretical basis and generic conventions of utopian and dystopian writing, including the specific characteristics of the recent wave of dystopian writing for young adults and its relevance for the foreign language classroom. The main focus of the seminar was then to explore the genre through detailed analysis of selected textual examples. These included Lois Lowry's *The Giver* (1993), *Feed* (2002) by Matthew T. Anderson, and Suzanne Collins' *The Hunger Games* (2008), which were read and discussed by the entire class. In addition, students were encouraged to bring in additional examples from the genre; this was done both through individual presentations required of some students for their module grade and the posters which were created by different groups. These examples included *Divergent* (2011) by Veronica Roth, Lauren Oliver's *Delirium* (2011), and James Dashner's *The Maze Runner* (2009). Despite the fact that the application to the EFL classroom was not the main focus of the seminar, some didactic elements and classroom activities were also included and tried out, since the vast majority of the participants were future teachers of English.

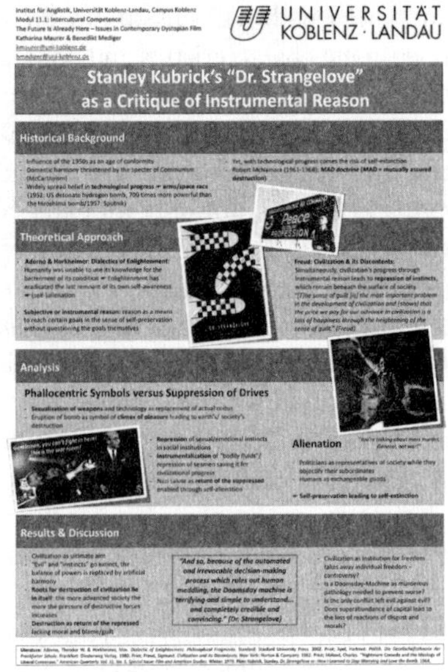

Fig. 1: A critique of instrumental reason in *Dr. Strangelove* (University of Koblenz-Landau)

While essays and term papers are a more or less regular text genre (and form of examination) in university courses, posters are – particularly in the humanities – still rather rarely used. Considering the fact that a poster is a medium in its own right with its own unique conventions and ways of getting a message across, creating an academic poster requires a myriad of skills and competences on behalf of both the students and the teacher. To name but a few examples, it involves traditional academic skills such as finding and evaluating (re)sources, developing a research question and thesis statement as well as building a coherent and cohesive argument but also contemporary skills such as bringing together written and visual language and fusing on- and offline materials, e.g. linking the poster content to relevant websites for further research.

Therefore, the participants of the film seminar in Koblenz were provided with a tutorial on the designing of academic posters, which took place three weeks before the conference.[19] In two 90-minute sessions, students were introduced, on the one hand, to the technical aspects of poster design (e.g., which programs to use or what kind of image resolution would be needed) and, on the other hand, to more content-oriented ones, including the question of which elements a poster should contain and how it can be structured. While a number of academic posters were used as both positive and negative examples in the tutorial, students were asked to bring their own projects (thesis statement, possible structure, film stills and other images that could be used etc.) to work on during the tutorial. Having already worked on thesis and basic structure of their project's argument, students had to assess their own ideas critically in view of the information provided by the tutorial. In discussions during the tutorial it became clear that the format of the poster challenged students to reconsider their argument and forced them to make it more concise and coherent. Space restrictions made it necessary, for instance, to select the most important information for inclusion on the poster, while the visual possibilities offered by a poster provided different, alternative ways of structuring one's argument. Next to technical skills, students' analytic and interpretive as well as their communicative competences were not simply enhanced but broadened. While this certainly challenged students, they came up with creative and convincing solutions for the poster presentation; moreover, the feedback after the conference suggests that they, in fact, enjoyed the preparation of the presentation despite the work that it meant.

Due to the limit of class time, the students in Karlsruhe merely received a crash-course in creating academic posters by drawing on freely available examples. Here the focus was on poster design by taking a critical look at layout issues, e.g. the use of colours and the relationship between text and images. Moreover, formatting issues such as spacing, margins as well as sizing and positioning photographs, images, and illustrations were addressed. Analysing already existing academic posters raised the students' awareness of the importance of a healthy balance of written text, graphics, and other visual images as well as the importance of linking the different areas and items of a poster. In addition, possibilities of designing a poster in such a way that its narrative can be understood with and without an accompanying presentation, e.g. facilitated through a pathway indicated by numbers, symbols, or colour signs, were discussed. In the following, we briefly describe two poster projects from each course in more detail, each focusing on different filmic or literary examples of dystopia.

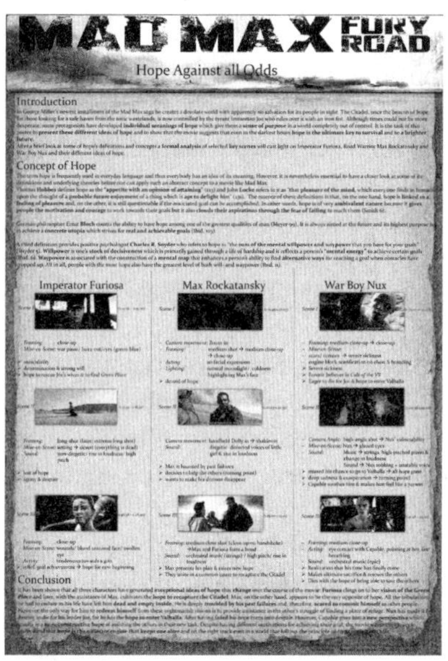

Fig. 2: The concept of hope in *Mad Max: Fury Road* (University of Koblenz-Landau)

Stanley Kubrick's *Dr. Strangelove or: How I Learned to Stop Worrying and Love the Bomb* (1964) is not a typical dystopian movie but a political satire whose plot and ending clearly reveal the dystopian elements and consequences of cold-war politics. In fact, most of the film is about the inability of the military and political 'elite' to stop the consequences set in motion by unhinged American General Jack D. Ripper, who single-handedly launches a nuclear attack on the Soviet Union, ending with the nuclear destruction of the earth. The students who chose this film focused on reading the movie as a "Critique of Instrumental Reason," using Adorno's and Horkheimer's notion of the dialectic of reason as well as Freud's ideas about (sexual) repression (fig. 1). Their poster contains not only the historical background of the cold war era (notably McNamara's MAD doctrine), it also highlights briefly the two main ideas used in the analysis of the film: instrumental reason and the repression of instincts it can lead to. Following this, the next section summarises the main ideas of the analysis, focusing on Kubrick's sexualisation of weapons and technology, which can be read as a sign of repression. As a conclusion, the poster's last part both discusses and evaluates the ideas sketched in the analytic part as a possible reading of the film. Using a more conventional structure, which is clearly marked with the help of headlines and coloured boxes, the poster shows that even the analysis of and argument about a film, including theoretical concepts, can be visualised and summarised on a poster. Moreover, the possibility to include film stills as well as to visually highlight central statements (such as a film quote or a theoretical concept) have been successfully utilised.

The next poster deals with the concept of hope in *Mad Max: Fury Road*, the latest instalment of the franchise directed by George Miller (2015). The film pictures earth's future as a dystopia in which almost all resources have been depleted and destroyed and in which lawless marauding bands controlling water and fuel rule the rest of humanity. The students decided to combine aspects from different concepts of hope (Hobbes, Locke, Bloch, and Snyder), thus working out its ambiguous nature which combines the desire of achieving a certain goal with the fear of not being able to do so. On the basis of a number of characteristics, they analysed three different protagonists, Mad Max, Imperator Furiosa, and Nux, and their development and function throughout the movie. Moreover, they combined the different characterisations with an analysis of filmic means to show how these underline differences and similarities between the characters as well as the changes they undergo. For this, they used one of the options that the poster format provides, namely the possibility of presenting the points and results of their analysis side-by-side in table form. Furthermore, the students used film stills to illustrate their analysis. In the conclusion, a flow text with highlighted key words, they put together the different results, coming to the conclusion that *Fury Road* insists on hope being a central element of both individuals and human communities, something which might be quite independent of any actual probability of a hopeful ending, even for a character as traumatised as Mad Max.

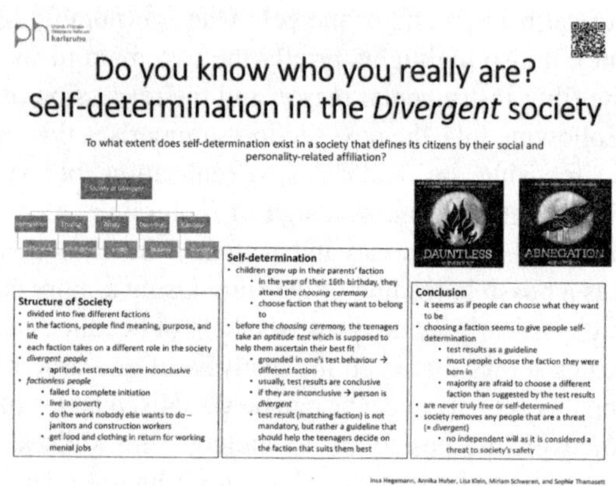

Fig. 3: Self-determination in the faction system of *Divergent* (University of Education Karlsruhe)

One of the most dominant characteristics of society in Veronica Roth's *Divergent* (2011) is the faction system: every citizen is a member of one of five factions, each of which represents and values a different human virtue and puts it at the service of the community by serving a particular civic function, depending on their strengths and abilities. This system, in turn, is strongly connected to questions of belonging, self-determination, and making choices. One of its ruling principles is that citizens actively decide which faction they want to become a member of, based on the results of an aptitude test taken at the age of sixteen, which is supposed to serve as a guideline for their decision.

The students who chose to work on *Divergent* for their research project decided to focus on these aspects and their mutual influence on one another when creating their poster. They developed a research question aiming to determine the extent to which self-determination plays a role in a society which defines its citizens by their social affiliations and personality. In order to develop an answer to the question, they first provided an overview of the different factions as well as general information on the structure of society. They then proceeded to consider the importance of self-determination within this framework, focusing in particular on the choosing ceremony during which all sixteen-year-olds decide which faction they want to belong to henceforth. Even though this procedure seems to offer a free choice to the characters in principle, in reality the number of options is limited and, more importantly, non-conformity (or *divergence*) is severely punished, as citizens whose test results are inconclusive are expelled from society. Thus, as is the case in many other dystopian societies as well, citizens are only given a *quasi-choice.* Accordingly, the group concluded that free will and self-determination are highly restricted in the social order presented in the novel. They successfully managed to display their result on the poster in a comprehensive manner by visually structuring it in three different sections, each focusing on a different aspect of the central research question.

Rather than work on a specific research question, the group of students who chose James Dashner's *The Maze Runner* (2009) for their poster presentation opted to give a more comprehensive overview of the novel's central elements. In doing so, they focused in particular on the microcosm of the Maze and the issues of manipulation and control which shape the life of the Gladers inside its walls. In addition to providing an overview of the character constellation and relationships between the Gladers, they also provided information on the conditions and regulations governing life inside the Maze by quoting central passages from the novel. An illustration provides an overview of what the Maze may look like; moreover, key vocabulary specific to the context of the Maze and, thus, unfamiliar to the reader, is also explained.

To a certain extent, exploring the material presented on the poster mirrors the situation that the characters find themselves in: in the novel, Thomas is thrown into the confinement of the Maze without having any information about his surroundings or memories of his previous life. Only gradually, through systematic observation and exploration of his new environment, is he able to decode the vocabulary the other Gladers use and piece together the information which can also be found on the poster. Thus, in a way, the audience is put in the protagonist's shoes when considering the different elements of the poster to form a comprehensive idea of the experiment conducted in the novel. This notion is supported further through the layout of the poster: The main body of information is displayed in the centre of the poster between an introductory paragraph outlining the plot, placed at the top, and a short conclusion which identifies the main themes of the novel at the bottom of the poster. The audience thus has to visually 'navigate' their way through the information, an impression which is strengthened by the outlines of a maze structure outlined in the background of the poster. The sense of confinement and confusion central to the Gladers' experiences is thus nicely transferred to the poster.

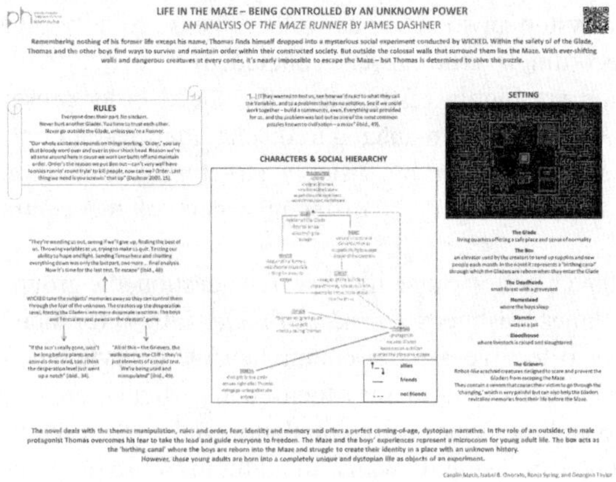

Fig. 4: Life in the maze: manipulation and control in *The Maze Runner* (University of Education Karlsruhe)

The posters from both universities were freely accessible during the whole conference day, while the official poster presentations took place during the assigned poster session slots as well as during the coffee breaks. At least one student from each group was required to stand with their poster while the others were allowed to move around and look at the other parts of the poster exhibition. Each group member was equally prepared to briefly present the content of the poster and answer questions from the audience.

As can be seen from these examples, posters and poster presentations can be successfully used in the university classroom. However, like everything, they come with certain advantages and disadvantages. As the various examples show, students are willing and able to use the alternative form of structuring and presenting their research project. Much less difficult and challenging than a full-fledged paper to be held in front of an audience of peers and – possibly – scholars, the poster and its presentation offers a more 'informal' way to present something in written and oral form. Moreover, it also provides an opportunity to make use of and enhance competences in the realm of multimodal communication and design as visual and language-based elements have to be combined. Particularly for the analysis of film scenes, this can be utilised in a variety of ways. Furthermore, the open format of the poster – less linear than a conventional written text – invites students to think and express themselves in alternative ways, helping to explore a topic from different angles. The fact that a poster presents the structure (if not the content) right at first glance also forces them to dwell on this point, maybe more than they would have to do in a term paper. However, the poster format is not without its pitfalls. Particularly the fact that it is so visually prominent might invite students to use images and illustrations as mere decorations devoid of real function or content. Moreover, because everything has to be designed and arranged on the page (type of font, colour and size of letters, decision on frames, to name but a few aspects), this can also be overwhelming, resulting in posters that are confusing and crowded simply because of their design. And while it is certainly possible to present results of research projects coming from literary and cultural studies in an academically adequate way on a poster, it is decidedly not easy. In disciplines that are based on analysis, interpretation, and argument (i.e. in which the way a text is written and phrased might be part of the argument), a brief enumeration of results is not as easy or as satisfactory as it might be when presenting, e.g., the results of a study. Hence, posters can easily contain too much text, which makes it hard to 'read' them in a way posters are supposed to be read.

As mentioned previously, academic student presentations are usually restricted to the classroom, with the audience being limited to the teacher and peers, and only offer limited options for dissemination of the students' research results. In contrast to this, the conference presentations did not occur in a vacuum but as part of a real and authentic context which situated students in authentic scholarly discussions, resulting in high levels of audience and speaker participation and forcing all student speakers to communicate in order to acquaint the audience with topics unfamiliar to them. In addition to this, the eclectic audience of scholars and students from two universities required the poster presenters to articulate their ideas within different discourses varying in formality and subject knowledge, training the presenters' skills to communicate effectively with diverse groups, particularly on an academically adequate level. Last but not least, the high number of posters (16 in total) allowed minimal time for shorter statements regarding research context and outcomes, stimulating concise communication and discussion with a regularly alternating audience.

4. Conclusion

As this contribution illustrates, preparing a poster and delivering it in a professional context beyond the four walls of the classroom engages students in a meaningful learning experience and stimulates them to develop their own academic voice as autonomous learners and researchers. From a content perspective, the posters as well as the input at the conference broadened the students' understanding of young adult dystopias in theory and practice. Furthermore, creating posters in a collaborative learning environment offers students the opportunity to engage in a dialogue about learning through which they share the responsibility for the outcome of a joint endeavour with their peers, which in turn creates an atmosphere of collaboration instead of competition. Moreover, in both courses the posters were not graded and could thus truly serve as an opportunity for students to creatively try out the role as a researcher as well as the possibilities of the poster format.[20] Last but not least, the research projects increase the participants' transferable skills and competences such as creating a poster, delivering a poster presentation as well as translating knowledge and content from one medium into another.

Notes

[1] The author was still a lecturer at the University of Education Karlsruhe at the time of the project and taught the seminar discussed in the article.

[2] The conference "'Tell Freedom I Said Hello': Issues in Contemporary Young Adult Dystopias" took place at the University of Koblenz-Landau, campus Koblenz, on January 22, 2016.

[3] Nancy Grimm, Michael Meyer, and Laurenz Volkmann (2015). *Teaching English.* Tübingen: Narr Francke Attempto, 176.

[4] The authors of this article are grateful to the University of Koblenz-Landau and the University of Education Karlsruhe for funding the project.

[5] Gunther Kress (1998). *Multimodality: A Social Semiotic Approach to Contemporary Communication.* Abingdon: Routledge.

[6] Henri Holec (1981). *Autonomy and Foreign Language Learning.* Oxford: Pergamon, 3.

[7] See Maria Eisenmann and Christian Ludwig (2016). "Authentische Lernprozesse in komplexen Web 2.0-basierten Kompetenzaufgaben zur Förderung von Lernerautonomie. *Web 2.0 und komplexe Kompetenzaufgaben im Fremdsprachenunterricht.* Ed. Carmen Becker et al. Frankfurt: Peter Lang, 98-108, 93-95, for a more detailed discussion of the role of authenticity in developing learner autonomy.

[8] David Little (2017). "Language Learner Autonomy: What, Why and How?" Web. 4 September 2017 <http://languagesinitiative.ie/images/Language_Learner_Autonomy_What WhyHow.pdf>, 5.

[9] Leo van Lier (2008). "Agency in the Classroom." *Sociocultural Theory and the Teaching of Second Languages*. Ed. James P. Lantolf and Matthew E. Poehner. London: Equinox, 163-186, 163.

[10] *Ibid.*, 163.

[11] Little (2017), 3.

[12] Carol J. Everhard (2015). "The Assessment-Autonomy Relationship." *Assessment and Autonomy in Language Learning* Ed. Everhard and L. Murphy. London: Palgrave Macmillan, 8-34, 11.

[13] Jean MacGregor and Barbara Leigh Smith (1992). "What Is Collaborative Learning?" *Collaborative Learning: A Sourcebook for Higher Education. National Center on Postsecondary Teaching, Learning, and Assessment.* Ed. Anne Goodsell et al. Pennsylvania State University. Web. 4 September 2017 <http://www.austincc.edu/pintutor/newsite/_source/WhatIsCollaborativeLearning.pdf>, n.pag.

[14] Anja Burkert (2017). "Two Heads Are Better than One: Collaborative Learning under Scrutiny." *Fostering Learner Autonomy – Learners, Teachers and Researchers in Action*. Ed. Annamaria Pinter et al. UK: IATEFL, n.pag.
[15] Leni Dam (1995). *Learner Autonomy 3: From Theory to Classroom Practice.* Dublin: Authentik, passim.
[16] Mick Healey and Alan Jenkins (2009). "Developing Undergraduate Research and Inquiry." York: Higher Education Academy. Web. 23 Aug. 2018 <https://www.heacademy.ac.uk/knowledge-hub/developing-undergraduate-research-and-inquiry>, 23.
[17] While the students from Karlsruhe were, indeed, undergraduates, the students at the University of Koblenz-Landau were graduate students.
[18] D.S. Handron (1994) qtd. in Lee Bracher, Jane Cantrell, and Kay Wilkie (1998). "The Process of Poster Presentation: A Valuable Learning Experience." *Medical Teacher* 20.6, 552-557, 553.
[19] This was only possible because the course (including its poster tutorial) was financed by the Hochschuldidaktische Arbeitsstelle of the University of Koblenz-Landau as an innovative teaching project.
[20] While the poster projects were not graded, students still received feedback in both courses. Based on the elements and characteristics to be considered when designing a poster, which were discussed beforehand, feedback was given during and after the creation of the posters regarding the poster's content (e.g., originality, complexity, clarity) as well as the way it was organised (neatness and correctness, layout and structure, colors, font size, use and relevance of images, text length etc.).

Bibliography

Primary Literature

Anderson, Matthew T. (2002). *Feed.* Somerville: Candlewick Press.
Bay, Michael (2005). *The Island.* DreamWorks.
Collins, Suzanne (2008). *The Hunger Games*. New York: Scholastic.
Dashner, James (2009). *The Maze Runner.* New York: Delacorte Press.
Hillcoat, John. (2009). *The Road.* Dimension Films.
Kubrick, Stanley (1964). *Dr. Strangelove or: How I learned to Stop Worrying and Love the Bomb.* Columbia Pictures Corporation.
Lang, Fritz (1927). *Metropolis.* Universum Film.
Lawrence, Francis. (2013). *The Hunger Games: Catching Fire.* Color Force.
--- (2014). *The Hunger Games: Mockingjay – Part I.* Color Force.
--- (2015). *The Hunger Games: Mockingjay – Part II.* Color Force.

Lowry, Lois (1993). *The Giver*. New York: Houghton Mifflin.
Miller, George (2015). *Mad Max: Fury Road*. Warner Bros. Pictures.
Niccol, Andrew (2011). *In Time*. Regency Enterprises.
Oliver, Lauren (2011). *Delirium*. New York: Harper Collins.
Ross, Gary (2012). *The Hunger Games*. Lionsgate.
Roth, Veronica (2011). *Divergent*. New York: Harper Collins.
Scott, Ridley (1982). *Blade Runner*. Ladd Company.
Spielberg, Steven (2002). *Minority Report*. Twentieth Century Fox Corporation.
Tykwer, Tom, Lana and Andy Wachowski (2012). *Cloud Atlas*. Cloud Atlas Productions.

Secondary Literature

Burkert, Anja (2017). "Two Heads Are Better than One: Collaborative Learning under Scrutiny." *Fostering Learner Autonomy – Learners, Teachers and Researchers in Action*. Ed. Annamaria Pinter, Tom Smits, Maria Giovanna Tassinari, and Kris Van de Poel. UK: IATEFL.
Dam, Leni (1995). *Learner Autonomy 3: From Theory to Classroom Practice*. Dublin: Authentik.
Eisenmann, Maria, and Christian Ludwig (2016). "Authentische Lernprozesse in komplexen Web 2.0-basierten Kompetenzaufgaben zur Förderung von Lernerautonomie." *Web 2.0 und komplexe Kompetenzaufgaben im Fremdsprachenunterricht*. Ed. Carmen Becker, Gabriele Blell, and Andrea Rössler. Frankfurt: Peter Lang, 89-108.
Everhard Carol J. (2015). "The Assessment-Autonomy Relationship." *Assessment and Autonomy in Language Learning*. Ed. Everhard and L. Murphy. London: Palgrave Macmillan, 8-34.
Grimm, Nancy, Michael Meyer, and Laurenz Volkmann (2015). *Teaching English*. Tübingen: Narr Francke Attempto.
Bracher, Lee, Jane Cantrell, and Kay Wilkie (1998). "The Process of Poster Presentation: A Valuable Learning Experience." *Medical Teacher* 20.6, 552-557.
Healey, Mick, and Alan Jenkins (2009). "Developing Undergraduate Research and Inquiry." York, Higher Education Academy. Web. 23 August 2018 <https:// www.heacademy. ac.uk/knowledge-hub/developing-undergraduate-research-and-inquiry>.
Holec, Henri (1981). *Autonomy and Foreign Language Learning*. Oxford: Pergamon.
Kress, Gunther (2009). *Multimodality: A Social Semiotic Approach to Contemporary Communication*. Abingdon: Routledge.

Little, David (n.d.). "Language Learner Autonomy: What, Why and How?" *Languages Initiative.* Web. 4 Sep. 2017 <http://languagesinitiative.ie/ images/ Language_Learner_Autonomy_WhatWhyHow.pdf>.

--- (2017). "Language Learner Autonomy: From Differentiation to Inclusion." *12th Nordic Conference on Developing Learner Autonomy in Language Learning and Teaching. 'Young Learners and Language Learner Autonomy – Practice, Teacher Education, Research.'* Ed. Hanne Thompson and Leni Dam. Copenhagen: University College Capital.

MacGregor, Jean, and Barbara Leigh Smith (1992). "What Is Collaborative Learning?" *Collaborative Learning: A Sourcebook for Higher Education. National Center on Postsecondary Teaching, Learning, and Assessment.* Ed. Anne Goodsell, Michelle Tinto, Vincent Maher, Barbara Leigh Smith, and Jean MacGregor. Pennsylvania State University. Web. 4 Sep. 2017 <http://www.austincc.edu/pintutor/newsite/_source/WhatIsCollaborativeLearning.pdf>.

van Lier, Leo (2008). "Agency in the Classroom." *Sociocultural Theory and the Teaching of Second Languages*. Ed. James P. Lantolf and Matthew E. Poehner. London: Equinox, 163-186.

Christian Ludwig (Karlsruhe)
Nicole Maruo-Schröder (Koblenz)

Teaching Young Adult Dystopian Fiction: A Bibliography

Primary Literature

Aguirre, Ann (2011). *Enclave (Razorland)*. New York: Feiwel & Friends.
Adams. John Joseph (ed.) (2012). *Brave New Worlds – Dystopian Stories*. San Francisco: Night Shade Books.
Aveyard, Victoria (2015). *Red Queen* (Red Queen 1). New York: HarperTeen.
--- (2016a). *Glass Sword* (Red Queen 2). New York: HarperTeen.
--- (2017). *King's Cage* (Red Queen 3). New York: HarperTeen.
--- (2018). *War Storm* (Red Queen 4). New York: HarperTeen.
--- (2015). *Queen Song* (Red Queen 0.1). New York: HarperTeen.
--- (2016b). *Steel Scars* (Red Queen 0.2). New York: HarperTeen.
--- (2016c). *Cruel Crown* (Red Queen 0.1 and 0.2). New York: HarperTeen.
Bacigalupi, Paolo (2010). *Ship Breaker*. New York: Little Brown Young Readers.
--- (2012). *The Drowned Cities*. London: Atom.
Baggott, Julianna (2012). *Pure*. New York: Grand Central Publishing.
--- (2013). *Fuse* (Pure Trilogy). New York: Grand Central Publishing.
--- (2014). *Burn* (Pure Trilogy). New York: Grand Central Publishing.
Bertagna, Julie (2008 [2002]). *Exodus*. Vol. 1. New York: Walker.
Bick, Ilsa J. (2011). *Ashes* (Ashes Trilogy). London: Quercus.
--- (2012). *Shadows* (Ashes Trilogy). London: Quercus.
--- (2013). *Monsters* (Ashes Trilogy). New York: Egmont USA.
Cass, Kiera (2012). *The Selection*. New York: HarperTeen.
--- (2013). *The Elite* (The Selection). New York: HarperTeen.
--- (2014). *The One* (The Selection). New York: HarperTeen.
Carey, Anna (2011). *Eve*. New York: HarperCollins.
--- (2012). *Once* (Eve). New York: HarperCollins.
--- (2013). *Rise* (Eve). New York: HarperCollins.
Card, Orson Scott (1985). *Ender's Game*. London: Century.
Collins, Suzanne (2008). *The Hunger Games*. New York: Scholastic Press.
--- (2009). *Catching Fire* (The Hunger Games). New York: Scholastic Press.
--- (2010). *Mockingjay* (The Hunger Games). New York: Scholastic Press.

Condie, Ally (2010). *Matched.* New York: Dutton Books.
--- (2011). *Crossed* (Matched). New York: Dutton Books.
--- (2012). *Reached* (Matched). New York: Dutton Books.
Dashner, James (2009). *The Maze Runner.* New York: Delacorte Press.
--- (2010). *The Scorch Trials* (The Maze Runner). New York: Delacorte Press
--- (2011). *The Death Cure* (The Maze Runner). New York: Delacorte Press.
DeStefano, Lauren (2011). *Wither* (The Chemical Garden). New York: Simon & Schuster Books.
--- (2012). *Fever* (The Chemical Garden). New York: Simon & Schuster Books.
--- (2013). *Sever* (The Chemical Garden). New York: Simon & Schuster Books.
Ee, Susan (2012). *Angelfall* (Penryn & the End of Days). New York: Skyscape.
Eggers, Dave (2013). *The Circle: A Novel.* New York: Alfred A. Knopf.
Fisher, Catherine (2007). *Incarceron.* London: Hodder Children's Books.
--- (2008). *Sapphique* (Incarceron). London: Hodder Children's Books.
Frisch, Aaron, and Robert Innocenti (2012). *The Girl in Red.* Mankato: Creative Editions & Paperbacks.
Grant, Michael (2008). *Gone.* New York: HarperCollins.
Hegland, Jean (1998 [1996]). *Into the Forest.* New York: Bantam Books.
Ishiguro, Kazuo (2005). *Never Let Me Go.* New York: Alfred A. Knopf.
Lloyd, Saci (2009). *The Carbon Diaries 2015* (Carbon Diaries). London: Hodder Children's Books.
--- (2010). *The Carbon Diaries 2017* (Carbon Diaries). London: Hodder Children's Books.
London, Alex (2013). *Proxy.* New York: Penguin Group.
--- (2014). *Guardian* (Proxy). New York: Penguin Group.
Lowry, Lois (1993). *The Giver,* Boston: Houghton Mifflin.
Lu, Marie (2011). *Legend.* New York: Penguin Group.
--- (2013a). *Prodigy* (Legend). New York: Penguin Group.
--- (2013b). *Champion* (Legend). New York: Penguin Group.
McGinnis, Mindy (2013). *Not a Drop to Drink.* New York: HarperCollins.
Mafi, Tahereh (2011). *Shatter Me.* New York: HarperCollins.
--- (2013). *Deravel Me* (Shatter Me). New York: HarperCollins.
--- (2014). *Ignite Me* (Shatter Me). New York: HarperCollins.
Meyer, Marissa (2012). *Cinder* (The Lunar Chronicles). New York: Feiwel & Friends.
--- (2014). *Cress* (The Lunar Chronicles). New York: Feiwel & Friends.
--- (2015). *Winter* (The Lunar Chronicles). New York: Feiwel & Friends.
Meyer, Stephanie (2008). *The Host.* London; Little Brown Book Group.
Morgan, Kass (2013). *The 100.* New York: Little, Brown and Company.
--- (2014). *Day 21* (The 100). New York: Little, Brown and Company.
--- (2015). *Homecoming* (The 100). New York: Little, Brown and Company.
--- (2016). *Rebellion* (The 100). New York: Little, Brown and Company.

O'Brien, Caragh M. (2010). *Birthmarked.* New York: Macmillan/Roaring Brook Press.
--- (2012). *Prized.* New York: Macmillan/Roaring Brook Press.
--- (2013). *Promised.* New York: Macmillan/Roaring Brook Press.
Orwell, George (1949). *Nineteen Eighty-Four.* New York: Harcourt Brace.
Oliver, Lauren (2012a). *Delirium.* New York: Harpercollins.
--- (2012b). *Pandemonium* (Delirium). New York: HarperCollins.
--- (2013). *Requiem* (Delirium). New York: HarperCollins.
Pfeffer, Susan Beth (2006). *Life as We Knew It* (Last Survivors). Orlando: Harcourt Books.
Price, Lissa (2012a). *Portrait of a Starter: An Unhidden Story* (Starters). New York: Delacorte Press for Young Readers.
--- (2012b). *Starters.* New York: Delacorte Press for Young Readers.
--- (2012c). *Portrait of a Marshal: The 2nd Unhidden Story* (Starters). New York: Delacorte Press for Young Readers.
--- (2013a). *Portrait of a Spore: The 3rd Unhidden Story* (Starters). New York: Delacorte Press for Young Readers.
--- (2013b). *Portrait of a Donor.* New York: Delacorte Press for Young Readers.
--- (2014). *Enders* (Starters). New York: Delacorte Press for Young Readers.
Roth, Veronica (2012a). *Divergent.* New York: HarperCollins/ Katherine Tegen Books.
--- (2012b). *Insurgent* (Divergent). New York: HarperCollins.
--- (2013). *Allegiant* (Divergent). New York: HarperCollins.
Rossi, Veronica (2012). *Under the Never Sky.* New York: HarperCollins.
--- (2013). *Through the Ever Night* (Under the Never Sky). New York: HarperCollins.
--- (2014). *Into the Still Blue* (Under the Never Sky). New York: HarperCollins.
Sandler, Karen (2013a). *Tankborn.* New York: Tu Books.
--- (2013b). *Awakening* (Tankborn). New York: Tu Books.
--- (2014). *Rebellion* (Tankborn). New York: Tu Books.
Shusterman, Neal (2007). *Unwind* (Unwind Dystology). New York: Simon & Schuster Books.
--- (2012). *UnWholly.* (Unwind Dystology). New York: Simon & Schuster Books.
--- (2013) *UnSouled.* (Unwind Dystology). New York: Simon & Schuster Books.
--- (2014). *UnDivided.* (Unwind Dystology). New York: Simon & Schuster Books.
Smith, Sherri L. (2013). *Orleans.* New York: Putnam Juvenile.
Taylor, Clark, ill. Jan T. Dicks (1992). *The House That Crack Built.* San Francisco: Chronicle Books.
The Grimm Brothers, ill. Anthony Brown (1981). *Hansel and Gretel.* London: Walker Books.
Terry, Teri (2012). *Slated.* London: Orchard Books.

--- (2013). *Fractured* (Slated). London: Orchard Books.
--- (2014). *Shattered* (Slated). London: Orchard Books.
Wells, Dan (2012a). *Isolation* (Partials). New York: Balzer + Bray.
--- (2012b). *Partials*. New York: Balzer + Bray.
--- (2013). *Fragments* (Partials). New York: Balzer + Bray.
--- (2014). *Ruins* (Partials). New York: Balzer + Bray.
Westerfeld, Scott (2005a). *Uglies*. New York: Simon & Schuster Books/ Simon Pulse.
--- (2005b). *Pretties* (Uglies). New York: Simon & Schuster Books/ Simon Pulse.
--- (2007). *Extras* (Uglies). New York: Simon & Schuster Books/ Simon Pulse.
Yancey, Rick (2013). *The 5th Wave*. London: Penguin Group.
Young, Moira (2011). *Blood Red Road* (Dust Lands). New York: Margaret K. McElderry Books.
--- (2012). *Rebel Heart* (Dust Lands). New York: Margaret K. McElderry Books.
--- (2014). *Raging Star* (Dust Lands). New York: Margaret K. McElderry Books.

Secondary Literature[1]

Young Adult Dystopian Literature

Aldridge, Alexandra (1984). *The Scientific World View in Dystopia*. Michigan: UMI Research Press. Web. 23 August 2018 <https://searchworks.stanford.edu/view/1562649>.
Applebaum, Noga (2010). *Representations of Technology in Science Fiction for Young People*. London and New York: Routledge.
Baccolini, Raffaella, and Tom Moylan (eds.) (2003). *Dark Horizons, Science Fiction and the Dystopian Imagination*. New York: Routledge.
--- (2004). "The Persistence of Hope in Dystopian Science Fiction." *PMLA* 119.3, 518-521.
Bartosch, Roman (2012). "Literary Quality and the Ethics of Reading: Some Thoughts on Literary Evolution and the Fiction of Margaret Atwood, Iija Trojanow, and Ian McEwan." *Literature, Ecology, Ethics. Recent Trends in Ecocriticism*. Ed. Timo Müller and Michael Sauter. Heidelberg: Winter, 113-128.
Basu, Balaka, Katherine R. Broad, and Carrie Hintz (eds.) (2015). *Contemporary Dystopian Fiction for Young Adults. Brave New Teenagers*. New York: Routledge.
Beck, Ulrich (2012 [2009]). *World at Risk*. Cambridge: Polity Press.
Bleich, David (1984). *Utopia: The Psychology of a Cultural Fantasy*. Michigan: UMI Research Press.
Booker, Keith M. (2013). *Contemporary Speculative Fiction*. Ipswich: Salem Press.

--- (1994a). *Dystopian Literature – A Theory and Research Guide*. Santa Barbara: Greenwood Press.

--- (1994b). *The Dystopian Impulse in Modern Literature: Fiction as Social Criticism.* Westport, CT: Greenwood Press.

--- (2012). *Dystopia.* Ipswich: Salem Press.

Bradford, Clare (2003). "Art, Pain, Children. Utopian and Dystopian Discourses in Picture Books." *Double Dialogues* 4 (Winter 2003), n.pag. Web. 2 November 2015 <http://www.doubledialogues.com/article/art-pain-children-utopian-and-dystopian-discourses-in-picture-books/>.

---, et al. (eds.) (2011). *New World Orders in Contemporary Children's Literature: Utopian Transformations.* New York: Palgrave Macmillan.

Braithwaite, Elizabeth (2010). "Post-Disaster Fiction for Young Adults: Some Trends and Variations." *Papers: Explorations into Children's Literature* 20.1, 5-19.

Brians, Paul (1990). "Nuclear War Fiction for Young Readers: A Commentary and Annotated Bibliography." *Science Fiction, Social Conflict and War.* Ed. Philip Davies. Manchester: Manchester University Press, 132-50.

Brown, Joanna, and Nancy St. Clair (2002). *Declarations of Independence: Empowered Girls in Young Adult Literature, 1990-2001*. Lanham: The Scarecrow Press.

Bucher, Katherine T., and KaaVonia M. Hinton (2013). *Young Adult Literature. Exploration, Evaluation, and Appreciation.* Cambridge: Pearson.

Buell, Frederick (2003). *From Apocalypse to Way of Life. Environmental Crisis in the American Century.* New York: Routledge.

Bullen, Elizabeth, and Elizabeth Parsons (2007). "Dystopian Visions of Global Capitalism: Philip Reeve's *Mortal Engines* and M. T. Anderson's *Feed.*" *Children's Literature in Education* 38.2, 127-139.

Burnett, G. Wesley, and Lucy Rollin (2000). "Anti-leisure in Dystopian Fiction: The Literature of Leisure in the Worst of all Possible Worlds." *Leisure Studies* 19.2, 77-90.

Campbell, Joseph (2010). *The Order and the Other: Power and Subjectivity in Young Adult Science Fiction and Dystopian Literature for Adolescents.* (Unpublished doctoral dissertation). Illinois State University.

Claeys, Gregory (ed.) (2010). *The Cambridge Companion to Utopian Literature.* Cambridge: Cambridge University Press.

--- (2017). *Dystopia: A Natural History.* Oxford: Oxford University Press.

Claeys, Gregory, and Lyman Tower Sargent (eds.) (2017). *The Utopia Reader.* New York: NYU Press.

Crew, Hillary S. (2004). "Not so Brave a World: The Representations of Human Cloning in Science Fiction for Young Adults." *The Lion and the Unicorn* 28.2, 203-21.

Curtis, Claire P. (2010). *Postapocalyptic Fiction and the Social Contract*. New York. Lexington Books.

Curwood, Jean Scott (2013). "'The Hunger Games': Literature, Literacy, and Online Affinity Spaces." *Language Arts* 90.6, 417-427.

Day, Sara K., Miranda A. Green-Barteet, and Amy L. Montz. (eds.) (2014). *Female Rebellion in Young Adult Dystopian Fiction*. London: Routledge.

Demerjian, Louisa MacKay (2016). *The Age of Dystopia. One Genre, Our Fears and Our Future*. Cambridge: Cambridge Scholars Pub.

Donawerth, Jane L., and Carol A. Kolmerten (eds.) (1994). *Utopian Science Fiction by Women: Worlds of Difference*. Liverpool: Liverpool University Press.

Dror, Stephanie (2013). "The Fairy Tale Dystopia." Web. 2 November 2015 <http://thebookwars.ca/2013/09/the-fairy-tale-dystopia/>. n.pag.

Dunn, George A., and Nicolas Michaud (2012). *The Hunger Games and Philosophy: A Critique of Pure Treason*. Hoboken: John Wiley & Sons.

Ferns, Chris (1999). *Narrating Utopia: Ideology, Gender, Form in Utopian Literature*. Liverpool: Liverpool University Press.

Flanagan, Victoria (2014). *Technology and Identity in Young Adult Fiction: The Posthuman Subject*. Basingstoke: Palgrave Macmillan.

Garforth, Lisa (2005). "Green Utopias: Beyond Apocalypse, Progress, and Pastoral." *Utopian Studies* 16.3, 393-427.

Geus, Marius de (1999). *Ecological Utopias: Envisioning the Sustainable Society*. Utrecht: International Books.

Gillis, Bryan, and Joanna Simpson (2015). "Sex and Romance in Dystopian Young Adult Fiction." *Sexual Content in Young Adult Literature*. Lanham: Rowman & Littlefield, 75-100.

Graham, Kathryn (1999). "Exodus from the City: Peter Dickinson's Eva." *The Lion and the Unicorn* 23.1, 79-85.

Grubisic, Brett Josef, Gisèle Baxter, and Tara Lee (eds.) (2014). *Blast, Corrupt, Dismantle, Erase. Contemporary North American Dystopian Literature*. Waterloo, Ontario: Wilfrid Laurier University Press.

Haraway, Donna J. (1990). *Simians, Cyborgs, and Women: The Reinvention of Nature*. New York: Routledge.

Heise, Ursula (2015). "What's the Matter with Dystopia?" *Public Books*. Web. 21 Feb. 2017 <http://www.publicbooks.org/whats-the-matter-with-dystopia/>.

Hemphill, Kara E. (2015). "Gender and the Popular Heroines (and Heroes) of the Young Adult Dystopia." *Honors Research Projects*. Paper 132. Web. 9. April 2017 <http://ideaexchange.uakron.edu/honors_research_projects/132>.

Hintz, Carrie, and Elaine Ostry (eds.) (2003). *Utopian and Dystopian Writing for Children and Young Adults*. New York: Routledge.

Hintz, Carrie (2002). "Monica Hughes, Lois Lowry, and Young Adult Dystopias." *The Lion and the Unicorn* 26.2, 254-264.

Hughes, Rowland, and Pat Wheeler (2013). "Introduction Eco-dystopias: Nature and the Dystopian Imagination." *Critical Survey* 25.2, 1-6.

Kouhestani, Maryam (2013). "Disciplining the Body: Power and Language in Margaret Atwood's Dystopian Novel *The Handmaid's Tale.*" *Journal of Educational and Social Research* 3.7, 610-613.

Layh, Susanna (2014). *Finstere neue Welten. Gattungsparadigmatische Transformationen der literarischen Utopie und Dystopie*. Würzburg: Königshausen & Neumann.

Levitas, Ruth (2010). *The Concept of Utopia*. Bern: Peter Lang.

Levy, Michael (2008). "'The Sublimation of Real Life': Malls, Shopping, and Advertising in Recent Young Adult SF." *The New York Review of Science Fiction* 18.7, 10-12.

Lewis, Courtland (ed.) (2016). *Divergent and Philosophy. The Factions of Life.* Chicago: Open Court.

Little, Judith A. (2007). *Feminist Philosophy and Science Fiction: Utopias and Dystopias*. Amherst: Prometheus Books.

Machat, Sibylle (2013). *In the Ruins of Civilization. Narrative Structures, World Constructions and Physical Realities in the Post-Apocalyptic Novel.* Trier: WVT.

Manuel, Frank E. (ed.) (1966). *Utopias and Utopian Thought*. Boston: Houghton Mufflin.

---, and Fritzie P. Manuel (1979). *Utopian Thought in the Western World.* Cambridge: The Belknap Press of Harvard University Press.

Marotta, Melanie (2016). "Sherri L. Smith's *Orleans* and Karen Sandler's *Tankborn*: The Female Leader, the Neo-Slave Narrative, and Twenty-first Century Young Adult Afrofuturism." *Journal of Science Fiction* 1.2, 56-70.

McCulloch, Fiona (2007). "A New Home in the World. Scottish Devolution, Nomadic Writing, and Supranational Citizenship in Julie Bertagna's *Exodus* and *Zenith*." *ARIEL* 38.4, 69-96.

McAlear, Rob (2010). "The Value of Fear: Toward a Rhetorical Model of Dystopia." *Interdisciplinary Humanities* 27.2, 24-42.

Moylan, Tom (2000). *Scraps of the Untainted Sky. Science Fiction, Utopia, Dystopia*. Boulder, CO: Westview Press.

--- (1986). *Demand the Impossible: Science Fiction and the Utopian Imagination.* London: Methuen.

Mohr, Dunja M. (2005) *Worlds Apart?: Dualism and Transgression in Contemporary Female Dystopias*. Jefferson: McFarland & Company.

Murphy, Graham J. (2009). "Dystopia." *The Routledge Companion to Science Fiction*. Ed. Mark Bould et al. London: Routledge, 473-477.

Nadir, Christine (2010). "Utopian Studies, Environmental Literature, and the Legacy of an Idea: Educating Desire in Miguel Abensour and Ursula K. Le Guin." *Utopian Studies* 21.1, 24-56.

Ostry, Elaine (2004). "Is He Still Human? Are You?: Young Adult Science Fiction in the Posthuman Age." *The Lion and the Unicorn* 28.2, 222-46.

Oziewicz, Marek C. (2015). *Justice in Young Adult Speculative Fiction: A Cognitive Reading.* London: Routledge.

Pearson, Carol (1981). "Coming Home: Four Feminist Utopias and Patriarchal Experience." *Future Females: A Critical Anthology*. Ed. Marleen S. Barr. Bowling Green, Ohio: Bowling Green State University Popular Press, 63-70.

Pharr, Mary, and Leisa Clark (eds.) (2012). *Of Bread, Blood and The Hunger Games. Critical Essays on the Suzanne Collins Trilogy*. Jefferson, N.C.: McFarland & Company.

Rau, Albert (2010). "Margaret Atwood's *The Handmaid's Tale*: A Dystopian Novel in the EFL Classroom." *Teaching the New English Cultures & Literatures.* Eds. Maria Eisenmann, Nancy Grimm, and Laurenz Volkmann. Heidelberg: Winter, 109-124.

Reeve, Philip (2011). "The Worst Is Yet to Come." *School Library Journal* 57.8, 34-36.

Rogan, Alcena Madeline Davis (2009). "Utopian Studies." *The Routledge Companion to Science Fiction.* Ed. Mark Bould et al. New York: Routledge, 308-316.

Sargisson, Lucy (2012). *Fool's Gold? Utopianism in the Twenty-First Century.* Basingstoke: Palgrave Macmillan.

--- (1996). *Contemporary Feminist Utopianism*. London: Routledge.

Sambell, Kay (2004). "Carnivalizing the Future: A New Approach to Theorizing Childhood and Adulthood in Science Fiction for Young Readers." *The Lion and the Unicorn* 28.2, 247-267.

Sargent, Lyman Tower (1994). "The Three Faces of Utopianism Revisited." *Utopian Studies* 5.1, 1-37.

--- (2004). "Utopian Literature in the United States 1990-2000." *Dreams of Paradise, Visions of Apocalypse: Utopia and Dystopia in American Culture.* Ed. Jaap Verheul. Amsterdam: VU University Press, 207-219.

Schaer, Roland, Gregory Claeys, and Lyman Tower Sargent (eds.) (2000). *Utopia: The Search for the Ideal Society in the Western World.* New York and Oxford: The New York Public Library/ Oxford University Press.

Schmeink, Lars (2016). *Biopunk Dystopias, Genetic Engineering, Society and Science Fiction*. Liverpool: Liverpool University Press.

SFE (2016). *The Encyclopedia of Science Fiction 2016*. Web. 23 August 2018 <http://www.sf-encyclopedia.com>.

Shostak, Arthur B. (ed.) (2003). *Viable Utopian Ideas: Shaping a Better World.* Armonk, NY: M. E. Sharpe.

Spisak, April (2012). "What Makes a Good YA Dystopian Novel?" *Horn Book Magazine* 88.3, 55-60.

Sullivan III, C. W. (ed.) (1999). *Young Adult Science Fiction.* Westport: Greenwood Press.

Thaler, Ingrid (ed.) (2010). *Black Atlantic Speculative Fictions*. London: Routledge.

Trites, Roberta (2000). *Disturbing the Universe: Power and Repression in Adolescent Literature*. Iowa City: University of Iowa Press.

Ventura, Abbie (2011). "Predicting a Better Situation? Three Young Adult Speculative Fiction Texts and the Possibilities for Social Change." *Children's Literature Association Quarterly* 36.1, 89-103.

Vieira, Fátima (2010). "The Concept of Utopia." *The Cambridge Companion to Utopian Literature*. Ed. Gregory Claeys. Cambridge: Cambridge University Press, 3-27.

Voigts, Eckart, and Alessandra Boller (eds.) (2015*). Dystopia, Science Fiction, Post-Apocalypse. Classics – New Tendencies – Model Interpretations*. Trier: WVT.

Wilson, D. Harlan (2009). *The Technologies of Desire: Selfhood and the Body in Postcapitalist Science Fiction.* Hyattsville, MD: Guided Dog Books.

Teaching Young Adult Dystopian Literature

Ames, Melissa A. (2013). "Engaging 'Apolitical' Adolescents: Analyzing the Popularity and Educational Potential of Dystopian Literature Post-9/11." *The High School Journal* 97.1, 3-20.

Bergmann, Harriet F. (1989). "Teaching Them to Read": A Fishing Expedition in *The Handmaid's Tale*." *College English*, 51.8, 847-854.

Bond, Gwenda (1994). "Honesty and Hope: Presenting Human Rights Issues to Teenagers Through Fiction." *Children's Literature in Education* 25.1, 41-53.

Freudenstein, Reinhold (1999). "Global Issues im Englischunterricht." *Praxis des neusprachlichen Unterrichts* 46.3, 237-249.

Groenke, Susan L., and Lisa Schwerff (2010). *Teaching YA Lit through Differentiated Instruction.* Urbana: National Council for Teachers of English.

Hayn, Judith A., and, Jeffrey S. Kaplan (eds.) (2012). *Teaching Young Adult Literature Today: Insights, Considerations, and Perspectives for the Classroom Teacher*. Lanham: Rowman & Littlefield.

Hesse, Mechthild (2009). *Teenage Fiction in the Active English Classroom.* Stuttgart: Klett.

Matz, Frauke (2014). "Dystopische Jugendromane: transkulturelle Themen und interkulturelle Bezüge." *Transkulturelles Lernen im Fremdsprachenunterricht. Theorie und Praxis*. Ed. Frauke Matz, Michael Rogge, and Philipp Siepman. Frankfurt: Peter Lang, 143-152.

--- (2015). "Alternative Worlds – Alternative Texts: Teaching (Young Adult) Dystopian Novels." *Learning with Literature in the EFL Classroom*. Ed. Werner Delanoy, Maria Eisenmann, and Frauke Matz. Frankfurt: Peter Lang, 263-282.

Parham, John (2006). "The Deficiency of Environmental Capital: Why Environmentalism Needs a Reflexive Pedagogy." *Ecodidactic Perspectives on English Language, Literatures and Cultures*. Ed. Sylvia Mayer and Graham Wilson. Trier: WVT, 7-22.

Siepmann, Philipp (2013). "Sharing Is Caring? Teaching Dave Eggers's Dystopian Novel 'The Circle.'" *Englisch betrifft uns* (March 2013), 12-19.

Simmons, Amber M. (2014). "Class on Fire: Using the Hunger Games Trilogy to Encourage Social Action." *Teaching towards Democracy with Postmodern and Popular Culture Texts*. Ed. Patricia Paugh, Tricia Kress, and Robert Lake. Rotterdam: Sense Publishers, 77-96.

Tearle, Oliver (2016). "Other Mothers and Fathers: Teaching Contemporary Dystopian Fiction." *Teaching 21st Century Genres*. Ed. Katy Shaw. London: Palgrave Macmillan, 109-128.

Volkmann, Laurenz (2012). "Ecodidactics als Antwort auf die planetarische Bedrohung? Zum Einsatz von Ecopoetry im Englischunterricht." *Anglophone Literaturdidaktik – Zukunftsperspektiven für den Englischunterricht*. Ed. Rüdiger Ahrens, Maria Eisenmann, and Julia Hammer. Heidelberg: Winter, 393-408.

Wilkinson, Rachel (2010). "Teaching Dystopian Literature to a Consumer Class." *The English Journal* 99.3, 22-26.

Wolk, Steven (2009). "Reading for a Better World: Teaching for Social Responsibility with Young Adult Literature." *Journal of Adolescent & Adult Literacy* 52.8, 664-673.

Note

[1] For a better overview, we have separated titles that are exclusively on young adult dystopian literature (including works about genre patterns and features of dystopian and related genres) from those that are about teaching (with) young adult dystopian texts. Of necessity, this is a selection that focuses on more recent titles as well as those that are particularly interesting for a German-language reader/ teacher.

Contibutors' Addresses

Dr. Grit Alter, Institut für Fachdidaktik, Bereich Didaktik der Sprachen, Universität Innsbruck, Innrain 52d, 6020 Innsbruck, Austria

Dr. Alessandra Boller, Philipps-Universität Marburg, Fachbereich 10: Fremdsprachliche Philologien, Institut für Anglistik und Amerikanistik, Wilhelm-Röpke-Straße 6, 35032 Marburg

Prof. Dr. Maria Eisenmann, Neuphilologisches Institut, Anglistik/ Amerikanistik, Julius-Maximilians-Universität Würzburg, Am Hubland, 97074 Würzburg

Miriam Gertzen, M.A., Institut für Anglistik, Amerikanistik und Keltologie, Rheinische Friedrich-Wilhelms-Universität Bonn, Regina-Pacis-Weg 5, 53113 Bonn

Prof. Dr. Rüdiger Heinze, Institut für Anglistik und Amerikanistik, Abt. Literatur- und Kulturwissenschaften, Technische Universität Braunschweig, Bienroder Weg 80, 38106 Braunschweig

Nadine Krüger, M.A., Neuphilologisches Institut, Anglistik/ Amerikanistik, Julius-Maximilians-Universität Würzburg, Am Hubland, 97074 Würzburg

Prof. (i.V.) Dr. Christian Ludwig, Institut für Mehrsprachigkeit, Abteilung Englisch, Pädagogische Hochschule Karlsruhe, Bismarckstr. 10, 76133 Karlsruhe

Prof. Dr. Nicole Maruo-Schröder, Institut für Anglistik, Universität Koblenz-Landau, Campus Koblenz, Universitätsstr. 1, 56070 Koblenz

Prof. Dr. Michael Meyer, Institut für Anglistik, Universität Koblenz-Landau, Campus Koblenz, Universitätsstr. 1, 56070 Koblenz

Dr. Sarah Schäfer-Althaus, Institut für Anglistik, Universität Koblenz-Landau, Campus Koblenz, Universitätsstr. 1, 56070 Koblenz